Deep Learning with Theano

Perform large-scale numerical and scientific
computations efficiently

Christopher Bourez

BIRMINGHAM - MUMBAI

Deep Learning with Theano

First published: July 2017

Production reference: 1280717

Published by Packt Publishing Ltd.
Livery Place
35 Livery Street
Birmingham B3 2PB, UK.

ISBN 978-1-78646-582-5

www.packtpub.com

Credits

Author
Christopher Bourez

Reviewers
Matthieu de Beaucorps
Frederic Bastien
Arnaud Bergeron
Pascal Lamblin

Commissioning Editor
Amey Varangaonkar

Acquisition Editor
Veena Pagare

Content Development Editor
Amrita Noronha

Technical Editor
Akash Patel

Copy Editor
Safis Editing

Project Coordinator
Shweta H Birwatkar

Proofreader
Safis Editing

Indexer
Pratik Shirodkar

Graphics
Tania Dutta

Production Coordinator
Shantanu Zagade

Cover Work
Shantanu N. Zagade

About the Author

Christopher Bourez graduated from Ecole Polytechnique and Ecole Normale Supérieure de Cachan in Paris in 2005 with a Master of Science in Math, Machine Learning and Computer Vision (MVA).

For 7 years, he led a company in computer vision that launched Pixee, a visual recognition application for iPhone in 2007, with the major movie theater brand, the city of Paris and the major ticket broker: with a snap of a picture, the user could get information about events, products, and access to purchase.

While working on missions in computer vision with Caffe, TensorFlow or Torch, he helped other developers succeed by writing on a blog on computer science. One of his blog posts, a tutorial on the Caffe deep learning technology, has become the most successful tutorial on the web after the official Caffe website.

On the initiative of Packt Publishing, the same recipes that made the sucess of his Caffe tutorial have been ported to write this book on Theano technology. In the meantime, a wide range of problems for Deep Learning are studied to gain more practice with Theano and its application.

Acknowledgments

This book has been written in less than a year, and I would like to thank Mohammed Jabreel for his help with writing texts and code examples for chapters 3 and 5.

Mohammed Hamood Jabreel is is a PhD student in Computer Science Engineering at the Department of Computer Science and Mathematics, Universitat Rovira i Virgili. He has received a Master degree in Computer Engineering: Computer Security and Intelligent Systems from Universitat Rovira i Virgili , Spain in2015 and a Bachelor's degree in Computer Science in 2009 from Hodiedha University. His main research interest is the Natural Language Processing, Text Mining and Sentiment Analysis.

Second, I would like to thank IBM for their tremendous support through the Global Entrepeneur Program. Their infrastructure of dedicated GPUs has been of uncomparable quality and performance to train the neural networks.

Last, I would like to thank the reviewers, Matthieu de Beaucorps and Pascal Lamblin, as well as the Packt employees Amrita and Vinay for their ideas and follow-up.

Happy reading.

About the Reviewers

Matthieu de Beaucorps is a machine learning specialist with an engineering background. Since 2012, he has been working on developing deep neural nets to enhance identification and recommendation tasks in computer vision, audio, and NLP.

Pascal Lamblin is a software analyst at MILA (Montreal Institute for Learning Algorithms). After completing his engineering degree at École Centrale Paris, Pascal has done some research under the supervision of Yoshua Bengio at Université de Montréal and is now working on the development of Theano.

www.PacktPub.com

eBooks, discount offers, and more

For support files and downloads related to your book, please visit www.PacktPub.com.

Did you know that Packt offers eBook versions of every book published, with PDF and ePub files available? You can upgrade to the eBook version at www.PacktPub.com and as a print book customer, you are entitled to a discount on the eBook copy. Get in touch with us at customercare@packtpub.com for more details.

At www.PacktPub.com, you can also read a collection of free technical articles, sign up for a range of free newsletters and receive exclusive discounts and offers on Packt books and eBooks.

https://www.packtpub.com/mapt

Get the most in-demand software skills with Mapt. Mapt gives you full access to all Packt books and video courses, as well as industry-leading tools to help you plan your personal development and advance your career.

Why subscribe?

- Fully searchable across every book published by Packt
- Copy and paste, print, and bookmark content
- On demand and accessible via a web browser

Customer Feedback

Thanks for purchasing this Packt book. At Packt, quality is at the heart of our editorial process. To help us improve, please leave us an honest review on this book's Amazon page at https://www.amazon.com/dp/1786465825. If you'd like to join our team of regular reviewers, you can e-mail us at customerreviews@packtpub.com. We award our regular reviewers with free eBooks and videos in exchange for their valuable feedback. Help us be relentless in improving our products!

Table of Contents

Preface

Gain insight and practice with neural net architecture design to solve problems with artificial intelligence. Understand the concepts behind the most advanced networks in deep learning. Leverage Python language with Theano technology, to easily compute derivatives and minimize objective functions of your choice.

What this book covers

Chapter 1, Theano Basics, helps the reader to reader learn main concepts of Theano to write code that can compile on different hardware architectures and optimize automatically complex mathematical objective functions.

Chapter 2, Classifying Handwritten Digits with a Feedforward Network, will introduce a simple, well-known and historical example which has been the starting proof of superiority of deep learning algorithms. The initial problem was to recognize handwritten digits.

Chapter 3, Encoding word into Vector, one of the main challenge with neural nets is to connect the real world data to the input of a neural net, in particular for categorical and discrete data. This chapter presents an example on how to build an embedding space through training with Theano.

Such embeddings are very useful in machine translation, robotics, image captioning, and so on because they translate the real world data into arrays of vectors that can be processed by neural nets.

Chapter 4, Generating Text with a Recurrent Neural Net, introduces recurrency in neural nets with a simple example in practice, to generate text.

Recurrent neural nets (RNN) are a popular topic in deep learning, enabling more possibilities for sequence prediction, sequence generation, machine translation, connected objects. Natural Language Processing (NLP) is a second field of interest that has driven the research for new machine learning techniques.

Chapter 5, Analyzing Sentiments with a Bidirectional LSTM, applies embeddings and recurrent layers to a new task of natural language processing, sentiment analysis. It acts as a kind of validation of prior chapters.

In the meantime, it demonstrates an alternative way to build neural nets on Theano, with a higher level library, Keras.

Chapter 6, Locating with Spatial Transformer Networks, applies recurrency to image, to read multiple digits on a page at once. This time, we take the opportunity to rewrite the classification network for handwritten digits images, and our recurrent models, with the help of Lasagne, a library of built-in modules for deep learning with Theano.

Lasagne library helps design neural networks for experimenting faster. With this help, we'll address object localization, a common computer vision challenge, with Spatial Transformer modules to improve our classification scores.

Chapter 7, Classifying Images with Residual Networks, classifies any type of images at the best accuracy. In the mean time, to build more complex nets with ease, we introduce a library based on Theano framework, Lasagne, with many already implemented components to help implement neural nets faster for Theano.

Chapter 8, Translating and Explaining through Encoding – decoding Networks, presents encoding-decoding techniques: applied to text, these techniques are heavily used in machine-translation and simple chatbots systems. Applied to images, they serve scene segmentations and object localization. Last, image captioning is a mixed, encoding images and decoding to texts.

This chapter goes one step further with a very popular high level library, Keras, that simplifies even more the development of neural nets with Theano.

Chapter 9, Selecting Relevant Inputs or Memories with the Mechanism of Attention, for solving more complicated tasks, the machine learning world has been looking for higher level of intelligence, inspired by nature: reasoning, attention and memory. In this chapter, the reader will discover the memory networks on the main purpose of artificial intelligence for natural language processing (NLP): the language understanding.

Chapter 10, *Predicting Times Sequence with Advanced RNN*, time sequences are an important field where machine learning has been used heavily. This chapter will go for advanced techniques with Recurrent Neural Networks (RNN), to get state-of-art results.

Chapter 11, *Learning from the Environment with Reinforcement*, reinforcement learning is the vast area of machine learning, which consists in training an agent to behave in an environment (such as a video game) so as to optimize a quantity (maximizing the game score), by performing certain actions in the environment (pressing buttons on the controller) and observing what happens.

Reinforcement learning new paradigm opens a complete new path for designing algorithms and interactions between computers and real world.

Chapter 12, *Learning Features with Unsupervised Generative Networks*, unsupervised learning consists in new training algorithms that do not require the data to be labeled to be trained. These algorithms try to infer the hidden labels from the data, called the factors, and, for some of them, to generate new synthetic data.

Unsupervised training is very useful in many cases, either when no labeling exists, or when labeling the data with humans is too expensive, or lastly when the dataset is too small and feature engineering would overfit the data. In this last case, extra amounts of unlabeled data train better features as a basis for supervised learning.

Chapter 13, *Extending Deep Learning with Theano*, extends the set of possibilities in Deep Learning with Theano. It addresses the way to create new operators for the computation graph, either in Python for simplicity, or in C to overcome the Python overhead, either for the CPU or for the GPU. Also, introduces the basic concept of parallel programming for GPU. Lastly, we open the field of General Intelligence, based on the first skills developed in this book, to develop new skills, in a gradual way, to improve itself one step further.

Why Theano?

Investing time and developments on Theano is very valuable and to understand why, it is important to explain that Theano belongs to the best deep learning technologies and is also much more than a deep learning library. Three reasons make of Theano a good choice of investment:

- It has comparable performance with other numerical or deep learning libraries

- It comes in a rich Python ecosystem

- It enables you to evaluate any function constraint by data, given a model, by leaving the freedom to compile a solution for any optimization problem

Let us first focus on the **performance** of the technology itself. The most popular libraries in deep learning are Theano (for Python), Torch (for Lua), Tensorflow (for Python) and Caffe (for C++ and with a Python wrapper). There has been lot's of benchmarks to compare deep learning technologies.

In Bastien et al 2012 (*Theano: new features and speed improvements, Frédéric Bastien, Pascal Lamblin, Razvan Pascanu, James Bergstra, Ian Goodfellow, Arnaud Bergeron, Nicolas Bouchard, David Warde-Farley, Yoshua Bengio, Nov 2012*), Theano made significant progress in speed, but the comparison on different tasks does not point a clear winner among the challenged technologies. Bahrampour et Al. 2016 (*Comparative Study of Deep Learning Software Frameworks, Soheil Bahrampour, Naveen Ramakrishnan, Lukas Schott, Mohak Shah, mars 2016*) conclude that:

- For GPU-based deployment of trained convolutional and fully connected networks, Torch is best suited, followed by Theano.

- For GPU-based training of convolutional and fully connected networks, Theano is fastest for small networks and Torch is fastest for larger networks

- For GPU-based training and deployment of recurrent networks (LSTM), Theano results in the best performance.

- For CPU-based training and deployment of any tested deep network architecture, Torch performs the best followed by Theano

These results are confirmed in the open-source *rnn-benchmarks* (`https://github.com/glample/rnn-benchmarks`) where for training (forward + backward passes), Theano outperforms Torch and TensorFlow. Also, Theano crushes Torch and TensorFlow for smaller batch sizes with larger numbers of hidden units. For bigger batch size and hidden layer size, the differences are smaller since they rely more on the performance of CUDA, the underlying NVIDIA graphic library common to all frameworks. Last, in up-to-date *soumith benchmarks* (`https://github.com/soumith/convnet-benchmarks`), the fftconv in Theano performs the best on CPU, while the best performing convolution implementations on GPU, cuda-convnet2 and fbfft, are CUDA extension, the underlying library. These results should convince the reader that, although results are mixed, Theano plays a leading role in the speed competition.

The second point to prefer Theano rather than Torch is that it comes with a **rich ecosystem**, taking benefit from the Python ecosystem, but also from a large number of libraries that have been developed for Theano. This book will present two of them, Lasagne, and Keras. Theano and Torch are the most extensible frameworks both in terms of supporting various deep architectures but also in terms of supported libraries. Last, Theano has not a reputation to be complex to debug, contrary to other deep learning libraries.

The third point makes Theano an uncomparable tool for the computer scientist because it is not specific to deep learning. Although Theano presents the same methods for deep learning than other libraries, its underlying principles are very different: in fact, Theano compiles the computation graph on the target architecture. This compilation step makes Theano's specificity, and it should be defined as a **mathematical expression compiler**, designed with machine learning in mind. The symbolic differentiation is one of the most useful features that Theano offers for implementing non-standard deep architectures. Therefore, Theano is able to address a much larger range of numerical problems, and can be used to find the solution that minimizes any problem expressed with a differentiable loss or energy function, given an existing dataset.

What you need for this book

Theano installation requires `conda` or `pip`, and the install process is the same under Windows, Mac OS and Linux.

The code has been tested under Mac OS and Linux Ubuntu. There might be some specificities for Windows, such as modifying the paths, that the Windows developer will solve quite easily.

Code examples suppose there exists on your computer a shared folder, where to download, uncompress, and preprocess database files that can be very voluminous and should not be left inside code repositories. This practice helps spare some disk space, while multiple code directories and users can use the same copy of the database. The folder is usually shared between user spaces:

```
sudo mkdir /sharedfiles
sudo chmod 777 /sharedfiles
```

Who this book is for

This book is indented to provide the widest overview of deep learning, with Theano as support technology. The book is designed for the beginner in deep learning and artificial intelligence, as well as the computer programmer who wants to get a cross domain experience and become familiar with Theano and its supporting libraries. This book helps the reader to begin with deep learning, as well as getting the relevant and practical informations in deep learning.

Are required some basic skills in Python programming and computer science, as well as skills in elementary algebra and calculus. The underlying technology for all experiments is Theano, and the book provides first an in-depth presentation of the core technology first, then introduces later on some libraries to do some reuse of existing modules.

The approach of this book is to introduce the reader to deep learning, describing the different types of networks and their applications, and in the meantime, exploring the possibilities offered by Theano, a deep learning technology, that will be the support for all implementations. This book sums up some of the best performing nets and state of the art results and helps the reader get the global picture of deep learning, taking her from the simple to the complex nets gradually.

Since Python has become the main programming language in data science, this book tries to cover all that a *Python programmer* needs to know to do deep learning with Python and Theano.

The book will introduce two abstraction frameworks on top of Theano, Lasagne and Keras, which can simplify the development of more complex nets, but do not prevent you from understanding the underlying concepts.

Conventions

In this book, you will find a number of text styles that distinguish between different kinds of information. Here are some examples of these styles and an explanation of their meaning.

Code words in text, database table names, folder names, filenames, file extensions, pathnames, dummy URLs, user input, and Twitter handles are shown as follows: "The operator is defined by a class deriving from the generic `theano.Op` class."

A block of code is set as follows:

```
import theano, numpy

class AXPBOp(theano.Op):
    """
    This creates an Op that takes x to a*x+b.
    """
    __props__ = ("a", "b")
```

Any command-line input or output is written as follows:

```
gsutil mb -l europe-west1 gs://keras_sentiment_analysis
```

New terms and **important words** are shown in bold. Words that you see on the screen, for example, in menus or dialog boxes, appear in the text like this: "Clicking the **Next** button moves you to the next screen."

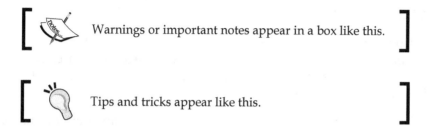

[Warnings or important notes appear in a box like this.]

[Tips and tricks appear like this.]

Reader feedback

Feedback from our readers is always welcome. Let us know what you think about this book—what you liked or disliked. Reader feedback is important for us as it helps us develop titles that you will really get the most out of.

To send us general feedback, simply e-mail feedback@packtpub.com, and mention the book's title in the subject of your message.

If there is a topic that you have expertise in and you are interested in either writing or contributing to a book, see our author guide at www.packtpub.com/authors.

Customer support

Now that you are the proud owner of a Packt book, we have a number of things to help you to get the most from your purchase.

Downloading the example code

You can download the example code files for this book from your account at http://www.packtpub.com. If you purchased this book elsewhere, you can visit http://www.packtpub.com/support and register to have the files e-mailed directly to you.

You can download the code files by following these steps:

1. Log in or register to our website using your e-mail address and password.
2. Hover the mouse pointer on the **SUPPORT** tab at the top.
3. Click on **Code Downloads & Errata**.

4. Enter the name of the book in the **Search** box.

5. Select the book for which you're looking to download the code files.

6. Choose from the drop-down menu where you purchased this book from.

7. Click on **Code Download**.

You can also download the code files by clicking on the **Code Files** button on the book's webpage at the Packt Publishing website. This page can be accessed by entering the book's name in the **Search** box. Please note that you need to be logged in to your Packt account.

Once the file is downloaded, please make sure that you unzip or extract the folder using the latest version of:

- WinRAR / 7-Zip for Windows

- Zipeg / iZip / UnRarX for Mac

- 7-Zip / PeaZip for Linux

The code bundle for the book is also hosted on GitHub at `https://github.com/PacktPublishing/Deep-Learning-with-Theano`. We also have other code bundles from our rich catalog of books and videos available at `https://github.com/PacktPublishing/`. Check them out!

Errata

Although we have taken every care to ensure the accuracy of our content, mistakes do happen. If you find a mistake in one of our books — maybe a mistake in the text or the code — we would be grateful if you could report this to us. By doing so, you can save other readers from frustration and help us improve subsequent versions of this book. If you find any errata, please report them by visiting `http://www.packtpub.com/submit-errata`, selecting your book, clicking on the **Errata Submission Form** link, and entering the details of your errata. Once your errata are verified, your submission will be accepted and the errata will be uploaded to our website or added to any list of existing errata under the Errata section of that title.

To view the previously submitted errata, go to `https://www.packtpub.com/books/content/support` and enter the name of the book in the search field. The required information will appear under the **Errata** section.

Piracy

Piracy of copyrighted material on the Internet is an ongoing problem across all media. At Packt, we take the protection of our copyright and licenses very seriously. If you come across any illegal copies of our works in any form on the Internet, please provide us with the location address or website name immediately so that we can pursue a remedy.

Please contact us at `copyright@packtpub.com` with a link to the suspected pirated material.

We appreciate your help in protecting our authors and our ability to bring you valuable content.

Questions

If you have a problem with any aspect of this book, you can contact us at `questions@packtpub.com`, and we will do our best to address the problem.

1
Theano Basics

This chapter presents Theano as a compute engine and the basics for symbolic computing with Theano. Symbolic computing consists of building graphs of operations that will be optimized later on for a specific architecture, using the computation libraries available for this architecture.

Although this chapter might appear to be a long way from practical applications, it is essential to have an understanding of the technology for the following chapters; what is it capable of and what value does it bring? All the following chapters address the applications of Theano when building all possible deep learning architectures.

Theano may be defined as a library for scientific computing; it has been available since 2007 and is particularly suited to deep learning. Two important features are at the core of any deep learning library: tensor operations, and the capability to run the code on CPU or **Graphical Computation Unit (GPU)**. These two features enable us to work with a massive amount of multi-dimensional data. Moreover, Theano proposes automatic differentiation, a very useful feature that can solve a wider range of numeric optimizations than deep learning problems.

The chapter covers the following topics:

- Theano installation and loading
- Tensors and algebra
- Symbolic programming
- Graphs
- Automatic differentiation
- GPU programming
- Profiling
- Configuration

The need for tensors

Usually, input data is represented with multi-dimensional arrays:

- **Images have three dimensions**: The number of channels, the width, and the height of the image

- **Sounds and times series have one dimension**: The duration

- **Natural language sequences can be represented by two-dimensional arrays**: The duration and the alphabet length or the vocabulary length

We'll see more examples of input data arrays in the future chapters.

In Theano, multi-dimensional arrays are implemented with an abstraction class, named **tensor**, with many more transformations available than traditional arrays in a computer language such as Python.

At each stage of a neural net, computations such as matrix multiplications involve multiple operations on these multi-dimensional arrays.

Classical arrays in programming languages do not have enough built-in functionalities to quickly and adequately address multi-dimensional computations and manipulations.

Computations on multi-dimensional arrays have a long history of optimizations, with tons of libraries and hardware. One of the most important gains in speed has been permitted by the massive parallel architecture of the GPU, with computation ability on a large number of cores, from a few hundred to a few thousand.

Compared to the traditional CPU, for example, a quadricore, 12-core, or 32-core engine, the gains with GPU can range from 5x to 100x, even if part of the code is still being executed on the CPU (data loading, GPU piloting, and result outputting). The main bottleneck with the use of GPU is usually the transfer of data between the memory of the CPU and the memory of the GPU, but still, when well programmed, the use of GPU helps bring a significant increase in speed of an order of magnitude. Getting results in days rather than months, or hours rather than days, is an undeniable benefit for experimentation.

The Theano engine has been designed to address the challenges of multi-dimensional arrays and architecture abstraction from the beginning.

There is another undeniable benefit of Theano for scientific computation: the automatic differentiation of functions of multi-dimensional arrays, a well-suited feature for model parameter inference via objective function minimization. Such a feature facilitates experimentation by releasing the pain to compute derivatives, which might not be very complicated, but are prone to many errors.

Installing and loading Theano

In this section, we'll install Theano, run it on the CPU and GPU devices, and save the configuration.

Conda package and environment manager

The easiest way to install Theano is to use `conda`, a cross-platform package and environment manager.

If `conda` is not already installed on your operating system, the fastest way to install `conda` is to download the `miniconda` installer from `https://conda.io/miniconda.html`. For example, for `conda under Linux 64 bit and Python 2.7`, use this command:

```
wget https://repo.continuum.io/miniconda/Miniconda2-latest-Linux-x86_64.sh
chmod +x Miniconda2-latest-Linux-x86_64.sh
bash ./Miniconda2-latest-Linux-x86_64.sh
```

Conda enables us to create new environments in which versions of Python (2 or 3) and the installed packages may differ. The `conda` root environment uses the same version of Python as the version installed on the system on which you installed `conda`.

Installing and running Theano on CPU

Let's install Theano:

```
conda install theano
```

Run a Python session and try the following commands to check your configuration:

```
>>> from theano import theano

>>> theano.config.device
'cpu'

>>> theano.config.floatX
'float64'

>>> print(theano.config)
```

The last command prints all the configuration of Theano. The `theano.config` object contains keys to many configuration options.

To infer the configuration options, Theano looks first at the ~/.theanorc file, then at any environment variables that are available, which override the former options, and lastly at the variable set in the code that are first in order of precedence:

```
>>> theano.config.floatX='float32'
```

Some of the properties might be read-only and cannot be changed in the code, but floatX, which sets the default floating point precision for floats, is among the properties that can be changed directly in the code.

 It is advised to use float32 since GPU has a long history without float64. float64 execution speed on GPU is slower, sometimes much slower (2x to 32x on latest generation Pascal hardware), and float32 precision is enough in practice.

GPU drivers and libraries

Theano enables the use of GPU, units that are usually used to compute the graphics to display on the computer screen.

To have Theano work on the GPU as well, a GPU backend library is required on your system.

The CUDA library (for NVIDIA GPU cards only) is the main choice for GPU computations. There is also the OpenCL standard, which is open source but far less developed, and much more experimental and rudimentary on Theano.

Most scientific computations still occur on NVIDIA cards at the moment. If you have an NVIDIA GPU card, download CUDA from the NVIDIA website, https://developer.nvidia.com/cuda-downloads, and install it. The installer will install the latest version of the GPU drivers first, if they are not already installed. It will install the CUDA library in the /usr/local/cuda directory.

Install the cuDNN library, a library by NVIDIA, that offers faster implementations of some operations for the GPU. To install it, I usually copy the /usr/local/cuda directory to a new directory, /usr/local/cuda-{CUDA_VERSION}-cudnn-{CUDNN_VERSION}, so that I can choose the version of CUDA and cuDNN, depending on the deep learning technology I use and its compatibility.

In your .bashrc profile, add the following line to set the $PATH and $LD_LIBRARY_ PATH variables:

export PATH=/usr/local/cuda-8.0-cudnn-5.1/bin:$PATH

export LD_LIBRARY_PATH=/usr/local/cuda-8.0-cudnn-5.1/lib64:/usr/local/ cuda-8.0-cudnn-5.1/lib:$LD_LIBRARY_PATH

Installing and running Theano on GPU

N-dimensional GPU arrays have been implemented in Python in six different GPU libraries (Theano/CudaNdarray, PyCUDA/ GPUArray, CUDAMAT/ CUDAMatrix, PYOPENCL/GPUArray, Clyther, Copperhead), are a subset of NumPy.ndarray. Libgpuarray is a backend library to have them in a common interface with the same property.

To install libgpuarray with conda, use this command:

conda install pygpu

To run Theano in GPU mode, you need to configure the config.device variable before execution since it is a read-only variable once the code is run. Run this command with the THEANO_FLAGS environment variable:

```
THEANO_FLAGS="device=cuda,floatX=float32" python
>>> import theano
Using cuDNN version 5110 on context None
Mapped name None to device cuda: Tesla K80 (0000:83:00.0)

>>> theano.config.device
'gpu'

>>> theano.config.floatX
'float32'
```

The first return shows that GPU device has been correctly detected, and specifies which GPU it uses.

By default, Theano activates CNMeM, a faster CUDA memory allocator. An initial pre-allocation can be specified with the `gpuarra.preallocate` option. At the end, my launch command will be as follows:

```
THEANO_FLAGS="device=cuda,floatX=float32,gpuarray.preallocate=0.8" python
>>> from theano import theano
Using cuDNN version 5110 on context None
Preallocating 9151/11439 Mb (0.800000) on cuda
Mapped name None to device cuda: Tesla K80 (0000:83:00.0)
```

The first line confirms that cuDNN is active, the second confirms memory pre-allocation. The third line gives the default **context name** (that is, `None` when flag `device=cuda` is set) and the model of GPU used, while the default context name for the CPU will always be `cpu`.

It is possible to specify a different GPU than the first one, setting the device to `cuda0`, `cuda1`,... for multi-GPU computers. It is also possible to run a program on multiple GPU in parallel or in sequence (when the memory of one GPU is not sufficient), in particular when training very deep neural nets, as for classification of full images as described in *Chapter 7, Classifying Images with Residual Networks*. In this case, the `contexts=dev0->cuda0;dev1->cuda1;dev2->cuda2;dev3->cuda3` flag activates multiple GPUs instead of one, and designates the context name to each GPU device to be used in the code. Here is an example on a 4-GPU instance:

```
THEANO_FLAGS="contexts=dev0->cuda0;dev1->cuda1;dev2->cuda2;dev3-
>cuda3,floatX=float32,gpuarray.preallocate=0.8" python
>>> import theano
Using cuDNN version 5110 on context None
Preallocating 9177/11471 Mb (0.800000) on cuda0
Mapped name dev0 to device cuda0: Tesla K80 (0000:83:00.0)
Using cuDNN version 5110 on context dev1
Preallocating 9177/11471 Mb (0.800000) on cuda1
Mapped name dev1 to device cuda1: Tesla K80 (0000:84:00.0)
Using cuDNN version 5110 on context dev2
Preallocating 9177/11471 Mb (0.800000) on cuda2
Mapped name dev2 to device cuda2: Tesla K80 (0000:87:00.0)
Using cuDNN version 5110 on context dev3
Preallocating 9177/11471 Mb (0.800000) on cuda3
Mapped name dev3 to device cuda3: Tesla K80 (0000:88:00.0)
```

To assign computations to a specific GPU in this multi-GPU setting, the names we choose, dev0, dev1, dev2, and dev3, have been mapped to each device (cuda0, cuda1, cuda2, cuda3).

This name mapping enables to write codes that are independent of the underlying GPU assignments and libraries (CUDA or others).

To keep the current configuration flags active at every Python session or execution without using environment variables, save your configuration in the ~/.theanorc file as follows:

```
[global]
floatX = float32
device = cuda0
[gpuarray]
preallocate = 1
```

Now you can simply run python command. You are now all set.

Tensors

In Python, some scientific libraries such as NumPy provide multi-dimensional arrays. Theano doesn't replace Numpy, but it works in concert with it. NumPy is used for the initialization of tensors.

To perform the same computation on CPU and GPU, variables are symbolic and represented by the tensor class, an abstraction, and writing numerical expressions consists of building a computation graph of variable nodes and apply nodes. Depending on the platform on which the computation graph will be compiled, tensors are replaced by either of the following:

- A TensorType variable, which has to be on CPU
- A GpuArrayType variable, which has to be on GPU

That way, the code can be written indifferently of the platform where it will be executed.

Here are a few tensor objects:

Object class	Number of dimensions	Example
theano.tensor.scalar	0-dimensional array	1, 2.5
theano.tensor.vector	1-dimensional array	[0,3,20]
theano.tensor.matrix	2-dimensional array	[[2,3][1,5]]
theano.tensor.tensor3	3-dimensional array	[[[2,3][1,5]],[[1,2],[3,4]]]

Playing with these Theano objects in the Python shell gives us a better idea:

```
>>> import theano.tensor as T

>>> T.scalar()
<TensorType(float32, scalar)>

>>> T.iscalar()
<TensorType(int32, scalar)>

>>> T.fscalar()
<TensorType(float32, scalar)>

>>> T.dscalar()
<TensorType(float64, scalar)>
```

With i, l, f, or d in front of the object name, you initiate a tensor of a given type, integer32, integer64, float32, or float64. For real-valued (floating point) data, it is advised to use the direct form T.scalar() instead of the f or d variants since the direct form will use your current configuration for floats:

```
>>> theano.config.floatX = 'float64'

>>> T.scalar()
<TensorType(float64, scalar)>

>>> T.fscalar()
<TensorType(float32, scalar)>

>>> theano.config.floatX = 'float32'

>>> T.scalar()
<TensorType(float32, scalar)>
```

Symbolic variables do either of the following:

- Play the role of placeholders, as a starting point to build your graph of numerical operations (such as addition, multiplication): they receive the flow of the incoming data during the evaluation once the graph has been compiled

- Represent intermediate or output results

Symbolic variables and operations are both part of a computation graph that will be compiled either on CPU or GPU for fast execution. Let's write our first computation graph consisting of a simple addition:

```
>>> x = T.matrix('x')

>>> y = T.matrix('y')

>>> z = x + y

>>> theano.pp(z)
'(x + y)'

>>> z.eval({x: [[1, 2], [1, 3]], y: [[1, 0], [3, 4]]})
array([[ 2.,    2.],
       [ 4.,    7.]], dtype=float32)
```

First, two symbolic variables, or *variable nodes*, are created, with the names x and y, and an addition operation, an *apply node*, is applied between both of them to create a new symbolic variable, z, in the computation graph.

The pretty print function, pp, prints the expression represented by Theano symbolic variables. Eval evaluates the value of the output variable, z, when the first two variables, x and y, are initialized with two numerical 2-dimensional arrays.

The following example shows the difference between the variables x and y, and their names x and y:

```
>>> a = T.matrix()

>>> b = T.matrix()

>>> theano.pp(a + b)
'(<TensorType(float32, matrix)> + <TensorType(float32, matrix)>)'.
```

Without names, it is more complicated to trace the nodes in a large graph. When printing the computation graph, names significantly help diagnose problems, while variables are only used to handle the objects in the graph:

```
>>> x = T.matrix('x')

>>> x = x + x

>>> theano.pp(x)
'(x + x)'
```

Here, the original symbolic variable, named x, does not change and stays part of the computation graph. x + x creates a new symbolic variable we assign to the Python variable x.

Note also that with the names, the plural form initializes multiple tensors at the same time:

```
>>> x, y, z = T.matrices('x', 'y', 'z')
```

Now, let's have a look at the different functions to display the graph.

Graphs and symbolic computing

Let's take back the simple addition example and present different ways to display the same information:

```
>>> x = T.matrix('x')

>>> y = T.matrix('y')

>>> z = x + y

>>> z

Elemwise{add,no_inplace}.0

>>> theano.pp(z)

'(x + y)'

>>> theano.printing.pprint(z)

'(x + y)'

>>> theano.printing.debugprint(z)
Elemwise{add,no_inplace} [id A] ''
 |x [id B]
 |y [id C]
```

Here, the `debugprint` function prints the pre-compilation graph, the unoptimized graph. In this case, it is composed of two variable nodes, x and y, and an apply node, the elementwise addition, with the `no_inplace` option. The `inplace` option will be used in the optimized graph to save memory and re-use the memory of the input to store the result of the operation.

If the `graphviz` and `pydot` libraries have been installed, the `pydotprint` command outputs a PNG image of the graph:

```
>>> theano.printing.pydotprint(z)
The output file is available at ~/.theano/compiledir_Linux-4.4--
generic-x86_64-with-Ubuntu-16.04-xenial-x86_64-2.7.12-64/theano.
pydotprint.gpu.png.
```

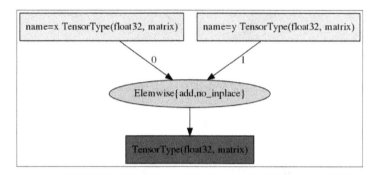

You might have noticed that the `z.eval` command takes while to execute the first time. The reason for this delay is the time required to optimize the mathematical expression and compile the code for the CPU or GPU before being evaluated.

The compiled expression can be obtained explicitly and used as a function that behaves as a traditional Python function:

```
>>> addition = theano.function([x, y], [z])

>>> addition([[1, 2], [1, 3]], [[1, 0], [3, 4]])
[array([[ 2.,   2.],
        [ 4.,   7.]], dtype=float32)]
```

The first argument in the function creation is a list of variables representing the input nodes of the graph. The second argument is the array of output variables. To print the post compilation graph, use this command:

```
>>> theano.printing.debugprint(addition)
HostFromGpu(gpuarray) [id A] ''   3
 |GpuElemwise{Add}[(0, 0)]<gpuarray> [id B] ''   2
   |GpuFromHost<None> [id C] ''   1
```

```
|  |x [id D]
|GpuFromHost<None> [id E] ''    0
   |y [id F]
```

```
>>> theano.printing.pydotprint(addition)
```

The output file is available at ~/.theano/compiledir_Linux-4.4--generic-x86_64-with-Ubuntu-16.04-xenial-x86_64-2.7.12-64/theano.pydotprint.gpu.png:

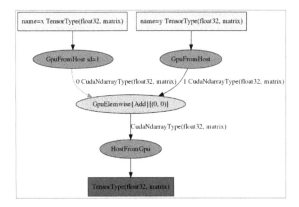

This case has been printed while using the GPU. During compilation, each operation has chosen the available GPU implementation. The main program still runs on CPU, where the data resides, but a GpuFromHost instruction performs a data transfer from the CPU to the GPU for input, while the opposite operation, HostFromGpu, fetches the result for the main program to display it:

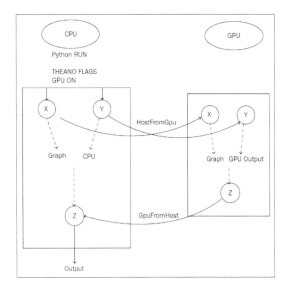

Theano performs some mathematical optimizations, such as grouping elementwise operations, adding a new value to the previous addition:

```
>>> z= z * x
```

```
>>> theano.printing.debugprint(theano.function([x,y],z))
HostFromGpu(gpuarray) [id A] ''    3
 |GpuElemwise{Composite{((i0 + i1) * i0)}}[(0, 0)]<gpuarray> [id B] ''
2
   |GpuFromHost<None> [id C] ''    1
   | |x [id D]
   |GpuFromHost<None> [id E] ''    0
     |y [id F]
```

The number of nodes in the graph has not increased: two additions have been merged into one node. Such optimizations make it more tricky to debug, so we'll show you at the end of this chapter how to disable optimizations for debugging.

Lastly, let's see a bit more about setting the initial value with NumPy:

```
>>> theano.config.floatX
'float32'
```

```
>>> x = T.matrix()
```

```
>>> x
<TensorType(float32, matrix)>
```

```
>>> y = T.matrix()
```

```
>>> addition = theano.function([x, y], [x+y])
```

```
>>> addition(numpy.ones((2,2)),numpy.zeros((2,2)))
Traceback (most recent call last):
  File "<stdin>", line 1, in <module>
  File "/usr/local/lib/python2.7/site-packages/theano/compile/
function_module.py", line 786, in __call__
    allow_downcast=s.allow_downcast)
```

```
  File "/usr/local/lib/python2.7/site-packages/theano/tensor/type.py",
line 139, in filter
    raise TypeError(err_msg, data)
TypeError: ('Bad input argument to theano function with name
"<stdin>:1" at index 0(0-based)', 'TensorType(float32, matrix) cannot
store a value of dtype float64 without risking loss of precision.
If you do not mind this loss, you can: 1) explicitly cast your data
to float32, or 2) set "allow_input_downcast=True" when calling
"function".', array([[ 1.,   1.],
       [ 1.,   1.]]))
```

Executing the function on the NumPy arrays throws an error related to loss of precision, since the NumPy arrays here have float64 and int64 dtypes, but x and y are float32. There are multiple solutions to this; the first is to create the NumPy arrays with the right dtype:

```
>>> import numpy

>>> addition(numpy.ones((2,2), dtype=theano.config.floatX),numpy.
zeros((2,2), dtype=theano.config.floatX))
[array([[ 1.,   1.],
       [ 1.,   1.]], dtype=float32)]
```

Alternatively, cast the NumPy arrays (in particular for numpy.diag, which does not allow us to choose the dtype directly):

```
>>> addition(numpy.ones((2,2)).astype(theano.config.floatX),numpy.
diag((2,3)).astype(theano.config.floatX))
[array([[ 3.,   1.],
       [ 1.,   4.]], dtype=float32)]
```

Or we could allow downcasting:

```
>>> addition = theano.function([x, y], [x+y],allow_input_
downcast=True)

>>> addition(numpy.ones((2,2)),numpy.zeros((2,2)))
[array([[ 1.,   1.],
       [ 1.,   1.]], dtype=float32)]
```

Operations on tensors

We have seen how to create a computation graph composed of symbolic variables and operations, and compile the resulting expression for an evaluation or as a function, either on GPU or on CPU.

As tensors are very important to deep learning, Theano provides lots of operators to work with tensors. Most operators that exist in scientific computing libraries such as NumPy for numerical arrays have their equivalent in Theano and have a similar name, in order to be more familiar to NumPy's users. But contrary to NumPy, expressions written with Theano can be compiled either on CPU or GPU.

This, for example, is the case for tensor creation:

- `T.zeros()`, `T.ones()`, `T.eye()` operators take a shape tuple as input
- `T.zeros_like()`, `T.one_like()`, `T.identity_like()` use the shape of the tensor argument
- `T.arange()`, `T.mgrid()`, `T.ogrid()` are used for range and mesh grid arrays

Let's have a look in the Python shell:

```
>>> a = T.zeros((2,3))

>>> a.eval()
array([[ 0.,   0.,   0.],
       [ 0.,   0.,   0.]])

>>> b = T.identity_like(a)

>>> b.eval()
array([[ 1.,   0.,   0.],
       [ 0.,   1.,   0.]])

>>> c = T.arange(10)

>>> c.eval()
array([0, 1, 2, 3, 4, 5, 6, 7, 8, 9])
```

Information such as the number of dimensions, `ndim`, and the type, `dtype`, are defined at tensor creation and cannot be modified later:

```
>>> c.ndim
1

>>> c.dtype
'int64'

>>> c.type
TensorType(int64, vector)
```

Some other information, such as shape, is evaluated by the computation graph:

```
>>> a = T.matrix()

>>> a.shape
Shape.0

>>> a.shape.eval({a: [[1, 2], [1, 3]]})
array([2, 2])

>>> shape_fct = theano.function([a],a.shape)

>>> shape_fct([[1, 2], [1, 3]])
array([2, 2])

>>> n = T.iscalar()

>>> c = T.arange(n)

>>> c.shape.eval({n:10})
array([10])
```

Dimension manipulation operators

The first type of operator on tensor is for **dimension manipulation**. This type of operator takes a tensor as input and returns a new tensor:

Operator	Description
T.reshape	Reshape the dimension of the tensor
T.fill	Fill the array with the same value
T.flatten	Return all elements in a 1-dimensional tensor (vector)
T.dimshuffle	Change the order of the dimension, more or less like NumPy's transpose method – the main difference is that it can be used to add or remove broadcastable dimensions (of length 1).
T.squeeze	Reshape by removing dimensions equal to 1
T.transpose	Transpose
T.swapaxes	Swap dimensions
T.sort, T.argsort	Sort tensor, or indices of the order

For example, the reshape operation's output represents a new tensor, containing the same elements in the same order but in a different shape:

```
>>> a = T.arange(10)

>>> b = T.reshape( a, (5,2) )

>>> b.eval()
array([[0, 1],
       [2, 3],
       [4, 5],
       [6, 7],
       [8, 9]])
```

The operators can be chained:

```
>>> T.arange(10).reshape((5,2))[::-1].T.eval()
array([[8, 6, 4, 2, 0],
       [9, 7, 5, 3, 1]])
```

Notice the use of traditional `[::-1]` array access by indices in Python and the `.T` for `T.transpose`.

Elementwise operators

The second type of operations on multi-dimensional arrays is elementwise operators.

The first category of elementwise operations takes two input tensors of the same dimensions and applies a function, `f`, elementwise, which means on all pairs of elements with the same coordinates in the respective tensors `f([a,b],[c,d]) = [ f(a,c), f(b,d)]`. For example, here's multiplication:

```
>>> a, b = T.matrices('a', 'b')

>>> z = a * b

>>> z.eval({a:numpy.ones((2,2)).astype(theano.config.floatX), b:numpy.
diag((3,3)).astype(theano.config.floatX)})
array([[ 3., 0.],
       [ 0., 3.]])
```

The same multiplication can be written as follows:

```
>>> z = T.mul(a, b)
```

`T.add` and `T.mul` accept an arbitrary number of inputs:

```
>>> z = T.mul(a, b, a, b)
```

Some elementwise operators accept only one input tensor `f([a,b]) = [f(a),f(b)])`:

```
>>> a = T.matrix()

>>> z = a ** 2

>>> z.eval({a:numpy.diag((3,3)).astype(theano.config.floatX)})
array([[ 9.,   0.],
       [ 0.,   9.]])
```

Lastly, I would like to introduce the mechanism of **broadcasting**. When the input tensors do not have the same number of dimensions, the missing dimension will be broadcasted, meaning the tensor will be repeated along that dimension to match the dimension of the other tensor. For example, taking one multi-dimensional tensor and a scalar (0-dimensional) tensor, the scalar will be repeated in an array of the same shape as the multi-dimensional tensor so that the final shapes will match and the elementwise operation will be applied, `f([a,b], c) = [ f(a,c), f(b,c) ]`:

```
>>> a = T.matrix()

>>> b = T.scalar()

>>> z = a * b

>>> z.eval({a:numpy.diag((3,3)).astype(theano.config.floatX),b:3})
array([[ 6.,   0.],
       [ 0.,   6.]])
```

Here is a list of elementwise operations:

Operator	Other form	Description
`T.add, T.sub, T.mul, T.truediv`	`+, -, *, /`	Add, subtract, multiply, divide
`T.pow, T.sqrt`	`**, T.sqrt`	Power, square root
`T.exp, T.log`		Exponential, logarithm
`T.cos, T.sin, T.tan`		Cosine, sine, tangent
`T.cosh, T.sinh, T.tanh`		Hyperbolic trigonometric functions
`T.intdiv, T.mod`	`//, %`	Int div, modulus

Operator	Other form	Description
`T.floor, T.ceil, T.round`		Rounding operators
`T.sgn`		Sign
`T.and_, T.xor, T.or_, T.invert`	`&, ^, |, ~`	Bitwise operators
`T.gt, T.lt, T.ge, T.le`	`>, <, >=, <=`	Comparison operators
`T.eq, T.neq, T.isclose`		Equality, inequality, or close with tolerance
`T.isnan`		Comparison with NaN (not a number)
`T.abs_`		Absolute value
`T.minimum, T.maximum`		Minimum and maximum elementwise
`T.clip`		Clip the values between a maximum and a minimum
`T.switch`		Switch
`T.cast`		Tensor type casting

The elementwise operators always return an array with the same size as the input array. `T.switch` and `T.clip` accept three inputs.

In particular, `T.switch` will perform the traditional `switch` operator elementwise:

```
>>> cond = T.vector('cond')

>>> x,y = T.vectors('x','y')

>>> z = T.switch(cond, x, y)

>>> z.eval({ cond:[1,0], x:[10,10], y:[3,2] })
array([ 10.,    2.], dtype=float32)
```

At the same position where `cond` tensor is true, the result has the x value; otherwise, if it is false, it has the y value.

For the `T.switch` operator, there is a specific equivalent, `ifelse`, that takes a scalar condition instead of a tensor condition. It is not an elementwise operation though, and supports lazy evaluation (not all elements are computed if the answer is known before it finishes):

```
>>> from theano.ifelse import ifelse

>>> z=ifelse(1, 5, 4)

>>> z.eval()
array(5, dtype=int8)
```

Reduction operators

Another type of operation on tensors is reductions, reducing all elements to a scalar value in most cases, and for that purpose, it is required to scan all the elements of the tensor to compute the output:

Operator	Description
`T.max, T.argmax, T.max_and_argmax`	Maximum, index of the maximum
`T.min, T.argmin`	Minimum, index of the minimum
`T.sum, T.prod`	Sum or product of elements
`T.mean, T.var, T.std`	Mean, variance, and standard deviation
`T.all, T.any`	AND and OR operations with all elements
`T.ptp`	Range of elements (minimum, maximum)

These operations are also available row-wise or column-wise by specifying an axis and the dimension along which the reduction is performed:

```
>>> a = T.matrix('a')

>>> T.max(a).eval({a:[[1,2],[3,4]]})
array(4.0, dtype=float32)

>>> T.max(a,axis=0).eval({a:[[1,2],[3,4]]})
array([ 3.,   4.], dtype=float32)

>>> T.max(a,axis=1).eval({a:[[1,2],[3,4]]})
array([ 2.,   4.], dtype=float32)
```

Linear algebra operators

A third category of operations are the linear algebra operators, such as matrix multiplication:

$$A \cdot B = \left[\; c_{i,j} \; \right] = \left[\sum_k a_{i,k} b_{k,j} \right]$$

Also called inner product for vectors:

$$V \cdot W = \sum_k v_k w_k$$

Operator	Description
T.dot	Matrix multiplication/inner product
T.outer	Outer product

There are some generalized (T.tensordot to specify the axis), or batched (batched_dot, batched_tensordot) versions of the operators.

Lastly, a few operators remain and can be very useful, but they do not belong to any of the previous categories: T.concatenate concatenates the tensors along the specified dimension, T.stack creates a new dimension to stack the input tensors, and T.stacklist creates new patterns to stack tensors together:

```
>>> a = T.arange(10).reshape((5,2))

>>> b = a[::-1]

>>> b.eval()
array([[8, 9],
       [6, 7],
       [4, 5],
       [2, 3],
       [0, 1]])
>>> a.eval()
array([[0, 1],
       [2, 3],
       [4, 5],
       [6, 7],
       [8, 9]])
```

```
>>> T.concatenate([a,b]).eval()
array([[0, 1],
       [2, 3],
       [4, 5],
       [6, 7],
       [8, 9],
       [8, 9],
       [6, 7],
       [4, 5],
       [2, 3],
       [0, 1]])
>>> T.concatenate([a,b],axis=1).eval()
array([[0, 1, 8, 9],
       [2, 3, 6, 7],
       [4, 5, 4, 5],
       [6, 7, 2, 3],
       [8, 9, 0, 1]])

>>> T.stack([a,b]).eval()
array([[[0, 1],
        [2, 3],
        [4, 5],
        [6, 7],
        [8, 9]],
       [[8, 9],
        [6, 7],
        [4, 5],
        [2, 3],
        [0, 1]]])
```

An equivalent of the NumPy expressions `a[5:] = 5` and `a[5:] += 5` exists as two functions:

```
>>> a.eval()
array([[0, 1],
       [2, 3],
       [4, 5],
       [6, 7],
       [8, 9]])

>>> T.set_subtensor(a[3:], [-1,-1]).eval()
```

```
array([[ 0,   1],
       [ 2,   3],
       [ 4,   5],
       [-1,  -1],
       [-1,  -1]])

>>> T.inc_subtensor(a[3:], [-1,-1]).eval()
array([[0, 1],
       [2, 3],
       [4, 5],
       [5, 6],
       [7, 8]])
```

Unlike NumPy's syntax, the original tensor is not modified; instead, a new variable is created that represents the result of that modification. Therefore, the original variable a still refers to the original value, and the returned variable (here unassigned) represents the updated one, and the user should use that new variable in the rest of their computation.

Memory and variables

It is good practice to always cast float arrays to the `theano.config.floatX` type:

- Either at the array creation with `numpy.array(array, dtype=theano.config.floatX)`
- Or by casting the array as `array.as_type(theano.config.floatX)` so that when compiling on the GPU, the correct type is used

For example, let's transfer the data manually to the GPU (for which the default context is None), and for that purpose, we need to use `float32` values:

```
>>> theano.config.floatX = 'float32'

>>> a = T.matrix()

>>> b = a.transfer(None)

>>> b.eval({a:numpy.ones((2,2)).astype(theano.config.floatX)})
gpuarray.array([[ 1.   1.]
 [ 1.   1.]], dtype=float32)
```

```
>>> theano.printing.debugprint(b)
GpuFromHost<None> [id A] ''
 |<TensorType(float32, matrix)> [id B]
```

The `transfer(device)` functions, such as `transfer('cpu')`, enable us to move the data from one device to another one. It is particularly useful when parts of the graph have to be executed on different devices. Otherwise, Theano adds the transfer functions automatically to the GPU in the optimization phase:

```
>>> a = T.matrix('a')

>>> b = a ** 2

>>> sq = theano.function([a],b)

>>> theano.printing.debugprint(sq)
HostFromGpu(gpuarray) [id A] ''    2
 |GpuElemwise{Sqr}[(0, 0)]<gpuarray> [id B] ''    1
   |GpuFromHost<None> [id C] ''    0
     |a [id D]
```

Using the transfer function explicitly, Theano removes the transfer back to CPU. Leaving the output tensor on the GPU saves a costly transfer:

```
>>> b = b.transfer(None)

>>> sq = theano.function([a],b)

>>> theano.printing.debugprint(sq)
GpuElemwise{Sqr}[(0, 0)]<gpuarray> [id A] ''    1
 |GpuFromHost<None> [id B] ''    0
   |a [id C]
```

The default context for the CPU is `cpu`:

```
>>> b = a.transfer('cpu')

>>> theano.printing.debugprint(b)
<TensorType(float32, matrix)> [id A]
```

A hybrid concept between numerical values and symbolic variables is the shared variables. They can also lead to better performance on the GPU by avoiding transfers. Initializing a shared variable with the scalar zero:

```
>>> state = shared(0)

>>> state
```

```
<TensorType(int64, scalar)>

>>> state.get_value()
array(0)

>>> state.set_value(1)

>>> state.get_value()
array(1)
```

Shared values are designed to be shared between functions. They can also be seen as an internal state. They can be used indifferently from the GPU or the CPU compile code. By default, shared variables are created on the default device (here, cuda), except for scalar integer values (as is the case in the previous example).

It is possible to specify another context, such as cpu. In the case of multiple GPU instances, you'll define your contexts in the Python command line, and decide on which context to create the shared variables:

```
PATH=/usr/local/cuda-8.0-cudnn-5.1/bin:$PATH THEANO_FLAGS="contexts=dev0-
>cuda0;dev1->cuda1,floatX=float32,gpuarray.preallocate=0.8" python

>>> from theano import theano
Using cuDNN version 5110 on context dev0
Preallocating 9151/11439 Mb (0.800000) on cuda0
Mapped name dev0 to device cuda0: Tesla K80 (0000:83:00.0)
Using cuDNN version 5110 on context dev1
Preallocating 9151/11439 Mb (0.800000) on cuda1
Mapped name dev1 to device cuda1: Tesla K80 (0000:84:00.0)

>>> import theano.tensor as T

>>> import numpy

>>> theano.shared(numpy.random.random((1024, 1024)).astype('float32'),
target='dev1')
<GpuArrayType<dev1>(float32, (False, False))>
```

Functions and automatic differentiation

The previous section introduced the `function` instruction to compile the expression. In this section, we develop some of the following arguments in its signature:

```
def theano.function(inputs,
    outputs=None, updates=None, givens=None,
  allow_input_downcast=None, mode=None, profile=None,
    )
```

We've already used the `allow_input_downcast` feature to convert data from `float64` to `float32`, `int64` to `int32` and so on. The `mode` and `profile` features are also displayed because they'll be presented in the optimization and debugging section.

Input variables of a Theano function should be contained in a list, even when there is a single input.

For outputs, it is possible to use a list in the case of multiple outputs to be computed in parallel:

```
>>> a = T.matrix()

>>> ex = theano.function([a],[T.exp(a),T.log(a),a**2])

>>> ex(numpy.random.randn(3,3).astype(theano.config.floatX))
[array([[ 2.33447003,   0.30287042,   0.63557744],
       [ 0.18511547,   1.34327984,   0.42203984],
       [ 0.87083125,   5.01169062,   6.88732481]], dtype=float32),
array([[-0.16512829,          nan,          nan],
       [         nan, -1.2203927 ,          nan],
       [         nan,   0.47733498,  0.65735561]], dtype=float32),
array([[ 0.71873927,   1.42671108,   0.20540957],
       [ 2.84521151,   0.08709242,   0.74417454],
       [ 0.01912885,   2.59781313,   3.72367549]], dtype=float32)]
```

The second useful attribute is the `updates` attribute, used to set new values to shared variables once the expression has been evaluated:

```
>>> w = shared(1.0)

>>> x = T.scalar('x')

>>> mul = theano.function([x],updates=[(w,w*x)])

>>> mul(4)
[]

>>> w.get_value()
array(4.0)
```

Such a mechanism can be used as an internal state. The shared variable `w` has been defined outside the function.

With the `givens` parameter, it is possible to change the value of any symbolic variable in the graph, without changing the graph. The new value will then be used by all the other expressions that were pointing to it.

The last and most important feature in Theano is the automatic differentiation, which means that Theano computes the derivatives of all previous tensor operators. Such a differentiation is performed via the `theano.grad` operator:

```
>>> a = T.scalar()

>>> pow = a ** 2

>>> g = theano.grad(pow,a)

>>> theano.printing.pydotprint(g)

>>> theano.printing.pydotprint(theano.function([a],g))
```

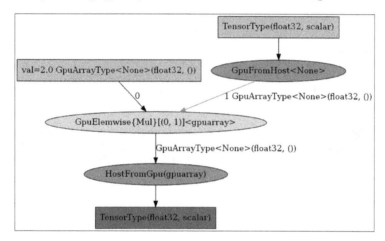

In the optimization graph, `theano.grad` has computed the gradient of a^2 with respect to a, which is a symbolic expression equivalent to 2 * a.

Note that it is only possible to take the gradient of a scalar, but the *wrt* variables can be arbitrary tensors.

Loops in symbolic computing

The Python `for` loop can be used outside the symbolic graph, as in a normal Python program. But outside the graph, a traditional Python `for` loop isn't compiled, so it will not be optimized with parallel and algebra libraries, cannot be automatically differentiated, and introduces costly data transfers if the computation subgraph has been optimized for GPU.

That's why a symbolic operator, T.scan, is designed to create a for loop as an operator inside the graph. Theano will unroll the loop into the graph structure and the whole unrolled loop is going to be compiled on the target architecture as the rest of the computation graph. Its signature is as follows:

```
def scan(fn,
          sequences=None,
          outputs_info=None,
          non_sequences=None,
          n_steps=None,
          truncate_gradient=-1,
          go_backwards=False,
          mode=None,
          name=None,
          profile=False,
          allow_gc=None,
          strict=False)
```

The scan operator is very useful to implement array loops, reductions, maps, multi-dimensional derivatives such as Jacobian or Hessian, and recurrences.

The scan operator is running the fn function repeatedly for n_steps. If n_steps is None, the operator will find out by the length of the sequences:

> The step fn function is a function that builds a symbolic graph, and that function will only get called once. However, that graph will then be compiled into another Theano function that will be called repeatedly. Some users try to pass a compile Theano function as fn, which is not possible.

Sequences are the lists of input variables to loop over. The number of steps will correspond to the shortest sequence in the list. Let's have a look:

```
>>> a = T.matrix()

>>> b = T.matrix()

>>> def fn(x): return x + 1

>>> results, updates = theano.scan(fn, sequences=a)

>>> f = theano.function([a], results, updates=updates)

>>> f(numpy.ones((2,3)).astype(theano.config.floatX))

array([[ 2.,   2.,   2.],
       [ 2.,   2.,   2.]], dtype=float32)
```

The scan operator has been running the function against all elements in the input tensor, a, and kept the same shape as the input tensor, (2,3).

 It is a good practice to add the updates returned by theano.scan in the theano.function, even if these updates are empty.

The arguments given to the fn function can be much more complicated. T.scan will call the fn function at each step with the following argument list, in the following order:

fn(**sequences** (if any), **prior results** (if needed), **non-sequences** (if any))

As shown in the following figure, three arrows are directed towards the fn step function and represent the three types of possible input at each time step in the loop:

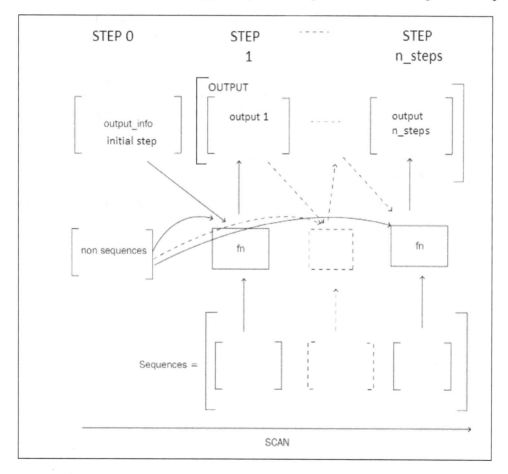

If specified, the `outputs_info` parameter is the initial state to use to start recurrence from. The parameter name does not sound very good, but the initial state also gives the shape information of the last state, as well as all other states. The initial state can be seen as the first output. The final output will be an array of states.

For example, to compute the cumulative sum in a vector, with an initial state of the sum at 0, use this code:

```
>>> a = T.vector()

>>> s0 = T.scalar("s0")

>>> def fn( current_element, prior ):
...     return prior + current_element

>>> results, updates = theano.scan(fn=fn,outputs_info=s0,sequences=a)

>>> f = theano.function([a,s0], results, updates=updates)

>>> f([0,3,5],0)
array([ 0., 3., 8.], dtype=float32)
```

When `outputs_info` is set, the first dimension of the `outputs_info` and sequence variables is the time step. The second dimension is the dimensionality of data at each time step.

In particular, `outputs_info` has the number of previous time-steps required to compute the first step.

Here is the same example, but with a vector at each time step instead of a scalar for the input data:

```
>>> a = T.matrix()

>>> s0 = T.scalar("s0")

>>> def fn( current_element, prior ):
...     return prior + current_element.sum()

>>> results, updates = theano.scan(fn=fn,outputs_info=s0,sequences=a)

>>> f = theano.function([a,s0], results, updates=updates)

>>> f(numpy.ones((20,5)).astype(theano.config.floatX),0)
```

```
array([   5.,    10.,    15.,    20.,    25.,    30.,    35.,    40.,    45.,
         50.,    55.,    60.,    65.,    70.,    75.,    80.,    85.,    90.,
         95.,   100.], dtype=float32)
```

Twenty steps along the rows (times) have accumulated the sum of all elements. Note that initial state (here 0) given by the `outputs_info` argument is not part of the output sequence.

The recurrent function, `fn`, may be provided with some fixed data, independent of the step in the loop, thanks to the `non_sequences` scan parameter:

```
>>> a = T.vector()

>>> s0 = T.scalar("s0")

>>> def fn( current_element, prior, non_seq ):
...     return non_seq * prior + current_element

>>> results, updates = theano.scan(fn=fn,n_
steps=10,sequences=a,outputs_info=T.constant(0.0),non_sequences=s0)

>>> f = theano.function([a,s0], results, updates=updates)

>>> f(numpy.ones((20)).astype(theano.),5)
array([   1.00000000e+00,    6.00000000e+00,    3.10000000e+01,
         1.56000000e+02,    7.81000000e+02,    3.90600000e+03,
         1.95310000e+04,    9.76560000e+04,    4.88281000e+05,
         2.44140600e+06], dtype=float32)
```

It is multiplying the prior value by 5 and adding the new element.

Note that `T.scan` in the optimized graph on GPU does not execute different iterations of the loop in parallel, even in the absence of recurrence.

Configuration, profiling and debugging

For debugging purpose, Theano can print more verbose information and offers different optimization modes:

```
>>> theano.config.exception_verbosity='high'

>>> theano.config.mode
'Mode'

>>> theano.config.optimizer='fast_compile'
```

In order for Theano to use the `config.optimizer` value, the mode has to be set to `Mode`, otherwise the value in `config.mode` will be used:

config.mode / function mode	config.optimizer (*)	Description
FAST_RUN	fast_run	Default; best run performance, slow compilation
FAST_RUN	None	Disable optimizations
FAST_COMPILE	fast_compile	Reduce the number of optimizations, compiles faster
None		Use the default mode, equivalent to FAST_RUN; optimizer=None
NanGuardMode		NaNs, Infs, and abnormally big value will raise errors
DebugMode		Self-checks and assertions during compilation

The same parameter as in `config.mode` can be used in the `Mode` parameter in the function compile:

```
>>> f = theano.function([a,s0], results, updates=updates, mode='FAST_COMPILE')
```

Disabling optimization and choosing high verbosity will help finding errors in the computation graph.

For debugging on the GPU, you need to set a synchronous execution with the environment variable `CUDA_LAUNCH_BLOCKING`, since GPU execution is by default, fully asynchronous:

```
CUDA_LAUNCH_BLOCKING=1 python
```

To find out the origin of the latencies in your computation graph, Theano provides a profiling mode.

Activate profiling:

```
>>> theano.config.profile=True
```

Activate memory profiling:

```
>>> theano.config.profile_memory=True
```

Activate profiling of optimization phase:

```
>>> theano.config.profile_optimizer=True
```

Or directly during compilation:

```
>>> f = theano.function([a,s0], results, profile=True)

>>> f.profile.summary()
Function profiling
==================
  Message: <stdin>:1
  Time in 1 calls to Function.__call__: 1.490116e-03s
  Time in Function.fn.__call__: 1.251936e-03s (84.016%)
  Time in thunks: 1.203537e-03s (80.768%)
  Total compile time: 1.720619e-01s
    Number of Apply nodes: 14
    Theano Optimizer time: 1.382768e-01s
       Theano validate time: 1.308680e-03s
    Theano Linker time (includes C, CUDA code generation/compiling):
2.405691e-02s
       Import time 1.272917e-03s
       Node make_thunk time 2.329803e-02s

Time in all call to theano.grad() 0.000000e+00s
Time since theano import 520.661s
Class
---
<% time> <sum %> <apply time> <time per call> <type> <#call> <#apply>
<Class name>
   58.2%    58.2%      0.001s        7.00e-04s     Py      1       1
theano.scan_module.scan_op.Scan
   27.3%    85.4%      0.000s        1.64e-04s     Py      2       2
theano.sandbox.cuda.basic_ops.GpuFromHost
    6.1%    91.5%      0.000s        7.30e-05s     Py      1       1
theano.sandbox.cuda.basic_ops.HostFromGpu
    5.5%    97.0%      0.000s        6.60e-05s      C      1       1
theano.sandbox.cuda.basic_ops.GpuIncSubtensor
    1.1%    98.0%      0.000s        3.22e-06s      C      4       4
theano.tensor.elemwise.Elemwise
    0.7%    98.8%      0.000s        8.82e-06s      C      1       1
theano.sandbox.cuda.basic_ops.GpuSubtensor
    0.7%    99.4%      0.000s        7.87e-06s      C      1       1
theano.sandbox.cuda.basic_ops.GpuAllocEmpty
    0.3%    99.7%      0.000s        3.81e-06s      C      1       1
theano.compile.ops.Shape_i
    0.3%   100.0%      0.000s        1.55e-06s      C      2       2
theano.tensor.basic.ScalarFromTensor
    ... (remaining 0 Classes account for   0.00%(0.00s) of the runtime)

Ops
---
```

```
<% time> <sum %> <apply time> <time per call> <type> <#call> <#apply>
<Op name>
    58.2%    58.2%      0.001s        7.00e-04s      Py      1        1
forall_inplace,gpu,scan_fn}
    27.3%    85.4%      0.000s        1.64e-04s      Py      2        2
GpuFromHost
     6.1%    91.5%      0.000s        7.30e-05s      Py      1        1
HostFromGpu
     5.5%    97.0%      0.000s        6.60e-05s       C      1        1
GpuIncSubtensor{InplaceSet;:int64:}
     0.7%    97.7%      0.000s        8.82e-06s       C      1        1
GpuSubtensor{int64:int64:int16}
     0.7%    98.4%      0.000s        7.87e-06s       C      1        1
GpuAllocEmpty
     0.3%    98.7%      0.000s        4.05e-06s       C      1        1
Elemwise{switch,no_inplace}
     0.3%    99.0%      0.000s        4.05e-06s       C      1        1
Elemwise{le,no_inplace}
     0.3%    99.3%      0.000s        3.81e-06s       C      1        1
Shape_i{0}
     0.3%    99.6%      0.000s        1.55e-06s       C      2        2
ScalarFromTensor
     0.2%    99.8%      0.000s        2.86e-06s       C      1        1
Elemwise{Composite{Switch(LT(i0, i1), i0, i1)}}
     0.2%   100.0%      0.000s        1.91e-06s       C      1        1
Elemwise{Composite{Switch(i0, i1, minimum(i2, i3))}}[(0, 2)]
   ... (remaining 0 Ops account for   0.00%(0.00s) of the runtime)


Apply
------

<% time> <sum %> <apply time> <time per call> <#call> <id> <Apply
name>
    58.2%    58.2%      0.001s        7.00e-04s        1     12    forall_
inplace,gpu,scan_fn}(TensorConstant{10}, GpuSubtensor{int64:int64:i
nt16}.0, GpuIncSubtensor{InplaceSet;:int64:}.0, GpuFromHost.0)
    21.9%    80.1%      0.000s        2.64e-04s        1      3    GpuFromHo
st(<TensorType(float32, vector)>)
     6.1%    86.2%      0.000s        7.30e-05s        1     13
HostFromGpu(forall_inplace,gpu,scan_fn}.0)
     5.5%    91.6%      0.000s        6.60e-05s        1      4    GpuIncS
ubtensor{InplaceSet;:int64:}(GpuAllocEmpty.0, CudaNdarrayConstant{[
0.]}, Constant{1})
     5.3%    97.0%      0.000s        6.41e-05s        1      0
GpuFromHost(s0)
     0.7%    97.7%      0.000s        8.82e-06s        1     11
GpuSubtensor{int64:int64:int16}(GpuFromHost.0, ScalarFromTensor.0,
ScalarFromTensor.0, Constant{1})
```

```
      0.7%    98.4%        0.000s      7.87e-06s       1      1    GpuAllocE
mpty(TensorConstant{10})
      0.3%    98.7%        0.000s      4.05e-06s       1      8
Elemwise{switch,no_inplace}(Elemwise{le,no_inplace}.0,
TensorConstant{0}, TensorConstant{0})
      0.3%    99.0%        0.000s      4.05e-06s       1      6
Elemwise{le,no_inplace}(Elemwise{Composite{Switch(LT(i0, i1), i0,
i1)}}.0, TensorConstant{0})
      0.3%    99.3%        0.000s      3.81e-06s       1      2
Shape_i{0}(<TensorType(float32, vector)>)
      0.3%    99.6%        0.000s      3.10e-06s       1     10    ScalarFro
mTensor(Elemwise{switch,no_inplace}.0)
      0.2%    99.8%        0.000s      2.86e-06s       1      5    Ele
mwise{Composite{Switch(LT(i0, i1), i0, i1)}}(TensorConstant{10},
Shape_i{0}.0)
      0.2%   100.0%        0.000s      1.91e-06s       1      7
Elemwise{Composite{Switch(i0, i1, minimum(i2, i3))}}[(0, 2)]
(Elemwise{le,no_inplace}.0, TensorConstant{0}, Elemwise{Composite{Swit
ch(LT(i0, i1), i0, i1)}}.0, Shape_i{0}.0)
      0.0%   100.0%        0.000s      0.00e+00s       1      9    Scalar
FromTensor(Elemwise{Composite{Switch(i0, i1, minimum(i2, i3))}}[(0,
2)].0)
      ... (remaining 0 Apply instances account for 0.00%(0.00s) of the
runtime)
```

Summary

The first concept is symbolic computing, which consists in building graph, that can be compiled and then executed wherever we decide in the Python code. A compiled graph is acting as a function that can be called anywhere in the code. The purpose of symbolic computing is to have an abstraction of the architecture on which the graph will be executed, and which libraries to compile it with. As presented, symbolic variables are typed for the target architecture during compilation.

The second concept is the tensor, and the operators provided to manipulate tensors. Most of these were already available in CPU-based computation libraries, such as NumPy or SciPy. They have simply been ported to symbolic computing, requiring their equivalents on GPU. They use underlying acceleration libraries, such as BLAS, Nvidia Cuda, and cuDNN.

The last concept introduced by Theano is automatic differentiation—a very useful feature in deep learning to backpropagate errors and adjust the weights following the gradients, a process known as *gradient descent*. Also, the `scan` operator enables us to program loops (`while...`, `for...`,) on the GPU, and, as other operators, available through backpropagation as well, simplifying the training of models a lot.

We are now ready to apply this to deep learning in the next few chapters and have a look at this knowledge in practice.

2
Classifying Handwritten Digits with a Feedforward Network

The first chapter presented Theano as a compute engine, with its different functions and specificities. With this knowledge, we'll go through an example and introduce some of the main concepts of deep learning, building three neural networks and training them on the problem of handwritten digit classification.

Deep learning is a field of machine learning in which layers of modules are stacked on top of each of other: this chapter introduces a simple single-linear-layer model, then adds a second layer on top of it to create a **multi-layer perceptron (MLP)**, and last uses multiple convolutional layers to create a **Convolutional Neural Network (CNN)**.

In the meantime, this chapter recaps the basic machine learning concepts, such as overfitting, validation, and loss analysis, for those who are not familiar with data science:

- Small image classification
- Handwritten digit recognition challenge
- Layer design to build a neural network
- Design of a classical objective/loss function
- Back-propagation with stochastic gradient descent
- Training on a dataset with validation
- Convolutional neural networks
- Towards state-of-art results for digit classification

The MNIST dataset

The **Modified National Institute of Standards and Technology (MNIST) dataset** is a very well-known dataset of handwritten digits {0,1,2,3,4,5,6,7,8,9} used to train and test classification models.

A classification model is a model that predicts the probabilities of observing a class, given an input.

Training is the task of *learning* the parameters to fit the model to the data as well as we can so that for any input image, the correct label is predicted. For this training task, the MNIST dataset contains 60,000 images with a target label (a number between 0 and 9) for each example.

To validate that the training is efficient and to decide when to stop the training, we usually split the training dataset into two datasets: 80% to 90% of the images are used for training, while the remaining 10-20% of images will not be presented to the algorithm for training but to validate that the model generalizes well on unobserved data.

There is a separate dataset that the algorithm should never see during training, named the test set, which consists of 10,000 images in the MNIST dataset.

In the MNIST dataset, the input data of each example is a 28x28 normalized monochrome image and a label, represented as a simple integer between 0 and 9 for each example. Let's display some of them:

1. First, download a pre-packaged version of the dataset that makes it easier to load from Python:

   wget http://www.iro.umontreal.ca/~lisa/deep/data/mnist/mnist.pkl.gz -P /sharedfiles

2. Then load the data into a Python session:

   ```
   import pickle, gzip
   with gzip.open("/sharedfiles/mnist.pkl.gz", 'rb') as f:
       train_set, valid_set, test_set = pickle.load(f)
   ```

   For Python3, we need pickle.load(f, encoding='latin1') due to the way it was serialized.

   ```
   train_set[0].shape
   (50000, 784)
   ```

   ```
   train_set[1].shape
   (50000,)
   ```

```python
import matplotlib

import numpy

import matplotlib.pyplot as plt

plt.rcParams['figure.figsize'] = (10, 10)

plt.rcParams['image.cmap'] = 'gray'

for i in range(9):
    plt.subplot(1,10,i+1)
    plt.imshow(train_set[0][i].reshape(28,28))
    plt.axis('off')
    plt.title(str(train_set[1][i]))

plt.show()
```

The first nine samples from the dataset are displayed with the corresponding label (the *ground truth*, that is, the correct answer expected by the classification algorithm) on top of them:

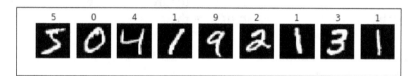

In order to avoid too many transfers to the GPU, and since the complete dataset is small enough to fit in the memory of the GPU, we usually place the full training set in shared variables:

```python
import theano
train_set_x = theano.shared(numpy.asarray(train_set[0], dtype=theano.config.floatX))
train_set_y = theano.shared(numpy.asarray(train_set[1], dtype='int32'))
```

Avoiding these data transfers allows us to train faster on the GPU, despite recent GPU and fast PCIe connections.

More information on the dataset is available at http://yann.lecun.com/exdb/mnist/.

Structure of a training program

The structure of a training program always consists of the following steps:

1. **Set the script environment**: Such as package imports, the use of the GPU, and so on.

2. **Load data**: A data loader class to access the data during training, usually in a random order to avoid too many similar examples of the same class, but sometimes in a precise order, for example, in the case of curriculum learning with simple examples first and complex ones last.

3. **Preprocess the data**: A set of transformations, such as swapping dimensions on images, adding blur or noise. It is very common to add some data augmentation transformations, such as random crop, scale, brightness, or contrast jittering to get more examples than the original ones, and reduce the risk of overfitting on data. If the number of free parameters in the model is too important with respect to the training dataset size, the model might learn from the available examples. Also, if the dataset is too small and too many iterations have been executed on the same data, the model might become too specific to the training examples and not generalize well on new unseen examples.

4. **Build a model**: Defining the model structure with the parameter in persistent variables (shared variables) to update their values during training in order to fit the training data

5. **Train**: There are different algorithms either training on the full dataset as a whole or training on each example step by step. The best convergence is usually achieved by training on a batch, a small subset of examples grouped together, from a few tens to a few hundreds.

    Another reason to use a batch is to improve the training speed of the GPU, because individual data transfers are costly and GPU memory is not sufficient to host the full dataset as well. The GPU is a parallel architecture, so processing a batch of examples is usually faster than processing the examples one by one, up to a certain point. Seeing more examples at the same time accelerates the convergence (in wall-time), up to a certain point. This is true even if the GPU memory is large enough to host the whole dataset: the diminishing returns on the batch size make it usually faster to have smaller batches than the whole dataset. Note that this is true for modern CPUs as well, but the optimal batch size is usually smaller.

 An iteration defines a training on one batch. An epoch is a number of iterations required for the algorithm to see the full dataset.

6. During training, after a certain number of iterations, there is usually a **validation** using a split of the training data or a validation dataset that has not been used for learning. The loss is computed on this validation set. Though the algorithm has the objective to reduce the loss given the training data, it does not ensure generalization with unseen data. Validation data is unseen data used to estimate the generalization performance. A lack of generalization might occur when the training data is not representative, or is an exception and has not been sampled correctly, or if the model overfits the training data.

   Validation data verifies everything is OK, and stops training when validation loss does not decrease any more, even if training loss might continue to decrease: further training is not worth it any more and leads to overfitting.

7. **Saving model parameters** and displaying results, such as best training/validation loss values, train loss curves for convergence analysis.

   In the case of classification, we compute the accuracy (the percentage of correct classification) or the error (the percentage of misclassification) during training, as well as the loss. At the end of training, a confusion matrix helps evaluate the quality of the classifier.

   Let's see these steps in practice and start a Theano session in a Python shell session:

```
from theano import theano
import theano.tensor as T
```

Classification loss function

The loss function is an objective function to minimize during training to get the best model. Many different loss functions exist.

In a classification problem, where the target is to predict the correct class among k classes, cross-entropy is commonly used as it measures the difference between the real probability distribution, q, and the predicted one, p, for each class:

$$\sum_{i=1}^{n}\sum_{c=1}^{k}q_i(c)\log p_i(c)$$

Here, i is the index of the sample in the dataset, n is the number of samples in the dataset, and k is the number of classes.

While the real probability $q(c|x_i)$ of each class is unknown, it can simply be approximated in practice by the empirical distribution, that is, randomly drawing a sample out of the dataset in the dataset order. The same way, the cross-entropy of any predicted probability, p, can be approximated by the empirical cross-entropy:

$$cross - entropy(p) = \frac{1}{n} \sum_{i=1}^{N} \log p_i$$

Here, p_i is the probability estimated by the model for the correct class of example x_i.

Accuracy and cross-entropy both evolve in the same direction but measure different things. Accuracy measures how much the predicted class is correct, while cross-entropy measure the distance between the probabilities. A decrease in cross-entropy explains that the probability to predict the correct class gets better, but the accuracy may remain constant or drop.

While accuracy is discrete and not differentiable, the cross-entropy loss is a differentiable function that can be easily used for training a model.

Single-layer linear model

The simplest model is the linear model, where for each class c, the output is a linear combination of the input values:

$$o_c : x \rightarrow W_c x + b_c$$

This output is unbounded.

To get a probability distribution, p_i, that sums to 1, the output of the linear model is passed into a softmax function:

$$softmax : \{o_c\}_c \rightarrow \left\{ \frac{e_c^o}{\sum_{\varsigma} e^{\varsigma}} \right\}_c$$

Hence, the estimated probability of class c for an input x is rewritten with vectors:

$$p = \text{softmax}\left(Wx + b\right)$$

Translated in Python with:

```
batch_size = 600
n_in = 28 * 28
n_out = 10

x = T.matrix('x')
y = T.ivector('y')
W = theano.shared(
            value=numpy.zeros(
                (n_in, n_out),
                dtype=theano.config.floatX
            ),
            name='W',
            borrow=True
        )
b = theano.shared(
        value=numpy.zeros(
            (n_out,),
            dtype=theano.config.floatX
        ),
        name='b',
        borrow=True
    )
model = T.nnet.softmax(T.dot(x, W) + b)
```

The prediction for a given input is given by the most probable class (maximum probability):

```
y_pred = T.argmax(model, axis=1)
```

In this model with a single linear layer, information moves from input to output: it is a **feedforward network**. The process to compute the output given the input is called **forward propagation**.

This layer is said fully connected because all outputs, o_c, are the sum of (are linked to) all inputs values through a multiplicative coefficient:

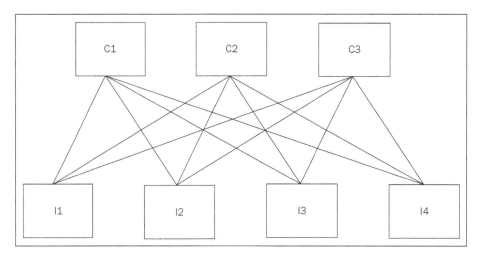

Cost function and errors

The cost function given the predicted probabilities by the model is as follows:

```
cost = -T.mean(T.log(model)[T.arange(y.shape[0]), y])
```

The error is the number of predictions that are different from the true class, averaged by the total number of values, which can be written as a mean:

```
error = T.mean(T.neq(y_pred, y))
```

On the contrary, accuracy corresponds to the number of correct predictions divided by the total number of predictions. The sum of error and accuracy is one.

For other types of problems, here are a few other loss functions and implementations:

Categorical cross entropy
 	
An equivalent implementation of ours
	`T.nnet.categorical_`
	`crossentropy(model, y_true).`
	`mean()`

Binary cross entropy For the case when output can take only two values {0,1} Typically used after a sigmoid activation predicting the probability, p	`T.nnet.binary_crossentropy(model,` `y_true).mean()`
Mean squared error L2 norm for regression problems	`T.sqr(model - y_true).mean()`
Mean absolute error L1 norm for regression problems	`T.abs_(model - y_true).mean()`

Smooth L1
 	
A mix between L1 for large values, and L2 for small values
 	
Known as an outlier resistant loss for regressions
	`T.switch(`
	`    T.lt(T.abs_(model - y_true) ,`
	`1. / sigma),`
	`    0.5 * sigma * T.sqr(model -`
	`y_true),`
	`    T.abs_(model - y_true) - 0.5`
	`/ sigma )`
	`.sum(axis=1).mean()`

Squared hinge loss Particularly used in unsupervised problems	`T.sqr(T.maximum(1. - y_true *` `model, 0.)).mean()`
Hinge loss	`T.maximum(1. - y_true * model,` `0.).mean()`

Backpropagation and stochastic gradient descent

Backpropagation, or the backward propagation of errors, is the most commonly used supervised learning algorithm for adapting the connection weights.

Considering the error or the cost as a function of the weights W and b, a local minimum of the cost function can be approached with a gradient descent, which consists of changing weights along the negative error gradient:

$$W \leftarrow W - \lambda \frac{\partial E}{\partial w}$$

Here, λ is the learning rate, a positive constant defining the speed of a descent.

The following compiled function updates the variables after each feedforward run:

```
g_W = T.grad(cost=cost, wrt=W)
g_b = T.grad(cost=cost, wrt=b)

learning_rate=0.13
index = T.lscalar()

train_model = theano.function(
    inputs=[index],
    outputs=[cost,error],
    updates=[(W, W - learning_rate * g_W),(b, b - learning_rate *
g_b)],
    givens={
        x: train_set_x[index * batch_size: (index + 1) * batch_size],
        y: train_set_y[index * batch_size: (index + 1) * batch_size]
    }
)
```

The input variable is the index of the batch, since all the dataset has been transferred in one pass to the GPU in shared variables.

Training consists of presenting each sample to the model iteratively (iterations) and repeating the operation many times (epochs):

```
n_epochs = 1000
print_every = 1000

n_train_batches = train_set[0].shape[0] // batch_size
n_iters = n_epochs * n_train_batches
train_loss = np.zeros(n_iters)
train_error = npzeros(n_iters)
```

```
for epoch in range(n_epochs):
    for minibatch_index in range(n_train_batches):
        iteration = minibatch_index + n_train_batches * epoch
        train_loss[iteration], train_error[iteration] = train_
model(minibatch_index)
        if (epoch * train_set[0].shape[0] + minibatch_index) % print_
every == 0 :
            print('epoch {}, minibatch {}/{}, training error {:02.2f}
%, training loss {}'.format(
                epoch,
                minibatch_index + 1,
                n_train_batches,
                train_error[iteration] * 100,
                train_loss[iteration]
            ))
```

This only reports the loss and error on one mini-batch, though. It would be good to also report the average over the whole dataset.

The error rate drops very quickly during the first iterations, then slows down.

Execution time on a GPU GeForce GTX 980M laptop is 67.3 seconds, while on an Intel i7 CPU, it is 3 minutes and 7 seconds.

After a long while, the model converges to a 5.3 - 5.5% error rate, and with a few more iterations could go further down, but could also lead to overfitting, Overfitting occurs when the model fits the training data well but does not get the same error rate on unseen data.

In this case, the model is too simple to overfit on this data.

A model that is too simple cannot learn very well. The principle of deep learning is to add more layers, that is, increase the depth and build deeper networks to gain better accuracy.

We'll see in the following section how to compute a better estimation of the model accuracy and the training stop.

Multiple layer model

A **multi-layer perceptron (MLP)** is a feedforward net with multiple layers. A second linear layer, named hidden layer, is added to the previous example:

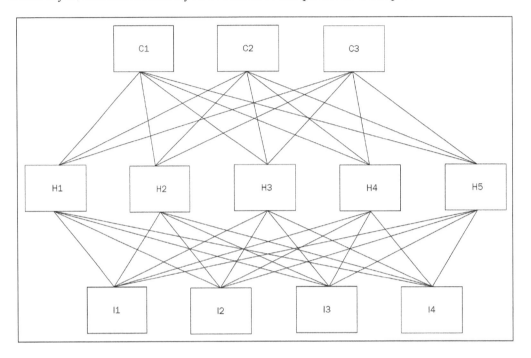

Having two linear layers following each other is equivalent to having a single linear layer.

With a *non-linear function or non-linearity or transfer function* between the linearities, the model does not simplify into a linear one any more, and represents more possible functions in order to capture more complex patterns in the data:

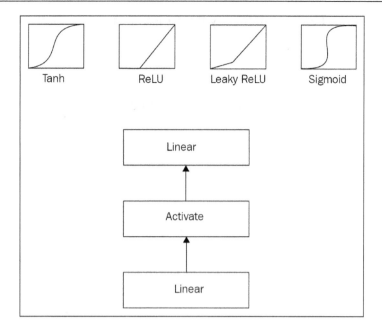

Activation functions helps saturating (ON-OFF) and reproduces the biological neuron activations.

The **Rectified Linear Unit (ReLU)** graph is given as follows:

(x + T.abs_(x)) / 2.0

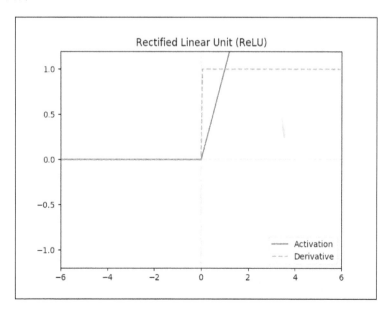

The **Leaky Rectifier Linear Unit** (**Leaky ReLU**) graph is given as follows:

((1 + leak) * x + (1 – leak) * T.abs_(x)) / 2.0

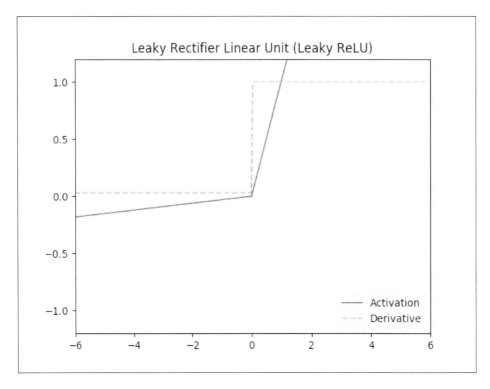

Here, `leak` is a parameter that defines the slope in the negative values. In leaky rectifiers, this parameter is fixed.

The activation named PReLU considers the `leak` parameter to be learned.

More generally speaking, a piecewise linear activation can be learned by adding a linear layer followed by a maxout activation of `n_pool` units:

```
T.max([x[:, n::n_pool] for n in range(n_pool)], axis=0)
```

This will output `n_pool` values or units for the underlying learned linearities:

Sigmoid (T.nnet.sigmoid)

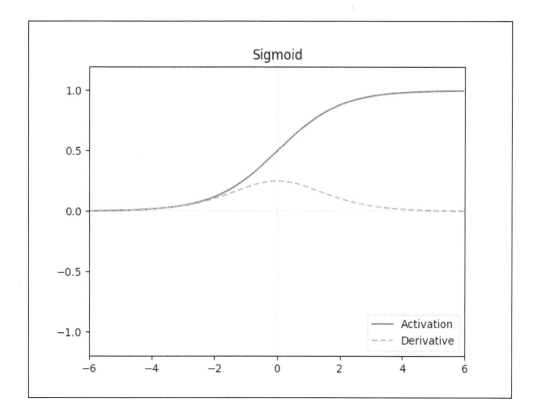

HardSigmoid function is given as:

T.clip(X + 0.5, 0., 1.)

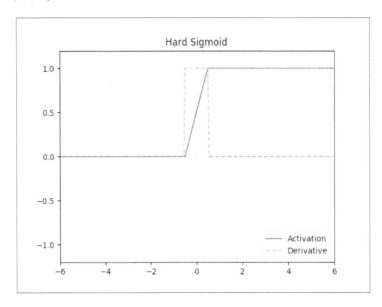

HardTanh function is given as:

T.clip(X, -1., 1.)

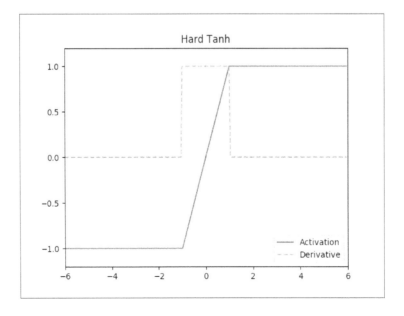

Tanh function is given as:

T.tanh(x)

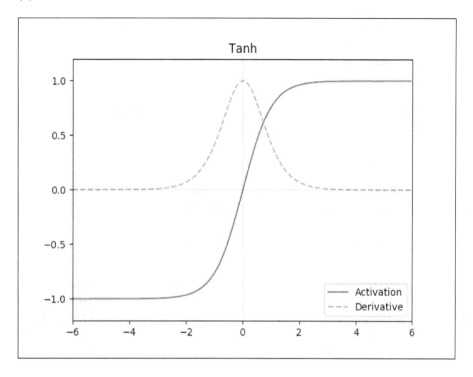

This two-layer network model written in Python will be as follows:

```
batch_size = 600
n_in = 28 * 28
n_hidden = 500
n_out = 10


def shared_zeros(shape, dtype=theano.config.floatX, name='', n=None):
    shape = shape if n is None else (n,) + shape
    return theano.shared(np.zeros(shape, dtype=dtype), name=name)


def shared_glorot_uniform(shape, dtype=theano.config.floatX, name='',
n=None):
    if isinstance(shape, int):
        high = np.sqrt(6. / shape)
    else:
```

```
        high = np.sqrt(6. / (np.sum(shape[:2]) * np.prod(shape[2:])))
    shape = shape if n is None else (n,) + shape
    return theano.shared(np.asarray(
        np.random.uniform(
            low=-high,
            high=high,
            size=shape),
        dtype=dtype), name=name)

W1 = shared_glorot_uniform( (n_in, n_hidden), name='W1' )
b1 = shared_zeros( (n_hidden,), name='b1' )

hidden_output = T.tanh(T.dot(x, W1) + b1)

W2 = shared_zeros( (n_hidden, n_out), name='W2' )
b2 = shared_zeros( (n_out,), name='b2' )

model = T.nnet.softmax(T.dot(hidden_output, W2) + b2)
params = [W1,b1,W2,b2]
```

In deep nets, if weights are initialized to zero with the `shared_zeros` method, the signal will not flow through the network correctly from end to end. If weights are initialized with values that are too big, after a few steps, most activation functions saturate. So, we need to ensure that the values can be passed to the next layer during propagation, as well as for the gradients to the previous layer during back-propagation.

We also need to break the symmetry between neurons. If the weights of all neurons are zero (or if they are all equal), they will all evolve exactly in the same way, and the model will not learn much.

The researcher Xavier Glorot studied an algorithm to initialize weights in an optimal way. It consists in drawing the weights from a Gaussian or uniform distribution of zero mean and the following variance:

$$v = 2 / \left(n_{in} + n_{out} \right)$$

Here are the variables from the preceding formula:

- n_{in} is the number of inputs the layer receives during feedforward propagation
- n_{out} is the number of gradients the layer receives during back-propagation

In the case of a linear model, the shape parameter is a tuple, and `v` is simply `numpy.sum( shape[:2] )` (in this case, `numpy.prod(shape[2:])` is 1).

The variance of a uniform distribution on *[-a, a]* is given by *a**2/3*, then the bound a can be computed as follows:

$$\sqrt{\frac{6}{\left(n_{in} + n_{out}\right)}}$$

The cost can be defined the same way as before, but the gradient descent needs to be adapted to deal with the list of parameters, `[W1,b1,W2,b2]`:

```
g_params = T.grad(cost=cost, wrt=params)
```

The training loop requires an updated training function:

```
learning_rate = 0.01
updates = [
        (param, param - learning_rate * gparam)
        for param, gparam in zip(params, g_params)
    ]

train_model = theano.function(
    inputs=[index],
    outputs=cost,
    updates=updates,
    givens={
        x: train_set_x[index * batch_size: (index + 1) * batch_size],
        y: train_set_y[index * batch_size: (index + 1) * batch_size]
    }
)
```

In this case, learning rate is global to the net, with all weights being updated at the same rate. The learning rate is set to 0.01 instead of 0.13. We'll speak about hyperparameter tuning in the training section.

The training loop remains unchanged. The full code is given in the `2-multi.py` file.

Execution time on the GPU is 5 minutes and 55 seconds, while on the CPU it is 51 minutes and 36 seconds.

After 1,000 iterations, the error has dropped to 2%, which is a lot better than the previous 5% error rate, but part of it might be due to overfitting. We'll compare the different models later.

Convolutions and max layers

A great improvement in image classification has been achieved with the invention of the convolutional layers on the MNIST database:

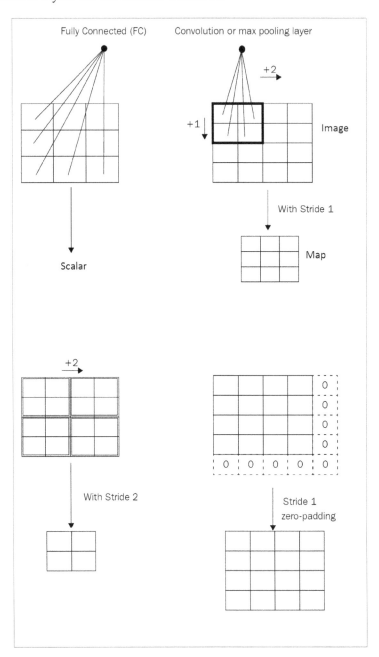

While previous fully-connected layers perform a computation with all input values (pixels in the case of an image) of the input, a 2D convolution layer will consider only a small patch or window or receptive field of NxN pixels of the 2D input image for each output unit. The dimensions of the patch are named kernel dimensions, N is the kernel size, and the coefficients/parameters are the kernel.

At each position of the input image, the kernel produces a scalar, and all position values will lead to a matrix (2D tensor) called a *feature map*. Convolving the kernel on the input image as a sliding window creates a new output image. The stride of the kernel defines the number of pixels to shift the patch/window over the image: with a stride of 2, the convolution with the kernel is computed every 2 pixels.

For example, on a 224 x 224 input image, we get the following:

- A 2x2 kernel with stride 1 outputs a 223 x 223 feature map
- A 3x3 kernel with stride 1 outputs a 222 x 222 feature map

In order to keep the output feature map the same dimension as the input image, there is a type of zero-padding called *same* or *half* that enables the following:

- Add a line and a column of zeros at the end of the input image in the case of a 2x2 kernel with stride 1
- Add two lines and two columns of zeros, one in front and one at the end of the input image vertically and horizontally in the case of a 3x3 kernel with stride 1

So, the output dimensions are the same as the original ones, that is, a 224 x 224 feature map.

With zero padding:

- A 2x2 kernel with stride 2 and zero padding will output a 112 x 112 feature map
- A 3x3 kernel with stride 2 will output a 112 x 112 feature map

Without zero-padding, it gets more complicated:

- A 2x2 kernel with stride 2 will output a 112 x 112 feature map
- A 3x3 kernel with stride 2 will output a 111 x 111 feature map

Note that kernel dimensions and strides can be different for each dimension. In this case, we say kernel width, kernel height, stride width, or stride height.

In one convolutional layer, it is possible to output multiple feature maps, each feature map being computed with a different kernel (and kernel weights) and representing one feature. We say outputs, neurons, kernels, features, feature maps, units, or output channels indifferently to give the number of these different convolutions with different kernels. To be precise, neuron usually refers to a specific position within a feature map. Kernels are the kernels themselves, and the other ones refer to the result of the convolution operation. The number of them is the same, which is why these words are often used to describe the same thing. I'll use the words channels, outputs, and features.

The usual convolution operators can be applied to multi-channel inputs. This enables to apply them to three-channel images (RGB images, for example) or to the output of another convolution in order to be chained.

Let's include two convolutions with a kernel size of 5 in front of the previous MLP mode:

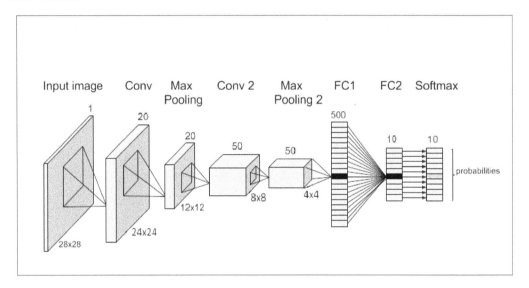

The 2D convolution operator requires a 4D tensor input. The first dimension is the batch size, the second the number of inputs or input channels (in the "channel-first format"), and the third and fourth the two dimensions of the feature map (in the "channel-last format", channels are the last dimension). MNIST gray images (one channel) stored in a one-dimensional vector need to be converted into a 28x28 matrix, where 28 is the image height and width:

```
layer0_input = x.reshape((batch_size, 1, 28, 28))
```

Then, adding a first convolution layer of 20 channels on top of the transformed input, we get this:

```
from theano.tensor.nnet import conv2d

n_conv1 = 20

W1 = shared_glorot_uniform( (n_conv1, 1, 5, 5) )

conv1_out = conv2d(
    input=layer0_input,
    filters=W1,
    filter_shape=(n_conv1, 1, 5, 5),
    input_shape=(batch_size, 1, 28, 28)
)
```

In this case, the Xavier initialization (from the name of its inventor, Xavier Glorot) multiplies the number of input/output channels by the number of parameters in the kernel, `numpy.prod(shape[2:])` = 5 x 5 = 25, to get the total number of incoming input/output gradients in the initialization formula.

The 20 kernels of size 5x5 and stride 1 on 28x28 inputs will produce 20 feature maps of size 24x24. So the first convolution output is (`batch_size,20,24,24`).

Best performing nets use max pooling layers to encourage translation invariance and stability to noise. A max-pooling layer performs a maximum operation over a sliding window/patch to keep only one value out of the patch. As well as increasing speed performance, it reduces the size of the feature maps, and the total computation complexity and training time decreases:

```
from theano.tensor.signal import pool
pooled_out = pool.pool_2d(input=conv1_out, ws=(2, 2), ignore_
border=True)
```

The output of the 2x2 max pooling layer will be (`batch_size,20,12,12`). The batch size and the number of channels stay constant. Only the feature map's size has changed.

Adding a second convolutional layer of 50 channels and max pooling layer on top of the previous one leads to an output of size (`batch_size,50,4,4`):

```
n_conv2 = 50

W2 = shared_glorot_uniform( (n_conv2, n_conv1, 5, 5) )

conv2_out = conv2d(
    input=pooled_out,
```

```
        filters=W2,
        filter_shape=(n_conv2, n_conv1, 5, 5),
        input_shape=(batch_size, n_conv1, 12, 12)
)

pooled2_out = pool.pool_2d(input=conv2_out, ds=(2, 2),ignore_
border=True)
```

To create a classifier, we connect on top the MLP with its two fully-connected linear layers and a softmax, as seen before:

```
hidden_input = pooled2_out.flatten(2)

n_hidden = 500

W3 = shared_zeros( (n_conv2 * 4 * 4, n_hidden), name='W3' )
b3 = shared_zeros( (n_hidden,), name='b3' )

hidden_output = T.tanh(T.dot(hidden_input, W3) + b3)

n_out = 10

W4 = shared_zeros( (n_hidden, n_out), name='W4' )
b4 = shared_zeros( (n_out,), name='b4' )

model = T.nnet.softmax(T.dot(hidden_output, W4) + b4)
params = [W1,W2,W3,b3,W4,b4]
```

Such a model is named a **Convolutional Neural Net (CNN)**.

The full code is given in the `3-cnn.py` file.

Training is much slower because the number of parameters has been multiplied again, and the use of the GPU makes a lot more sense: total training time on the GPU has increased to 1 hour, 48 min and 27 seconds. Training on the CPU would take days.

The training error is zero after a few iterations, part of it due to overfitting. Let's see in the next section how to compute a testing loss and accuracy that better explains the model's efficiency.

Training

In order to get a good measure of how the model behaves on data that's unseen during training, the validation dataset is used to compute a validation loss and accuracy during training.

The validation dataset enables us to choose the best model, while the test dataset is only used at the end to get the final test accuracy/error of the model. The training, test, and validation datasets are discrete datasets, with no common examples. The validation dataset is usually 10 times smaller than the test dataset to slow the training process as little as possible. The test dataset is usually around 10-20% of the training dataset. Both the training and validation datasets are part of the training program, since the first one is used to learn, and the second is used to select the best model on unseen data at training time.

The test dataset is completely outside the training process and is used to get the accuracy of the produced model, resulting from training and model selection.

If the model overfits the training set because it has been trained too many times on the same images, for example, then the validation and test sets will not suffer from this behavior and will provide a real estimation of the model's accuracy.

Usually, a validation function is compiled without a gradient update of the model to simply compute only the cost and error on the input batch.

Batches of data *(x,y)* are commonly transferred to the GPU at every iteration because the dataset is usually too big to fit in the GPU's memory. In this case, we could still use the trick with the shared variables to place the whole validation dataset in the GPU's memory, but let's see how we would do if we had to transfer the batches to the GPU at each step and not use the previous trick. We would use the more usual form:

```
validate_model = theano.function(
    inputs=[x,y],
    outputs=[cost,error]
)
```

It requires the transfer of batch inputs. Validation is computed not at every iteration, but at `validation_interval` iterations in the training `for` loop:

```
if iteration % validation_interval == 0 :
    val_index = iteration // validation_interval
    valid_loss[val_index], valid_error[val_index] = np.mean([
            validate_model(
                valid_set[0][i * batch_size: (i + 1) * batch_size],
                numpy.asarray(valid_set[1][i * batch_size: (i + 1) *
batch_size], dtype="int32")
                )
            for i in range(n_valid_batches)
        ], axis=0)
```

Let's see the simple first model:

```
epoch 0, minibatch 1/83, validation error 40.05 %, validation loss
2.16520105302

epoch 24, minibatch 9/83, validation error 8.16 %, validation loss
0.288349323906
epoch 36, minibatch 13/83, validation error 7.96 %, validation loss
0.278418215923
epoch 48, minibatch 17/83, validation error 7.73 %, validation loss
0.272948684171
epoch 60, minibatch 21/83, validation error 7.65 %, validation loss
0.269203903154
epoch 72, minibatch 25/83, validation error 7.59 %, validation loss
0.26624627877
epoch 84, minibatch 29/83, validation error 7.56 %, validation loss
0.264540277421
...
epoch 975, minibatch 76/83, validation error 7.10 %, validation loss
0.258190142922
epoch 987, minibatch 80/83, validation error 7.09 %, validation loss
0.258411859162
```

In a full training program, a validation interval corresponding to the total number of epochs, with an average validation score for the epoch, would make more sense.

To better estimate how the training performs, let's plot the training and valid loss. In order to display the descent in early iterations, I'll stop the drawing at 100 iterations. If I use 1,000 iterations in the plot, I won't see the early iterations:

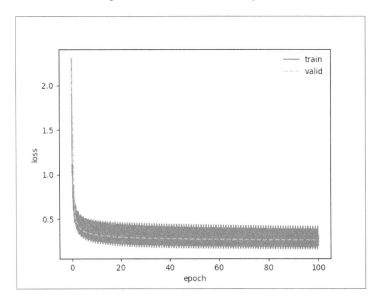

The training loss looks like a wide band because it oscillates between different values. Each of the values corresponds to one batch. The batch might be too small to provide a stable loss value. The mean value of the training loss over the epoch would provide a more stable value to compare with the valid loss and show overfitting.

Also note that the loss plot provides information on how the network converges, but does not give any valuable information on the error. So, it is also very important to plot the training error and the valid error.

For the second model:

```
epoch 0, minibatch 1/83, validation error 41.25 %, validation loss
2.35665753484
epoch 24, minibatch 9/83, validation error 10.20 %, validation loss
0.438846310601
epoch 36, minibatch 13/83, validation error 9.40 %, validation loss
0.399769391865
epoch 48, minibatch 17/83, validation error 8.85 %, validation loss
0.379035864025
epoch 60, minibatch 21/83, validation error 8.57 %, validation loss
0.365624915808
epoch 72, minibatch 25/83, validation error 8.31 %, validation loss
0.355733696371
epoch 84, minibatch 29/83, validation error 8.25 %, validation loss
0.348027150147
epoch 96, minibatch 33/83, validation error 8.01 %, validation loss
0.34150374867
epoch 108, minibatch 37/83, validation error 7.91 %, validation loss
0.335878048092
...
epoch 975, minibatch 76/83, validation error 2.97 %, validation loss
0.167824191041
epoch 987, minibatch 80/83, validation error 2.96 %, validation loss
0.167092795949
```

Again, the training curves give better insights:

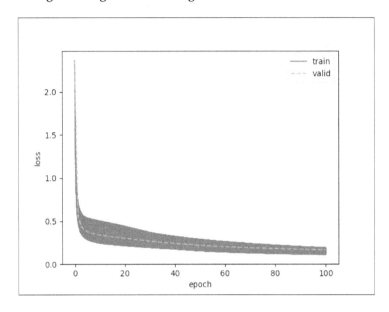

For the third model:

```
epoch 0, minibatch 1/83, validation error 53.81 %, validation loss
2.29528842866
epoch 24, minibatch 9/83, validation error 1.55 %, validation loss
0.048202780541
epoch 36, minibatch 13/83, validation error 1.31 %, validation loss
0.0445762014715
epoch 48, minibatch 17/83, validation error 1.29 %, validation loss
0.0432346871821
epoch 60, minibatch 21/83, validation error 1.25 %, validation loss
0.0425786205451
epoch 72, minibatch 25/83, validation error 1.20 %, validation loss
0.0413943211024
epoch 84, minibatch 29/83, validation error 1.20 %, validation loss
0.0416557886347
epoch 96, minibatch 33/83, validation error 1.19 %, validation loss
0.0414686980075
...
epoch 975, minibatch 76/83, validation error 1.08 %, validation loss
0.0477593478863
epoch 987, minibatch 80/83, validation error 1.08 %, validation loss
0.0478142946085
```

Refer to the following graph:

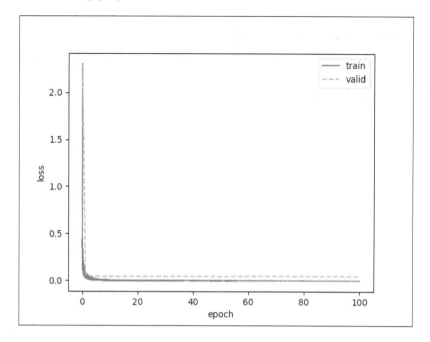

Here we see the difference between train and valid, losses either due to a slight overfitting to the training data, or a difference between the training and test datasets.

The main causes of overfitting are as follows:

- **Too small a dataset**: Collect more data
- **Too high a learning rate**: The network is learning too quickly on earlier examples
- **A lack of regularization**: Add more dropout (see next section), or a penalty on the norm of the weights in the loss function
- **Too small model**: Increase the number of filters/units in different layers

Validation loss and error gives a better estimate than training loss and error, which are more noisy, and during training, they are also used to decide which model parameters are the best:

- **Simple model**: 6.96 % at epoch 518
- **MLP model**: 2.96 % at epoch 987
- **CNN model**: 1.06 % at epoch 722

These results also indicate that the models might not improve much with further training.

Here's a comparison of the three models' validation losses:

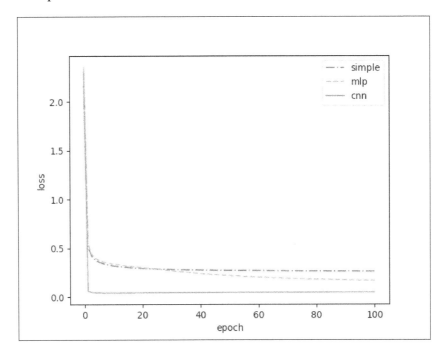

Note that the MLP is still improving and the training has not finished, while the CNN and simple networks have converged.

With the selected model, you can easily compute the test loss and error on the test dataset to finalize it.

The last important concept of machine learning is hyperparameter tuning. An hyperparameter defines a parameter of the model that is not learned during training. Here are examples:

```
learning rate
number of hidden neurons
batch size
```

For the learning rate, too slow a descent might prevent finding a more global minimum, while too fast a descent damages the final convergence. Finding the best initial learning rate is crucial. Then, it is common to decrease the learning rate after many iterations in order to have more precise fine-tuning of the model.

Hyperparameter selection requires us to run the previous runs many times for different values of the hyperparameters; testing all combinations of hyperparameters can be done in a simple grid search, for example.

Here is an exercise for the reader:

- Train the models with different hyperparameters and draw the training loss curves to see how hyperparameters influence the final loss.

- Visualize the content of the neurons of the first layer, once the model has been trained, to see what the features capture from the input image. For this task, compile a specific visualization function:

```
visualize_layer1 = theano.function(
    inputs=[x,y],
    outputs=conv1_out
)
```

Dropout

Dropout is a widely used technique to improve convergence and robustness of a neural net and prevent neural nets from overfitting. It consists of setting some random values to zero for the layers on which we'd like it to apply. It introduces some randomness in the data at every epoch.

Usually, dropout is used before the fully connected layers and not used very often in convolutional layers. Let's add the following lines before each of our two fully connected layers:

```
dropout = 0.5

if dropout > 0 :
    mask = srng.binomial(n=1, p=1-dropout, size=hidden_input.shape)
    # The cast is important because
    # int * float32 = float64 which make execution slower
    hidden_input = hidden_input * T.cast(mask, theano.config.floatX)
```

The full script is in 5-cnn-with-dropout.py. After 1,000 iterations, the validation error of the CNN with dropout continues to drops down to 1.08%, while the validation error of the CNN without dropout will not go down by 1.22%.

Readers who would like to go further with dropout should have a look at maxout units. They work well with dropout and replace the tanh non-linearities to get even better results. As dropout does a kind of model averaging, maxout units try to find the optimal non-linearity to the problem.

Inference

Inference is the process of using the model to produce predictions.

For inference, the weight parameters do not need to be updated, so the inference function is simpler than the training function:

```
infer_model = theano.function(
    inputs=[x],
    outputs=[y_pred]
)
```

Optimization and other update rules

Learning rate is a very important parameter to set correctly. Too low a learning rate will make it difficult to learn and will train slower, while too high a learning rate will increase sensitivity to outlier values, increase the amount of noise in the data, train too fast to learn generalization, and get stuck in local minima:

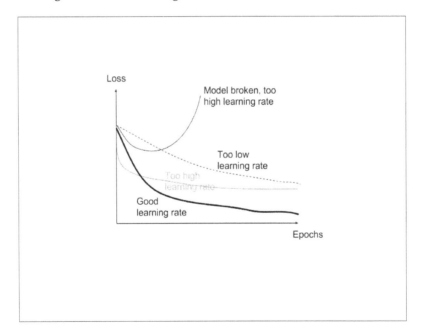

When training loss does not improve anymore for one or a few more iterations, the learning rate can be reduced by a factor:

$$\lambda \leftarrow \lambda \times 0.1$$

It helps the network learn fine-grained differences in the data, as shown when training residual networks (*Chapter 7, Classifying Images with Residual Networks*):

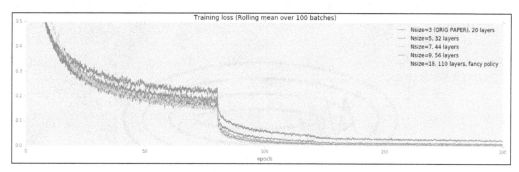

To check the training process, it is usual to print the norm of the parameters, the gradients, and the updates, as well as NaN values.

The update rule seen in this chapter is the simplest form of update, known as **Stochastic Gradient Descent (SGD)**. It is a good practice to clip the norm to avoid saturation and NaN values. The updates list given to the theano function becomes this:

```python
def clip_norms(gs, c):
    norm = T.sqrt(sum([T.sum(g**2) for g in gs]))
    return [ T.switch(T.ge(norm, c), g*c/norm, g) for g in gs]

updates = []
grads = T.grad(cost, params)
grads = clip_norms(grads, 50)
for p,g in zip(params,grads):
    updated_p = p - learning_rate * g
    updates.append((p, updated_p))
```

Some very simple variants have been experimented with in order to improve the descent, and are proposed in many deep learning libraries. Let's see them in Theano.

Momentum

For each parameter, a momentum (v, as velocity) is computed from the gradients accumulated over the iterations with a time decay. The previous momentum value is multiplied by a decay parameter between 0.5 and 0.9 (to be cross-validated) and added to the current gradient to provide the new momentum value.

The momentum of the gradients plays the role of a moment of inertia in the updates, in order to learn faster. The idea is also that oscillations in successive gradients will be canceled in the momentum, to move the parameter in a more direct path towards the solution:

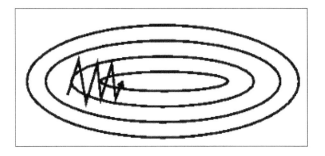

The decay parameter between 0.5 and 0.9 is a hyperparameter usually referred to as the momentum, in an abuse of language:

```
updates = []
grads = T.grad(cost, params)
grads = clip_norms(grads, 50)
for p,g in zip(params,grads):
    m = theano.shared(p.get_value() * 0.)
    v = (momentum * m) - (learning_rate * g)
    updates.append((m, v))
    updates.append((p, p + v))
```

Nesterov Accelerated Gradient

Instead of adding v to the parameter, the idea is to add directory the future value of the momentum momentum v - learning_rate g, in order to have it compute the gradients in the next iteration directly at the next position:

```
updates = []
grads = T.grad(cost, params)
grads = clip_norms(grads, 50)
for p, g in zip(params, grads):
    m = theano.shared(p.get_value() * 0.)
    v = (momentum * m) - (learning_rate * g)
    updates.append((m,v))
    updates.append((p, p + momentum * v - learning_rate * g))
```

Adagrad

This update rule, as well as the following rules consists of adapting the learning rate **parameter-wise** (differently for each parameter). The element-wise sum of squares of the gradients is accumulated into a shared variable for each parameter in order to decay the learning rate in an element-wise fashion:

```
updates = []
grads = T.grad(cost, params)
grads = clip_norms(grads, 50)
for p,g in zip(params,grads):
    acc = theano.shared(p.get_value() * 0.)
    acc_t = acc + g ** 2
    updates.append((acc, acc_t))
    p_t = p - (learning_rate / T.sqrt(acc_t + 1e-6)) * g
    updates.append((p, p_t))
```

Adagrad is an aggressive method, and the next two rules, AdaDelta and RMSProp, try to reduce its aggression.

AdaDelta

Two accumulators are created per parameter to accumulate the squared gradients and the updates in moving averages, parameterized by the decay rho:

```
updates = []
grads = T.grad(cost, params)
grads = clip_norms(grads, 50)
for p,g in zip(params,grads):
    acc = theano.shared(p.get_value() * 0.)
    acc_delta = theano.shared(p.get_value() * 0.)
    acc_new = rho * acc + (1 - rho) * g ** 2
    updates.append((acc,acc_new))
    update = g * T.sqrt(acc_delta + 1e-6) / T.sqrt(acc_new + 1e-6)
    updates.append((p, p - learning_rate * update))
    updates.append((acc_delta, rho * acc_delta + (1 - rho) * update **
2))
```

RMSProp

This updates rule is very effective in many cases. It is an improvement of the `Adagrad` update rule, using a moving average (parameterized by `rho`) to get a less aggressive decay:

```
updates = []
grads = T.grad(cost, params)
grads = clip_norms(grads, 50)
for p,g in zip(params,grads):
    acc = theano.shared(p.get_value() * 0.)
    acc_new = rho * acc + (1 - rho) * g ** 2
    updates.append((acc, acc_new))
    updated_p = p - learning_rate * (g / T.sqrt(acc_new + 1e-6))
    updates.append((p, updated_p))
```

Adam

This is `RMSProp` with momemtum, one of the best choices for the learning rule. The time step is kept track of in a shared variable, `t`. Two moving averages are computed, one for the past squared gradients, and the other for past gradient:

```
b1=0.9, b2=0.999, l=1-1e-8
updates = []
grads = T.grad(cost, params)
grads = clip_norms(grads, 50)
t = theano.shared(floatX(1.))
b1_t = b1 * l **(t-1)

for p, g in zip(params, grads):
    m = theano.shared(p.get_value() * 0.)
    v = theano.shared(p.get_value() * 0.)
    m_t = b1_t * m + (1 - b1_t) * g
    v_t = b2 * v + (1 - b2) * g**2
    updates.append((m, m_t))
    updates.append((v, v_t))
    updates.append((p, p - (learning_rate * m_t / (1 - b1**t)) /
(T.sqrt(v_t / (1 - b2**t)) + 1e-6)) )
updates.append((t, t + 1.))
```

To conclude on update rules, many recent research papers still prefer the simple SGD rule, and work the architecture and the initialization of the layers with the correct learning rate. For more complex networks, or if the data is sparse, the adaptive learning rate methods are better, sparing you the pain of finding the right learning rate.

Related articles

You can refer to the following documents for more insights into the topics covered in this chapter:

- *Deeplearning.net Theano tutorials*: *Single layer* (`http://deeplearning.net/tutorial/logreg.html`), MLP (`http://deeplearning.net/tutorial/mlp.html`), Convolutions (`http://deeplearning.net/tutorial/lenet.html`)

- All loss functions: for classification, regression, and joint embedding (`http://christopher5106.github.io/deep/learning/2016/09/16/about-loss-functions-multinomial-logistic-logarithm-cross-entropy-square-errors-euclidian-absolute-frobenius-hinge.html`)

- The last example corresponds to Yann Lecun's five-5 layer network as in Gradient based learning applied to document recognition (`http://yann.lecun.com/exdb/publis/pdf/lecun-98.pdf`)

- Understanding the difficulty of training deep feedforward neural networks, Xavier Glorot, Yoshua Bengio, 2010

- Maxout Networks: Ian J. Goodfellow, David Warde-Farley, Mehdi Mirza, Aaron Courville, Yoshua Bengio 2013

- An overview of gradient descent algorithms: `http://sebastianruder.com/optimizing-gradient-descent/`

- CS231n Convolutional Neural Networks for Visual Recognition, `http://cs231n.github.io/neural-networks-3/`

- Yes you should understand backprop, Andrej Karpathy, 2016, `https://medium.com/@karpathy/`

- Striving for Simplicity: The All Convolutional Net, Jost Tobias Springenberg, Alexey Dosovitskiy, Thomas Brox, Martin Riedmiller, 2014

- Fractional Max-Pooling, Benjamin Graham, 2014

- Batch Normalization: Accelerating Deep Network Training by Reducing Internal Covariate Shift, Sergey Ioffe, Christian Szegedy, 2015

- Visualizing and Understanding Convolutional Networks, Matthew D Zeiler, Rob Fergus, 2013

- Going Deeper with Convolutions, Christian Szegedy, Wei Liu, Yangqing Jia, Pierre Sermanet, Scott Reed, Dragomir Anguelov, Dumitru Erhan, Vincent Vanhoucke, Andrew Rabinovich, 2014

Summary

Classification is a very wide topic in machine learning. It consists of predicting a class or a category, as we have shown with our handwritten digits example. In *Chapter 7, Classifying Images with Residual Networks,* we'll see how to classify a wider set of natural images and objects.

Classification can be applied to different problems and the cross-entropy/negative log likelihood is the common loss function to solve them through gradient descent. There are many other loss functions for problems such as regression (mean square error loss) or unsupervised joint learning (hinge loss).

In this chapter, we have been using a very simple update rule as gradient descent named stochastic gradient descent, and presented some other gradient descent variants (`Momentum`, `Nesterov`, `RMSprop`, `ADAM`, `ADAGRAD`, `ADADELTA`). There has been some research into second order optimizations, such as Hessian Free, or K-FAC, which provided better results in deep or recurrent networks but remain complex and costly, and have not be widely adopted until now. Researchers have been looking for new architectures that perform better without the need for such optimization techniques.

When training networks, I would strongly encourage you to use the following two Linux commands:

- **Screen**: To detach your shell, run scripts on the server and reconnect later, since training usually takes a few days.
- **Tee**: To which you pipe the output of your running program, in order to save the displayed results to a file, while continuing to visualize the output in your shell. This will spare your code the burden of log functions and frameworks.

3
Encoding Word into Vector

In the previous chapter, inputs to neural nets were images, that is, vectors of continuous numeric values, the **natural language** for neural nets. But for many other machine learning fields, inputs may be categorical and discrete.

In this chapter, we'll present a technique known as embedding, which learns to transform discrete input signals into vectors. Such a representation of inputs is an important first step for compatibility with the rest of neural net processing.

Such embedding techniques will be illustrated with an example of natural language texts, which are composed of words belonging to a finite vocabulary.

We will present the different aspects of embedding:

- The principles of embedding
- The different types of word embedding
- One hot encoding versus index encoding
- Building a network to translate text into vectors
- Training and discovering the properties of embedding spaces
- Saving and loading the parameters of a model
- Dimensionality reduction for visualization
- Evaluating the quality of embeddings
- Applications of embedding spaces
- Weight tying

Encoding and embedding

Each word can be represented by an index in a vocabulary:

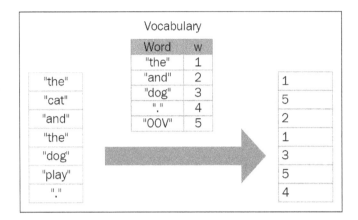

Encoding words is the process of representing each word as a vector.
The simplest method of encoding words is called one-hot or 1-of-K vector
representation. In this method, each word is represented as an $\mathbb{R}^{|V| \times 1}$ vector with
all 0s and one 1 at the index of that word in the sorted vocabulary. In this notation,
$|V|$ is the size of the vocabulary. Word vectors in this type of encoding for
vocabulary {**King, Queen, Man, Woman, Child**} appear as in the following example
of encoding for the word **Queen**:

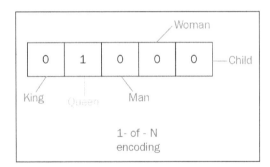

In the one-hot vector representation method, every word is equidistant from the
other. However, it fails to preserve any relationship between them and leads to
data sparsity. Using word embedding does overcome some of these drawbacks.

Word embedding is an approach to distributional semantics that represents words as
vectors of real numbers. Such representation has useful clustering properties, since it
groups together words that are semantically and syntactically similar.

For example, the words **seaworld** and **dolphin** will be very close in the created space. The main aim of this step is to map each word into a continuous, low-dimensional, and real-valued vector and use it as input to a model such as a **Recurrent Neural Network (RNN)**, a **Convolutional Neural Network (CNN)**, and so on:

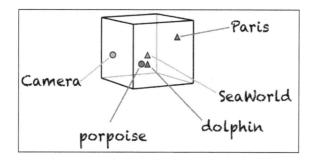

Such a representation is **dense**. We would expect synonyms and interchangeable words to be close in that space.

In this chapter, we will present the very popular model of word embedding, Word2Vec, which was initially developed by Mikolov et al. in 2013. Word2Vec has two different models: **Continuous Bag of Words (CBOW)** and **Skip-gram**.

In the CBOW method, the goal is to predict a word given a surrounding context. A Skip-gram predicts a surrounding context of words given a single word (see the following figure):

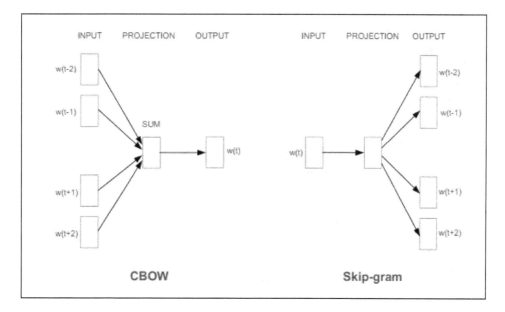

For this chapter, we will focus on the CBOW model. We will start by presenting the dataset, then we will explain the idea behind the method. Afterwards, we will show a simple implementation of it using Theano. Finally, we will end with referring to some applications of word embedding.

Dataset

Before we explain the model part, let us start by processing the text corpus by creating the vocabulary and integrating the text with it so that each word is represented as an integer. As a dataset, any text corpus can be used, such as Wikipedia or web articles, or posts from social networks such as Twitter. Frequently used datasets include PTB, text8, BBC, IMDB, and WMT datasets.

In this chapter, we use the text8 corpus. It consists of a pre-processed version of the first 100 million characters from a Wikipedia dump. Let us first download the corpus:

wget http://mattmahoney.net/dc/text8.zip -O /sharedfiles/text8.gz

gzip -d /sharedfiles/text8.gz -f

Now, we construct the vocabulary and replace the rare words with tokens for **UNKNOWN**. Let us start by reading the data into a list of strings:

1. Read the data into a list of strings:

```
words = []
with open('data/text8') as fin:
  for line in fin:
    words += [w for w in line.strip().lower().split()]

data_size = len(words)
print('Data size:', data_size)
```

From the list of strings, we can now build the dictionary. We start by counting the frequency of the words in the word_freq dictionary. Afterwards, we replace the words that are infrequent, that have a number of ocurrences in the corpus less than max_df, with tokens.

2. Build the dictionary and replace rare words with the UNK token:

```
unkown_token = '<UNK>'
pad_token = '<PAD>' # for padding the context
max_df = 5 # maximum number of freq
word_freq = [[unkown_token, -1], [pad_token, 0]]
word_freq.extend(Counter(words).most_common())
```

```
word_freq = OrderedDict(word_freq)
word2idx = {unkown_token: 0, pad_token: 1}
idx2word = {0: unkown_token, 1: pad_token}
idx = 2
for w in word_freq:
  f = word_freq[w]
  if f >= max_df:
    word2idx[w] = idx
    idx2word[idx] = w
    idx += 1
  else:
    word2idx[w] = 0 # map the rare word into the unkwon token
    word_freq[unkown_token] += 1 # increment the number of unknown
tokens

data = [word2idx[w] for w in words]

del words # for reduce mem use

vocabulary_size = len(word_freq)
most_common_words = list(word_freq.items())[:5]
print('Most common words (+UNK):', most_common_words)
print('Sample data:', data[:10], [idx2word[i] for i in data[:10]])
```

Data size: 17005207
Most common words (+UNK): [('<UNK>', 182564), ('the', 1061396), ('of', 593677), ('and', 416629), ('one', 411764)]
Sample data: [5239, 3084, 12, 6, 195, 2, 3137, 46, 59, 156] ['anarchism', 'originated', 'as', 'a', 'term', 'of', 'abuse', 'first', 'used', 'against']

3. Now, let us define the functions of creating the dataset (that is, the contexts and targets):

```
def get_sample(data, data_size, word_idx, pad_token, c = 1):

  idx = max(0, word_idx - c)
  context = data[idx:word_idx]
  if word_idx + 1 < data_size:
    context += data[word_idx + 1 : min(data_size, word_idx + c +
1)]
  target = data[word_idx]
  context = [w for w in context if w != target]
  if len(context) > 0:
    return target, context + (2 * c - len(context)) * [pad_token]
  return None, None

def get_data_set(data, data_size, pad_token, c=1):
  contexts = []
```

```
        targets = []
        for i in xrange(data_size):
          target, context =  get_sample(data, data_size, i, pad_token,
c)
          if not target is None:
            contexts.append(context)
            targets.append(target)

        return np.array(contexts, dtype='int32'), np.array(targets,
dtype='int32')
```

Continuous Bag of Words model

The design of the neural network to predict a word given its surrounding context is shown in the following figure:

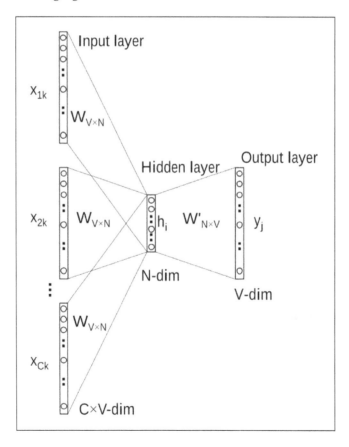

The input layer receives the context while the output layer predicts the target word. The model we'll use for the CBOW model has three layers: input layer, hidden layer (also called the projection layer or embedding layer), and output layer. In our setting, the vocabulary size is V and the hidden layer size is N. Adjacent units are fully connected.

The input and the output can be represented either by an index (an integer, 0-dimensional) or a one-hot-encoding vector (1-dimensional). Multiplying with the one-hot-encoding vector v consists simply of taking the j-th row of the embedding matrix:

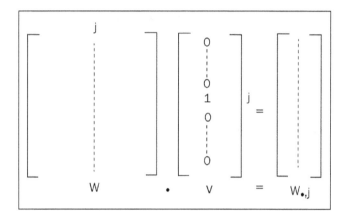

Since the index representation is more efficient than the one-hot encoding representation in terms of memory usage, and Theano supports indexing symbolic variables, it is preferable to adopt the index representation as much as possible.

Therefore, input (context) will be 2-dimensional, represented by a matrix, with two dimensions: the batch size and the context length. The output (target) is 1-dimensional, represented by a vector with one dimension: the batch size.

Let's define the CBOW model:

```python
import theano
import theano.tensor as T
import numpy as np
import math
context = T.imatrix(name='context')
target = T.ivector('target')
```

The context and target variables are the known parameters of this model. The unknown parameters of the CBOW model are the connection matrix W_{in}, between the input layer and the hidden layer, and the connection matrix W_{out}, between the hidden layer and the output layer:

```
vocab_size = len(idx2word)
emb_size = 128
W_in_values = np.asarray(np.random.uniform(-1.0, 1.0,
    (vocab_size, emb_size)),
dtype=theano.config.floatX)

W_out_values = np.asarray(np.random.normal(
    scale=1.0 / math.sqrt(emb_size),
    size=(emb_size, vocab_size)),
    dtype=theano.config.floatX)

W_in = theano.shared(value=W_in_values,
                     name='W_in',
                     borrow=True)

W_out = theano.shared(value=W_out_values,
                      name='W_out',
                      borrow=True)



params = [W_in, W_out]
```

Each row of W_{in} is the N-dimension vector representation v_{wj} of the associated word, i, of the input layer, where N is the hidden layer size. Given a context, when computing the hidden layer output, the CBOW model takes the average of the vectors of the input context words, and uses the product of the input -> hidden weight matrix and the average vector as the output:

$$h = \frac{1}{C}\left(v_{w_1} + v_{w_2} + \cdots + v_{w_c}\right)$$
(1)

Here, c is the number of words in the context, w1, w2, w3, ..., wc are the words in the context, and v_{w_j} is the input vector of a word w_j. The activation function of the output layer is the softmax layer. Equations 2 and 3 show how we compute the output layer:

$$u_j = v_{w_j}^T \cdot h \quad (2)$$

$$p\left(w_j | w_1, w_2, \cdots w_C\right) = p\left(w_j | h\right) = \frac{\exp\left(u_j\right)}{\sum_{i=1}^{V} \exp\left(u_i\right)} \quad (3)$$

Here, v_{w_j} is the j-th column of the matrix W_{out} and v is the vocabulary size. In our settings, the vocabulary size is vocab_size and the hidden layer size is emb_size. The loss function is as follows:

$$E = -\log p\left(w_j | w_1, w_2, \cdots w_C\right) = -\log p\left(w_j | h\right) \quad (4)$$

Now, let us translate equations 1, 2, 3, and 4 in Theano.

To compute the hidden (projection) layer output: input -> hidden (eq. 1)

```
h = T.mean(W_in[context], axis=1)
```

For the hidden -> output layer (eq. 2)
```
uj = T.dot(h, W_out)
```

The softmax activation (eq. 3) :

```
p_target_given_contex = T.nnet.softmax(uj).dimshuffle(1, 0)
```

The loss function (eq. 4):

```
loss = -T.mean(T.log(p_target_given_contex)[T.arange(target.shape[0]), target])
```

Update the parameters of the model using SGD:

```
g_params = T.grad(cost=loss, wrt=params)
updates = [
        (param, param - learning_rate * gparam)
        for param, gparam in zip(params, g_params)
]
```

Finally, we need to define the training and evaluation functions.

Let's make the dataset shared to pass it to the GPU. For simplicity, we assume that we have a function called `get_data_set` that returns the set of targets and its surrounding context:

```
contexts, targets = get_data_set(data, data_size, word2idx[pad_token],
c=2)

contexts = theano.shared(contexts)
targets = theano.shared(targets)

index = T.lscalar('index')

train_model = theano.function(
    inputs=[index],
    outputs=[loss],
    updates=updates,
    givens={
        context: contexts[index * batch_size: (index + 1) * batch_
size],
        target: targets[index * batch_size: (index + 1) * batch_size]
    }
)
```

The input variable of `train_model` is the index of the batch, since the whole dataset has been transferred in one pass to the GPU thanks to shared variables.

For validation during training, we evaluate the model using the cosine similarity between a mini batch of examples and all embeddings.

Let's use a `theano` variable to place the input to the validation model:

```
valid_samples = T.ivector('valid_samples')
```

Normalized word embedding of the validation input:

```
embeddings = params[0]
norm = T.sqrt(T.sum(T.sqr(embeddings), axis=1, keepdims=True))
normalized_embeddings = W_in / norm


valid_embeddings = normalized_embeddings[valid_samples]
```

Similarity is given by the cosine similarity function:

```
similarity = theano.function([valid_samples], T.dot(valid_embeddings,
normalized_embeddings.T))
```

Training the model

Now we can start training the model. In this example, we chose to train the model using SGD with a batch size of 64 and 100 epochs. To validate the model, we randomly selected 16 words and used the similarity measure as an evaluation metric:

1. Let's begin training:

```
valid_size = 16      # Random set of words to evaluate similarity
on.
valid_window = 100  # Only pick dev samples in the head of the
distribution.
valid_examples = np.array(np.random.choice(valid_window, valid_
size, replace=False), dtype='int32')

n_epochs = 100
n_train_batches = data_size // batch_size
n_iters = n_epochs * n_train_batches
train_loss = np.zeros(n_iters)
average_loss = 0

for epoch in range(n_epochs):
    for minibatch_index in range(n_train_batches):

        iteration = minibatch_index + n_train_batches * epoch
        loss = train_model(minibatch_index)
        train_loss[iteration] = loss
        average_loss += loss


        if iteration % 2000 == 0:

            if iteration > 0:
                average_loss /= 2000
                # The average loss is an estimate of the loss over the
last 2000 batches.
                print("Average loss at step ", iteration, ": ",
average_loss)
                average_loss = 0


            # Note that this is expensive (~20% slowdown if computed
every 500 steps)
            if iteration % 10000 == 0:
```

```
        sim = similarity(valid_examples)
    for i in xrange(valid_size):
        valid_word = idx2word[valid_examples[i]]
        top_k = 8 # number of nearest neighbors
        nearest = (-sim[i, :]).argsort()[1:top_k+1]
        log_str = "Nearest to %s:" % valid_word
        for k in xrange(top_k):
            close_word = idx2word[nearest[k]]
            log_str = "%s %s," % (log_str, close_word)
        print(log_str)
```

2. Lastly, let us create two generic functions that will help us save any model parameters in a reusable `utils.py` utility file:

```
def save_params(outfile, params):
    l = []
    for param in params:
        l = l + [ param.get_value() ]
    numpy.savez(outfile, *l)
    print("Saved model parameters to {}.npz".format(outfile))


def load_params(path, params):
    npzfile = numpy.load(path+".npz")
    for i, param in enumerate(params):
        param.set_value( npzfile["arr_" +str(i)] )
    print("Loaded model parameters from {}.npz".format(path))
```

3. Running on a GPU, the preceding code prints the following results:

Using gpu device 1: Tesla K80 (CNMeM is enabled with initial size: 80.0% of memory, cuDNN 5105)

Data size 17005207

Most common words (+UNK) [('<UNK>', 182565), ('<PAD>', 0), ('the', 1061396), ('of', 593677), ('and', 416629)]

Sample data [5240, 3085, 13, 7, 196, 3, 3138, 47, 60, 157] ['anarchism', 'originated', 'as', 'a', 'term', 'of', 'abuse', 'first', 'used', 'against']

Average loss at step 0 : 11.2959747314

Average loss at step 2000 : 8.81626828802

Average loss at step 4000 : 7.63789177912

Average loss at step 6000 : 7.40699760973

Average loss at step 8000 : 7.20080085599

Average loss at step 10000 : 6.85602856147

Average loss at step 12000 : 6.88123817992

Average loss at step 14000 : 6.96217652643
Average loss at step 16000 : 6.53794862854

...

Average loss at step 26552000 : 4.52319500107
Average loss at step 26554000 : 4.55709513521
Average loss at step 26556000 : 4.62755958384
Average loss at step 26558000 : 4.6266620369
Average loss at step 26560000 : 4.82731778347
Nearest to system: systems, network, device, unit, controller, schemes, vessel, scheme,
Nearest to up: off, out, alight, forth, upwards, down, ordered, ups,
Nearest to first: earliest, last, second, next, oldest, fourth, third, newest,
Nearest to nine: apq, nineteenth, poz, jyutping, afd, apod, eurocents, zoolander,
Nearest to between: across, within, involving, with, among, concerning, through, from,
Nearest to state: states, provincial, government, nation, gaeltachta, reservation, infirmity, slates,
Nearest to are: were, is, aren, was, include, have, weren, contain,
Nearest to may: might, should, must, can, could, would, will, cannot,
Nearest to zero: hundred, pounders, hadza, cest, bureaus, eight, rang, osr,
Nearest to that: which, where, aurea, kessai, however, unless, but, although,
Nearest to can: could, must, cannot, should, may, will, might, would,
Nearest to s: his, whose, its, castletown, cide, codepoint, onizuka, brooklands,
Nearest to will: would, must, should, could, can, might, shall, may,
Nearest to their: its, his, your, our, her, my, the, whose,
Nearest to but: however, though, although, which, while, whereas, moreover, unfortunately,
Nearest to not: never, indeed, rarely, seldom, almost, hardly, unable, gallaecia,
Saved model parameters to model.npz

Let us note:

- Rare words are updated only a small number of times, while frequent words appear more often in inputs and context windows. Subsampling of frequent words can remedy to this.

- All weights are updated in the output embedding, and only a few of them, those corresponding to the words in the context window, are updated positively. Negative sampling can help rebalance the positives and negatives in the update.

Visualizing the learned embeddings

Let us visualize the embedding in a 2D figure in order to get an understanding of how well they capture similarity and semantics. For that purpose, we need to reduce the number of dimension of the embedding, which is highly dimensional, to two dimensions without altering the structure of the embeddings.

Reducing the number of dimension is called manifold learning, and many different techniques exist, some of them linear, such as **Principal Component Analysis (PCA)**, **Independent Component Analysis (ICA)**, **Linear Discriminant Analysis (LDA)**, and **Latent Sementic Analysis / Indexing (LSA / LSI)**, and some are non-linear, such as **Isomap**, **Locally Linear Embedding (LLE)**, **Hessian Eigenmapping**, **Spectral embedding**, **Local tangent space embedding**, **Multi Dimensional Scaling (MDS)**, and **t-distributed Stochastic Neighbor Embedding (t-SNE)**.

To display the word embedding, let us use t-SNE, a great technique adapted to high dimensional data to reveal local structures and clusters, without crowding points together:

1. Visualize the embeddings:

```python
def plot_with_labels(low_dim_embs, labels, filename='tsne.png'):
  assert low_dim_embs.shape[0] >= len(labels), "More labels than
embeddings"
  plt.figure(figsize=(18, 18))  #in inches
  for i, label in enumerate(labels):
    x, y = low_dim_embs[i,:]
    plt.scatter(x, y)
    plt.annotate(label,
                 xy=(x, y),
                 xytext=(5, 2),
                 textcoords='offset points',
                 ha='right',
                 va='bottom')

  plt.savefig(filename)

from sklearn.manifold import TSNE
import matplotlib.pyplot as plt

tsne = TSNE(perplexity=30, n_components=2, init='pca', n_iter=5000)
```

```
plot_only = 500
low_dim_embs = tsne.fit_transform(final_embeddings[:plot_only,:])
labels = [idx2word[i] for i in xrange(plot_only)]
plot_with_labels(low_dim_embs, labels)
```

The plotted map displays the words with similar embeddings close to each other:

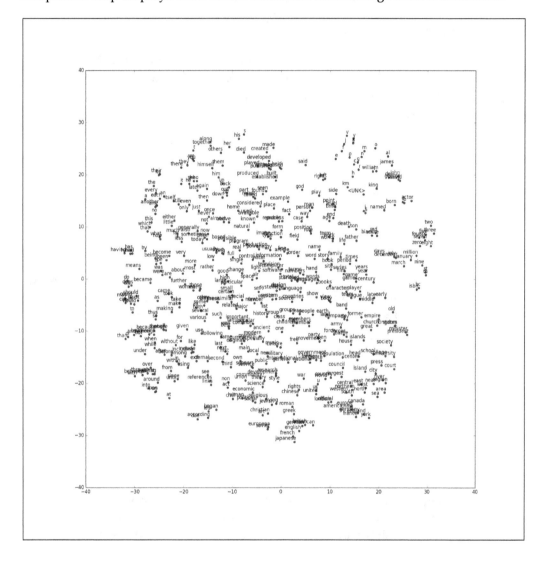

Evaluating embeddings – analogical reasoning

Analogical reasoning is a simple and efficient way to evaluate embeddings by predicting syntactic and semantic relationships of the form *a is to b as c is to _?*, denoted as $a : b \rightarrow c : ?$. The task is to identify the held-out fourth word, with only exact word matches deemed correct.

For example, the word *woman* is the best answer to the question *king is to queen as man is to?*. Assume that $\vec{w}$ is the representation vector for the word w normalized to unit norm. Then, we can answer the question $a : b \rightarrow c : ?$, by finding the word d' with the representation closest to:

$$\vec{b} - \vec{a} + \vec{c}$$

According to cosine similarity:

$$d' = \underset{x}{argmax} \left(\vec{b} - \vec{a} + \vec{c} \right)^T \cdot \vec{x}$$

Now let us implement the analogy prediction function using Theano. First, we need to define the input of the function. The analogy function receives three inputs, which are the word indices of a, b, and c:

```
analogy_a = T.ivector('analogy_a')
analogy_b = T.ivector('analogy_b')
analogy_c = T.ivector('analogy_c')
```

Then, we need to map each input to the word embedding vector. Each row of a_emb, b_emb, c_emb is a word's embedding vector:

```
a_emb = embeddings[analogy_a]    # a's embs
b_emb = embeddings[analogy_b]    # b's embs
c_emb = embeddings[analogy_c]    # c's embs
```

Now we can compute the cosine distance between each target and vocab pair. We expect that d's embedding vectors on the unit hyper-sphere is near: c_emb + (b_emb - a_emb), which has the shape [bsz, emb_size]. dist has shape [bsz, vocab_size].

```
dist = T.dot(target, embeddings.T)
```

In this example, we consider that the prediction function takes the top four words. Thus, we can define the function in Theano as the following:

```
pred_idx = T.argsort(dist, axis=1)[:, -4:]
prediction = theano.function([analogy_a, analogy_b, analogy_c], pred_
idx)
```

To run the preceding function, we need to load the evaluation data, which is in this example the set of analogy questions defined by Google. Each question contains four words separated by spaces. The first question can be interpreted as *Athens is to Greece as Baghdad is to _?* and the correct answer should be *Iraq*:

```
Athens Greece Baghdad Iraq
Athens Greece Bangkok Thailand
Athens Greece Beijing China
```

Let us load the analogy questions using the read_analogies function that is defined in the following code:

```
def read_analogies(fname, word2idx):
    """Reads through the analogy question file.
    Returns:
      questions: a [n, 4] numpy array containing the analogy
question's
                 word ids.
      questions_skipped: questions skipped due to unknown words.
    """
    questions = []
    questions_skipped = 0
    with open(fname, "r") as analogy_f:
      for line in analogy_f:
        if line.startswith(":"):  # Skip comments.
          continue
        words = line.strip().lower().split(" ")
        ids = [word2idx.get(w.strip()) for w in words]
        if None in ids or len(ids) != 4:
          questions_skipped += 1
        else:
          questions.append(np.array(ids))
    print("Eval analogy file: ", fname)
```

```
print("Questions: ", len(questions))
print("Skipped: ", questions_skipped)

return np.array(questions, dtype=np.int32)
```

Now, we can run the evaluation model:

```
"""Evaluate analogy questions and reports accuracy."""

# How many questions we get right at precision@1.
correct = 0
analogy_data = read_analogies(args.eval_data, word2idx)
analogy_questions = analogy_data[:, :3]
answers = analogy_data[:, 3]
del analogy_data
total = analogy_questions.shape[0]
start = 0

while start < total:
  limit = start + 200
  sub_questions = analogy_questions[start:limit, :]
  sub_answers = answers[start:limit]
  idx = prediction(sub_questions[:,0], sub_questions[:,1], sub_
questions[:,2])

  start = limit
  for question in xrange(sub_questions.shape[0]):
    for j in xrange(4):
      if idx[question, j] == sub_answers[question]:
        # Bingo! We predicted correctly. E.g., [italy, rome, france,
paris].
        correct += 1
        break
      elif idx[question, j] in sub_questions[question]:
        # We need to skip words already in the question.
        continue
      else:
        # The correct label is not the precision@1
        break
  print()
  print("Eval %4d/%d accuracy = %4.1f%%" % (correct, total,
                                            correct * 100.0 / total))
```

This results in:

> *Eval analogy file: questions-words.txt*
> *Questions: 17827*
> *Skipped: 1717*
> *Eval 831/17827 accuracy = 4.7%*

Evaluating embeddings – quantitative analysis

A few words might be enough to indicate that the quantitative analysis of embeddings is also possible.

Some word similarity benchmarks propose human-based distances between concepts: Simlex999 (Hill et al., 2016), Verb-143 (Baker et al., 2014), MEN (Bruni et al., 2014), RareWord (Luong et al., 2013), and MTurk- 771 (Halawi et al., 2012).

Our similarity distance between embeddings can be compared to these human distances, using Spearman's rank correlation coefficient to quantitatively evaluate the quality of the learned embeddings.

Application of word embeddings

Word embeddings capture the meaning of the words. They translate a discrete input into an input that can be processed by neural nets.

Embeddings are the start of many applications linked to language:

- Generating texts, as we'll see in the next chapter
- Translation systems, where input and target sentences are sequences of words and whose embeddings can be processed by end-to-end neural nets (*Chapter 8, Translating and Explaining with Encoding – decoding Networks*)
- Sentiment analysis (*Chapter 5, Analyzing Sentiment with a Bidirectional LSTM*)
- Zero-shot learning in computer vision; the structure in the word language enables us to find classes for which no training images exist
- Image annotation/captioning
- Neuro-psychiatry, for which neural nets can predict with 100% accuracy some psychiatric disorders in human beings
- Chatbots, or answering questions from a user (*Chapter 9, Selecting Relevant Inputs or Memories with the Mechanism of Attention*)

As with words, the principle of semantic embedding can be used on any problem with categorical variables (classes of images, sounds, films, and so on), where the learned embedding for the activation of categorical variables can be used as input to neural nets for further classification challenges.

As language structures our mind, word embeddings help structure or improve the performance of neural net based systems.

Weight tying

Two weight matrices, W_{in} and W_{out} have been used for input or output respectively. While all weights of W_{out} are updated at every iteration during back propagation, W_{in} is only updated on the column corresponding to the current training input word.

Weight tying (**WT**) consists of using only one matrix, W, for input and output embedding. Theano then computes the new derivatives with respect to these new weights and all weights in W are updated at every iteration. Fewer parameters leads to less overfitting.

In the case of Word2Vec, such a technique does not give better results for a simple reason: in the Word2Vec model, the probability of finding the input word in the context is given as:

$$\left(W \cdot i\right)^{T} \cdot \left(W \cdot i\right)$$

It should be as close to zero but cannot be zero except if W = 0.

But in other applications, such as in **Neural Network Language Models** (**NNLM**) in *Chapter 4, Generating Text with a Recurrent Neural Net* and **Neural Machine Translation** (**NMT**) in *Chapter 8, Translating and Explaining with Encoding-decoding Networks*), it can be shown [*Using the output embedding to improve the language models*] that:

- Input embeddings are usually worse than output embeddings
- WT solves this problem
- The common embedding learned with WT is close in quality to the output embedding without WT
- Inserting a regularized projection matrix P before the output embedding helps the networks use the same embedding and leads to even better results under WT

Further reading

Please refer to the following articles:

- Efficient Estimation of Word Representations in Vector Space, Tomas Mikolov, Kai Chen, Greg Corrado, Jeffrey Dean, Jan 2013

- Factor-based Compositional Embedding Models, Mo Yu, 2014

- Character-level Convolutional Networks for Text Classification, Xiang Zhang, Junbo Zhao, Yann LeCun, 2015

- Distributed Representations of Words and Phrases and their Compositionality, Tomas Mikolov, Ilya Sutskever, Kai Chen, Greg Corrado, Jeffrey Dean, 2013

- Using the Output Embedding to Improve Language Models, Ofir Press, Lior Wolf, Aug 2016

Summary

This chapter presented a very common way to transform discrete inputs in particular texts into numerical embeddings, in the case of natural language processing.

The technique to train these word representations with neural networks does not require us to label the data and infers its embedding directly from natural texts. Such training is named *unsupervised learning*.

One of the main challenges with deep learning is to convert input and output signals into representations that can be processed by nets, in particular vectors of floats. Then, neural nets give all the tools to process these vectors, to learn, decide, classify, reason, or generate.

In the next chapters, we'll use these embeddings to work with texts and more advanced neural networks. The first application presented in the next chapter is about automatic text generation.

4
Generating Text with a Recurrent Neural Net

In the previous chapter, you learned how to represent a discrete input into a vector so that neural nets have the power to understand discrete inputs as well as continuous ones.

Many real-world applications involve variable-length inputs, such as connected objects and automation (sort of Kalman filters, much more evolved); natural language processing (understanding, translation, text generation, and image annotation); human behavior reproduction (text handwriting generation and chat bots); and reinforcement learning.

Previous networks, named feedforward networks, are able to classify inputs of fixed dimensions only. To extend their power to variable-length inputs, a new category of networks has been designed: the **recurrent neural networks** (**RNN**) that are well suited for machine learning tasks on variable-length inputs or sequences.

Three well-known recurrent neural nets (simple RNN, GRU, and LSTM) are presented for the example of text generation. The topics covered in this chapter are as follows:

- The case of sequences
- The mechanism of recurrent networks
- How to build a simple recurrent network
- Backpropagation through time
- Different types of RNN, LSTM, and GRU
- Perplexity and word error rate
- Training on text data for text generation
- Applications of recurrent networks

Need for RNN

Deep learning networks for natural language is numerical and deals well with multidimensional arrays of floats and integers, as input values. For categorical values, such characters or words, the previous chapter demonstrated a technique known as embedding for transforming them into numerical values as well.

So far, all inputs have been fixed-sized arrays. In many applications, such as texts in natural language processing, inputs have one semantic meaning but can be represented by sequences of variable length.

There is a need to deal with variable-length sequences as shown in the following diagram:

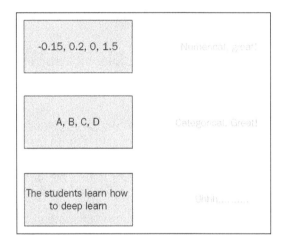

Recurrent Neural Networks (RNN) are the answer to variable-length inputs.

Recurrence can be seen as applying a feedforward network more than once at different time steps, with different incoming input data, but with a major difference, the presence of connections to the past, previous time steps, and in one goal, to refine the representation of input through time.

At each time step, the hidden layer output values represent an intermediate state of the network.

Recurrent connections define the transition for moving from one state to another, given an input, in order to refine the representation:

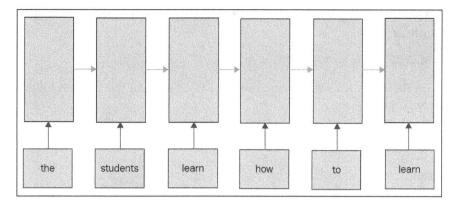

Recurrent neural networks are suited for challenges involving sequences, such as texts, sounds and speech, hand writing, and time series.

A dataset for natural language

As a dataset, any text corpus can be used, such as Wikipedia, web articles, or even with symbols such as code or computer programs, theater plays, and poems; the model will catch and reproduce the different patterns in the data.

In this case, let's use tiny Shakespeare texts to predict new Shakespeare texts or at least, new texts written in a style inspired by Shakespeare; two levels of predictions are possible, but can be handled in the same way:

- **At the character level**: Characters belong to an alphabet that includes punctuation, and given the first few characters, the model predicts the next characters from an alphabet, including spaces to build words and sentences. There is no constraint for the predicted word to belong to a dictionary and the objective of training is to build words and sentences close to real ones.

- **At the word level**: Words belong to a dictionary that includes punctuation, and given the first few words, the model predicts the next word out of a vocabulary. In this case, there is a strong constraint on the words since they belong to a dictionary, but not on sentences. We expect the model to focus more on capturing the syntax and meaning of the sentences than on the character level.

In both modes, token designates character/word; dictionary, alphabet, or vocabulary designates (the list of possible values for the token);

The popular NLTK library, a Python module, is used to split texts into sentences and tokenize into words:

```
conda install nltk
```

In a Python shell, run the following command to download the English tokenizer in the book package:

```
import nltk
nltk.download("book")
```

Let's parse the text to extract words:

```
from load import parse_text
X_train, y_train, index_to_word = parse_text("data/tiny-shakespear.
txt", type="word")

for i in range(10):
  print "x", " ".join([index_to_word[x] for x in X_train[i]])
  print "y"," ".join([index_to_word[x] for x in y_train[i]])
```

Vocabulary size 9000
Found 12349 unique words tokens.
The least frequent word in our vocabulary is 'a-fire' and appeared 1 times.
x START first citizen : before we proceed any further , hear me speak .
y first citizen : before we proceed any further , hear me speak . END
x START all : speak , speak .
y all : speak , speak . END
x START first citizen : you are all resolved rather to die than to famish ?
y first citizen : you are all resolved rather to die than to famish ? END
x START all : resolved .
y all : resolved . END
x START resolved .
y resolved . END
x START first citizen : first , you know caius marcius is chief enemy to the people .
y first citizen : first , you know caius marcius is chief enemy to the people . END
x START all : we know't , we know't .
y all : we know't , we know't . END
x START first citizen : let us kill him , and we 'll have corn at our own price .
y first citizen : let us kill him , and we 'll have corn at our own price . END
x START is't a verdict ?
y is't a verdict ? END
x START all : no more talking o n't ; let it be done : away , away !
y all : no more talking o n't ; let it be done : away , away ! END

Or the `char` library:

```
from load import parse_text
X_train, y_train, index_to_char = parse_text("data/tiny-shakespear.
txt",
    type="char")

for i in range(10):
  print "x",''.join([index_to_char[x] for x in X_train[i]])
  print "y",''.join([index_to_char[x] for x in y_train[i]])
```

x ^first citizen: before we proceed any further, hear me speak
y irst citizen: before we proceed any further, hear me speak.$
x ^all: speak, speak
y ll: speak, speak.$
x ^first citizen: you are all resolved rather to die than to famish
y irst citizen: you are all resolved rather to die than to famish?$
x ^all: resolved
y ll: resolved.$
x ^resolved
y esolved.$
x ^first citizen: first, you know caius marcius is chief enemy to the people
y irst citizen: first, you know caius marcius is chief enemy to the people.$
x ^all: we know't, we know't
y ll: we know't, we know't.$
x ^first citizen: let us kill him, and we'll have corn at our own price
y irst citizen: let us kill him, and we'll have corn at our own price.$
x ^is't a verdict
y s't a verdict?$
x ^all: no more talking on't; let it be done: away, away
y ll: no more talking on't; let it be done: away, away!$

The additional start token (the START word and the ^ character) avoids having a void hidden state when the prediction starts. Another solution is to initialize the first hidden state with $h_0 = W_{h0}$.

The additional end token (the END word and the $ character) helps the network learn to predict a stop when the sequence generation is predicted to be finished.

Last, the out of vocabulary token (the UNKNOWN word) replaces words that do not belong to the vocabulary to avoid big dictionaries.

In this example, we'll omit the validation dataset, but for any real-world application, keeping a part of the data for validation is a good practice.

Also, note that functions from *Chapter 2, Classifying Handwritten Digits with a Feedforward Network* for layer initialization `shared_zeros` and `shared_glorot_uniform` and from *Chapter 3, Encoding Word into Vector* for model saving and loading `save_params` and `load_params` have been packaged into the `utils` package:

```
from theano import *
import theano.tensor as T
from utils import shared_zeros,
    shared_glorot_uniform,
    save_params,
    load_params
```

Simple recurrent network

An RNN is a network applied at multiple time steps but with a major difference: a connection to the previous state of layers at previous time steps named hidden states h_t:

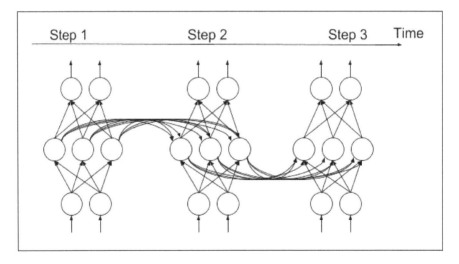

This can be written in the following form:

$$h_t = \tanh\left(W_{in} \cdot x + W \cdot h_{t-1} + b_h\right)$$
$$y_t = W_{out} \cdot h_t + b_y$$

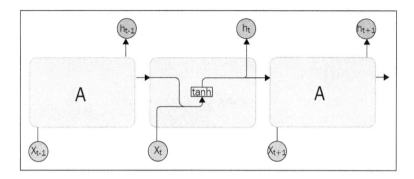

An RNN can be unrolled as a feedforward network applied on the sequence $\left[x(t)\right]_t$ as input and with shared parameters between different time steps.

Input and output's first dimension is time, while next dimensions are for the data dimension inside each step. As seen in the previous chapter, the value at a time step (a word or a character) can be represented either by an index (an integer, 0-dimensional) or a one-hot-encoding vector (1-dimensional). The former representation is more compact in memory. In this case, input and output sequences will be 1-dimensional represented by a vector, with one dimension, the time:

```
x = T.ivector()
y = T.ivector()
```

The structure of the training program remains the same as in *Chapter 2, Classifying Handwritten Digits with a Feedforward Network* with feedforward network, except the model that we'll define with a recurrent module shares the same weights at different time steps:

```
embedding_size = len(index_)
n_hidden=500
```

Let's define the hidden and input weights:

```
U = shared_glorot_uniform(( embedding_size,n_hidden), name="U")
W = shared_glorot_uniform((n_hidden, n_hidden), name="W")
bh = shared_zeros((n_hidden,), name="bh")
```

And the output weights:

```
V = shared_glorot_uniform(( n_hidden, embedding_size), name="V")
by = shared_zeros((embedding_size,), name="by")

params = [U,V,W,by,bh]

def step(x_t, h_tm1):
    h_t = T.tanh(U[x_t] + T.dot( h_tm1, W) + bh)
    y_t = T.dot(h_t, V) + by
    return h_t, y_t
```

Initial state can be set to zero while using the start tokens:

```
h0 = shared_zeros((n_hidden,), name='h0')
[h, y_pred], _ = theano.scan(step, sequences=x, outputs_info=[h0,
None], truncate_gradient=10)
```

It returns two tensors, where the first dimension is time and the second dimension is data values (0-dimensional in this case).

Gradient computation through the scan function is automatic in Theano and follows both direct and recurrent connections to the previous time step. Therefore, due to the recurrent connections, the error at a particular time step is propagated to the previous time step, a mechanism named **Backpropagation Through Time** (BPTT).

It has been observed that the gradients either explode or vanish after too many time steps. This is why the gradients are truncated after 10 steps in this example, and errors will not be backpropagated to further past time steps.

For the remaining steps, we keep the classification as before:

```
model = T.nnet.softmax(y_pred)
y_out = T.argmax(model, axis=-1)
cost = -T.mean(T.log(model)[T.arange(y.shape[0]), y])
```

This returns a vector of values at each time step.

LSTM network

One of the main difficulties with RNN is to capture long-term dependencies due to the vanishing/exploding gradient effect and truncated backpropagation.

To overcome this issue, researchers have been looking at a long list of potential solutions. A new kind of recurrent network was designed in 1997 with a memory unit, named a cell state, specialized in keeping and transmitting long-term information.

At each time step, the cell value can be updated partially with a candidate cell and partially erased thanks to a gate mechanism. Two gates, the update gate and the forget gate, decide how to update the cell, given the previously hidden state value and current input value:

$$g_u = \sigma\left(W_{ui}x_t + W_{uh}h_{t-1} + W_{uc}c_{t-1}\right)$$
$$g_f = \sigma\left(W_{fi}x_t + W_{fh}h_{t-1} + W_{fc}c_{t-1}\right)$$

The candidate cell is computed in the same way:

$$\varsigma = \tanh\left(W_{ci}x_t + W_{ch}h_{t-1}\right)$$

The new cell state is computed as follows:

$$c_t = g_f * c_{t-1} + g_u * \varsigma$$

For the new hidden state, an output gate decides what information in the cell value to output:

$$g_o = \sigma\left(W_{oi}x_t + W_{oh}h_{t-1} + W_{oc}c_{t-1}\right)$$
$$h_t = \tanh\left(c_t\right) * g_o$$

The remaining stays equal with the simple RNN:

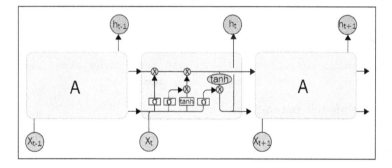

This mechanism allows the network to store some information to use a lot further in future than it was possible with a simple RNN.

Many variants of design for LSTM have been designed and it is up to you to test these variants on your problems to see how they behave.

In this example, we'll use a variant, where gates and candidates use both the previously hidden state and previous cell state.

In Theano, let's define the weights for:

- the input gate:

```
W_xi = shared_glorot_uniform(( embedding_size,n_hidden))
W_hi = shared_glorot_uniform(( n_hidden,n_hidden))
W_ci = shared_glorot_uniform(( n_hidden,n_hidden))
b_i = shared_zeros((n_hidden,))
```

- the forget gate:

```
W_xf = shared_glorot_uniform(( embedding_size, n_hidden))
W_hf = shared_glorot_uniform(( n_hidden,n_hidden))
W_cf = shared_glorot_uniform(( n_hidden,n_hidden))
b_f = shared_zeros((n_hidden,))
```

- the output gate:

```
W_xo = shared_glorot_uniform(( embedding_size, n_hidden))
W_ho = shared_glorot_uniform(( n_hidden,n_hidden))
W_co = shared_glorot_uniform(( n_hidden,n_hidden))
b_o = shared_zeros((n_hidden,))
```

- the cell:

```
W_xc = shared_glorot_uniform(( embedding_size, n_hidden))
W_hc = shared_glorot_uniform(( n_hidden,n_hidden))
b_c = shared_zeros((n_hidden,))
```

- the output layer:

```
W_y = shared_glorot_uniform(( n_hidden, embedding_size), name="V")
b_y = shared_zeros((embedding_size,), name="by")
```

The array of all trainable parameters:

```
params = [W_xi,W_hi,W_ci,b_i,W_xf,W_hf,W_cf,b_f,W_xo,W_ho,W_co,b_o,W_xc,W_hc,b_c,W_y,b_y]
```

The step function to be placed inside the recurrent loop :

```
def step(x_t, h_tm1, c_tm1):
    i_t = T.nnet.sigmoid(W_xi[x_t] + T.dot(W_hi, h_tm1) + T.dot(W_ci, c_tm1) + b_i)
```

```
    f_t = T.nnet.sigmoid(W_xf[x_t] + T.dot(W_hf, h_tm1) + T.dot(W_cf,
c_tm1) + b_f)
    c_t = f_t * c_tm1 + i_t * T.tanh(W_xc[x_t] + T.dot(W_hc, h_tm1) +
b_c)
    o_t = T.nnet.sigmoid(W_xo[x_t] + T.dot(W_ho, h_tm1) + T.dot(W_co,
c_t) + b_o)
    h_t = o_t * T.tanh(c_t)
    y_t = T.dot(h_t, W_y) + b_y
    return h_t, c_t, y_t
```

Let's create the recurrent loop with the scan operator :

```
h0 = shared_zeros((n_hidden,), name='h0')
c0 = shared_zeros((n_hidden,), name='c0')
[h, c, y_pred], _ = theano.scan(step,
    sequences=x,
    outputs_info=[h0, c0, None],
    truncate_gradient=10)
```

Gated recurrent network

The GRU is an alternative to LSTM, simplifying the mechanism without the use of an extra cell:

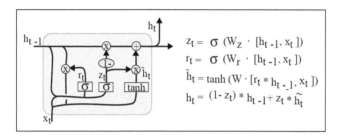

$$z_t = \sigma (W_z \cdot [h_{t-1}, x_t])$$
$$r_t = \sigma (W_r \cdot [h_{t-1}, x_t])$$
$$\tilde{h}_t = \tanh (W \cdot [r_t * h_{t-1}, x_t])$$
$$h_t = (1 - z_t) * h_{t-1} + z_t * \tilde{h}_t$$

The code to build a gated recurrent network consists simply of defining the weights and the `step` function, as before:

- Weights for the Update gate:

```
W_xz = shared_glorot_uniform(( embedding_size,n_hidden))
W_hz = shared_glorot_uniform(( n_hidden,n_hidden))
b_z = shared_zeros((n_hidden,))
```

- Weights for the Reset gate:

```
W_xr = shared_glorot_uniform(( embedding_size,n_hidden))
W_hr = shared_glorot_uniform(( n_hidden,n_hidden))
b_r = shared_zeros((n_hidden,))
```

- Weight for the Hidden layer:

```
W_xh = shared_glorot_uniform(( embedding_size,n_hidden))
W_hh = shared_glorot_uniform(( n_hidden,n_hidden))
b_h = shared_zeros((n_hidden,))
```

- Weight for the Output layer:

```
W_y = shared_glorot_uniform(( n_hidden, embedding_size), name="V")
b_y = shared_zeros((embedding_size,), name="by")
```

The trainable parameters:

```
params = [W_xz, W_hz, b_z, W_xr, W_hr, b_r, W_xh, W_hh, b_h, W_y, b_y]
```

The step function:

```
def step(x_t, h_tm1):
    z_t = T.nnet.sigmoid(W_xz[x_t] + T.dot(W_hz, h_tm1) + b_z)
    r_t = T.nnet.sigmoid(W_xr[x_t] + T.dot(W_hr, h_tm1) + b_r)
    can_h_t = T.tanh(W_xh[x_t] + r_t * T.dot(W_hh, h_tm1) + b_h)
    h_t = (1 - z_t) * h_tm1 + z_t * can_h_t
    y_t = T.dot(h_t, W_y) + b_y
    return h_t, y_t
```

The recurrent loop:

```
h0 = shared_zeros((n_hidden,), name='h0')
[h, y_pred], _ = theano.scan(step,
    sequences=x,
    outputs_info=[h0, None],
    truncate_gradient=10)
```

Having introduced the major nets, we'll see how they perform on the text generation task.

Metrics for natural language performance

The **Word Error Rate (WER)** or **Character Error Rate (CER)** is equivalent to the designation of the accuracy error for the case of natural language.

Evaluation of language models is usually expressed with perplexity, which is simply:

$$e^{cross-entropy}$$

Training loss comparison

During training, the learning rate might be strong after a certain number of epochs for fine-tuning. Decreasing the learning rate when the loss does not decrease anymore will help during the last steps of training. To decrease the learning rate, we need to define it as an input variable during compilation:

```
lr = T.scalar('learning_rate')
train_model = theano.function(inputs=[x,y,lr],
                            outputs=cost,
                            updates=updates)
```

During training, we adjust the learning rate, decreasing it if the training loss is not better:

```
if (len(train_loss) > 1 and train_loss[-1] > train_loss[-2]):
    learning_rate = learning_rate * 0.5
```

As a first experiment, let's see the impact of the size of the hidden layer on the training loss for a simple RNN:

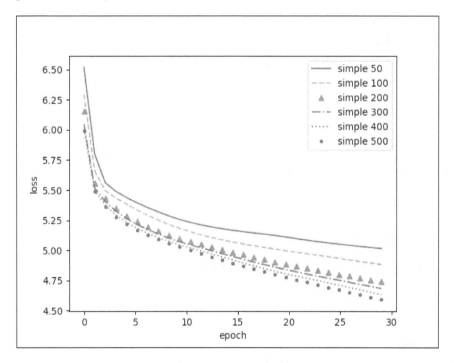

More hidden units improve training speed and might be better in the end. To check this, we should run it for more epochs.

Comparing the training of the different network types, in this case, we do not observe any improvement with LSTM and GRU:

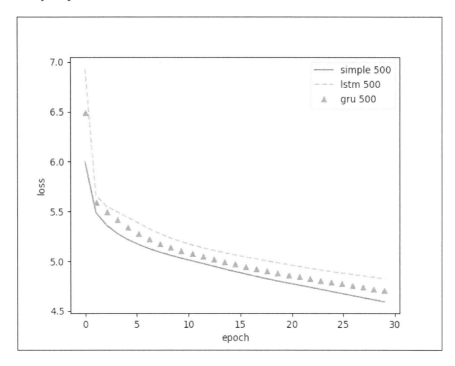

This might be due to the `truncate_gradient` option or because the problem is too simple and not so memory-dependent.

Another parameter to tune is the minimum number of occurrences for a word to be a part of the dictionary. A higher number will learn on words that are more frequent, which is better.

Example of predictions

Let's predict a sentence with the generated model:

```
sentence = [0]
while sentence[-1] != 1:
    pred = predict_model(sentence)[-1]
    sentence.append(pred)
print(" ".join([ index_[w] for w in sentence[1:-1]]))
```

Note that we take the most probable next word (argmax), while we must, in order to get some randomness, draw the next word following the predicted probabilities.

At 150 epochs, while the model has still not converged entirely with learning our Shakespeare writings, we can play with the predictions, initiating it with a few words, and see the network generate the end of the sentences:

- **First citizen**: A word , i know what a word
- **How** now!
- **Do** you not this asleep , i say upon this?
- **Sicinius**: What, art thou my master?
- **Well,** sir, come.
- **I have been** myself
- **A most** hose, you in thy hour, sir
- **He shall** not this
- **Pray you,** sir
- **Come**, come, you
- **The crows?**
- **I'll give** you
- **What,** ho!
- **Consider you,** sir
- **No more!**
- **Let us** be gone, or your UNKNOWN UNKNOWN, i do me to do
- **We are** not now

From these examples, we notice that the model has learned to position punctuation correctly, adding a point, comma, question mark, or an exclamation mark at the right place to order direct objects, indirect objects, and adjectives correctly.

The original texts are composed of short sentences in a Shakespeare style. Bigger articles such as Wikipedia pages, as well as pushing the training further with a validation split to control overfitting will produce longer texts. *Chapter 10, Predicting Times Sequence with Advanced RNN*: will teach how to predict time sequences with Advanced RNN and present an advanced version of this chapter.

Applications of RNN

This chapter introduced the simple RNN, LSTM, and GRU models. Such models have a wide range of applications in sequence generation or sequence understanding:

- Text generation, such as automatic generation of Obama political speech (obama-rnn), for example with a text seed on jobs:

    Good afternoon. God bless you. The United States will step up to the cost of a new challenges of the American people that will share the fact that we created the problem. They were attacked and so that they have to say that all the task of the final days of war that I will not be able to get this done. The promise of the men and women who were still going to take out the fact that the American people have fought to make sure that they have to be able to protect our part. It was a chance to stand together to completely look for the commitment to borrow from the American people. And the fact is the men and women in uniform and the millions of our country with the law system that we should be a strong stretcks of the forces that we can afford to increase our spirit of the American people and the leadership of our country who are on the Internet of American lives. Thank you very much. God bless you, and God bless the United States of America.

    You can check this example out in detail at `https://medium.com/@ samim/obama-rnn-machine-generated-political-speeches-c8abd18a2ea0#.4nee5wafe`.

- Text annotation, for example, the **Part of Speech** (**POS**) tags: noun, verb, particle, adverb, and adjective.

- Generating human handwriting: `http://www.cs.toronto.edu/~graves/ handwriting.html`

- Drawing with Sketch-RNN (`https://github.com/hardmaru/sketch-rnn`)

- **Speech synthesis**: A recurrent network will generate parameters for generating each phoneme in a speech or voice speaking. In the following image, time-frequency homogeneous blocs are classified in phonemes (or graphemes or letters):

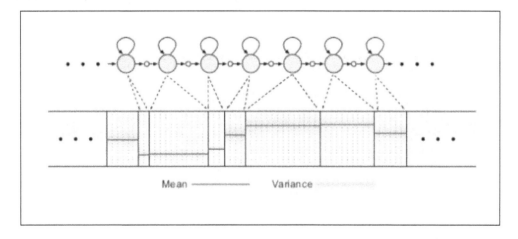

- Music generation:
    - Melody generation at `https://github.com/tensorflow/magenta/tree/master/magenta/models/melody_rnn`.
    - Mozart style music generation with Mozart-RNN at `http://www.hexahedria.com/2015/08/03/composing-music-with-recurrent-neural-networks/`.

- Any classification of sequences, such as sentiment analysis (positive, negative, or neutral sentiments) that we'll address in *Chapter 5, Analyzing Sentiment with a Bidirectional LSTM*.

- Sequence encoding or decoding that we'll address in *Chapter 6, Locating with Spatial Transformer Networks*.

Related articles

You can refer to the following links for more insight:

- *The Unreasonable Effectiveness of Recurrent Neural Networks*, Andrej Karpathy May 21, 2015(`http://karpathy.github.io/2015/05/21/rnn-effectiveness/`)

- *Understanding LSTM Networks* on Christopher Colah's blog's, 2015 (`http://colah.github.io/posts/2015-08-Understanding-LSTMs/`)

- Use of LSTM for audio classification: *Connectionist Temporal Classification* and *Deep Speech: Scaling up end-to-end speech recognition* (`https://arxiv.org/abs/1412.5567`)

- Handwriting demo at `http://www.cs.toronto.edu/~graves/handwriting.html`

- *General Sequence Learning using Recurrent Neural Networks* tutorial at `https://www.youtube.com/watch?v=VINCQghQRuM`

- On the difficulty of training Recurrent Neural Networks Razvan Pascanu, Tomas Mikolov, Yoshua Bengio 2012

- Recurrent Neural Networks Tutorial:
    - ° Introduction to RNNS
    - ° Implementing RNN with Python, NumPy, and Theano
    - ° Backpropagation through time and vanishing gradients
    - ° Implementing a GRU/LSTM RNN with Python and Theano Denny Britz 2015 at `http://www.wildml.com/2015/09/recurrent-neural-networks-tutorial-part-1-introduction-to-rnns/`

- LONG SHORT-TERM MEMORY, Sepp Hochreiter, Jürgen Schmidhuber, 1997

Summary

Recurrent Neural Networks provides the ability to process variable-length inputs and outputs of discrete or continuous data.

While the previous feedforward networks were able to process only one input to one output (one-to-one scheme), recurrent neural nets introduced in this chapter offered the possibility to make conversions between variable-length and fixed-length representations adding new operating schemes for deep learning input/output: one-to-many, many-to-many, or many-to-one.

The range of applications of RNN is wide. For this reason, we'll study them more in depth in the further chapters, in particular how to enhance the predictive power of these three modules or how to combine them to build multi-modal, question-answering, or translation applications.

In particular, in the next chapter, we'll see a practical example using text embedding and recurrent networks for sentiment analysis. This time, there will also be an opportunity to review these recurrence units under another library Keras, a deep learning library that simplifies writing models for Theano.

5
Analyzing Sentiment with a Bidirectional LSTM

This chapter is a bit more practical to get a better sense of the commonly used recurrent neural networks and word embeddings presented in the two previous chapters.

It is also an opportunity to introduce the reader to a new application of deep learning, sentiment analysis, which is another field of **Natural Language Processing (NLP)**. It is a many-to-one scheme, where a variable-length sequence of words has to be assigned to one class. An NLP problem where such a scheme can be used similarly is language detection (english, french, german, italian, and so on).

While the previous chapter demonstrated how to build a recurrent neural network from scratch, this chapter shows how a high-level library built on top of Theano, Keras, can help implement and train the model with prebuilt modules. Thanks to this example, the reader should be able to decide when to use Keras in their projects.

The following points are developed in this chapter:

- A recap of recurrent neural networks and word embeddings
- Sentiment analysis
- The Keras library
- Bidirectional recurrent networks

Automated sentiment analysis is the problem of identifying opinions expressed in text. It normally involves the classification of text into categories such as *positive*, *negative*, and *neutral*. Opinions are central to almost all human activities and they are key influencers of our behaviors.

Recently, neural networks and deep learning approaches have been used to build sentiment analysis systems. Such systems have the ability to automatically learn a set of features to overcome the drawbacks of handcrafted approaches.

Recurrent Neural Networks (**RNN**) have been proved in the literature to be a very useful technique to represent sequential inputs, such as text. A special extension of recurrent neural networks called **Bi-directional Recurrent Neural Networks** (**BRNN**) can capture both the preceding and the following contextual information in a text.

In this chapter, we'll present an example to show how a bidirectional recurrent neural network using the **Long Short Term Memory** (**LSTM**) architecture can be used to deal with the problem of the sentiment analysis. We aim to implement a model in which, given an input of text (that is, a sequence of words), the model attempts to predict whether it is positive, negative, or neutral.

Installing and configuring Keras

Keras is a high-level neural network API, written in Python and capable of running on top of either TensorFlow or Theano. It was developed to make implementing deep learning models as fast and easy as possible for research and development. You can install Keras easily using conda, as follows:

```
conda install keras
```

When writing your Python code, importing Keras will tell you which backend is used:

```
>>> import keras
Using Theano backend.
Using cuDNN version 5110 on context None
Preallocating 10867/11439 Mb (0.950000) on cuda0
Mapped name None to device cuda0: Tesla K80 (0000:83:00.0)
Mapped name dev0 to device cuda0: Tesla K80 (0000:83:00.0)
Using cuDNN version 5110 on context dev1
Preallocating 10867/11439 Mb (0.950000) on cuda1
Mapped name dev1 to device cuda1: Tesla K80 (0000:84:00.0)
```

If you have installed Tensorflow, it might not use Theano. To specify which backend to use, write a Keras configuration file, `~/.keras/keras.json`:

```
{
    "epsilon": 1e-07,
    "floatx": "float32",
    "image_data_format": "channels_last",
    "backend": "theano"
}
```

It is also possible to specify the Theano backend directly with the environment variable:

```
KERAS_BACKEND=theano python
```

Note that the device used is the device we specified for Theano in the `~/.theanorc` file. It is also possible to modify these variables with Theano environment variables:

```
KERAS_BACKEND=theano THEANO_FLAGS=device=cuda,floatX=float32,mode=FAST_
RUN python
```

Programming with Keras

Keras provides a set of methods for data preprocessing and for building models.

Layers and models are callable functions on tensors and return tensors. In Keras, there is no difference between a layer/module and a model: a model can be part of a bigger model and composed of multiple layers. Such a sub-model behaves as a module, with inputs/outputs.

Let's create a network with two linear layers, a ReLU non-linearity in between, and a softmax output:

```python
from keras.layers import Input, Dense
from keras.models import Model

inputs = Input(shape=(784,))

x = Dense(64, activation='relu')(inputs)
predictions = Dense(10, activation='softmax')(x)
model = Model(inputs=inputs, outputs=predictions)
```

The `model` module contains methods to get input and output shape for either one or multiple inputs/outputs, and list the submodules of our module:

```
>>> model.input_shape
(None, 784)

>>> model.get_input_shape_at(0)
(None, 784)

>>> model.output_shape
(None, 10)

>>> model.get_output_shape_at(0)
(None, 10)

>>> model.name
'sequential_1'

>>> model.input
/dense_3_input

>>> model.output
Softmax.0

>>> model.get_output_at(0)
Softmax.0

>>> model.layers
[<keras.layers.core.Dense object at 0x7f0abf7d6a90>, <keras.layers.core.Dense object at 0x7f0abf74af90>]
```

In order to avoid specify inputs to every layer, Keras proposes a functional way of writing models with the `Sequential` module, to build a new module or model composed.

The following definition of the model builds exactly the same model as shown previously, with `input_dim` to specify the input dimension of the block that would be unknown otherwise and generate an error:

```
from keras.models import Sequential
from keras.layers import Dense, Activation

model = Sequential()
model.add(Dense(units=64, input_dim=784, activation='relu'))
model.add(Dense(units=10, activation='softmax'))
```

The `model` is considered a module or layer that can be part of a bigger model:

```
model2 = Sequential()
model2.add(model)
model2.add(Dense(units=10, activation='softmax'))
```

Each module/model/layer can be compiled then and trained with data :

```
model.compile(optimizer='rmsprop',
              loss='categorical_crossentropy',
              metrics=['accuracy'])
model.fit(data, labels)
```

Let us see Keras in practice.

SemEval 2013 dataset

Let us start by preparing the data. In this chapter, we will use the standard dataset used in the supervised task of Twitter sentiment classification (message-level) presented in the SemEval 2013 competition. It contains 3662 tweets as a training set, 575 tweets as a development set, and 1572 tweets as a testing set. Each sample in this dataset consists of the tweet ID, the polarity (positive, negative, or neutral) and the tweet.

Let's download the dataset:

```
wget http://alt.qcri.org/semeval2014/task9/data/uploads/semeval2013_
task2_train.zip
wget http://alt.qcri.org/semeval2014/task9/data/uploads/semeval2013_
task2_dev.zip
wget http://alt.qcri.org/semeval2014/task9/data/uploads/semeval2013_
task2_test_fixed.zip
unzip semeval2013_task2_train.zip
unzip semeval2013_task2_dev.zip
unzip semeval2013_task2_test_fixed.zip
```

A refers to subtask A, which is message-level sentiment classification *our aim of study in this chapter*, where **B** refers to subtask B term level sentiment analysis.

The `input` directories do not contain the labels, just the tweets. `full` contains one more level of classification, *subjective* or *objective*. Our interest is in the `gold` or `cleansed` directories.

Let's use the script to convert them:

```
pip install bs4
python download_tweets.py train/cleansed/twitter-train-cleansed-A.tsv
> sem_eval2103.train
python download_tweets.py dev/gold/twitter-dev-gold-A.tsv > sem_
eval2103.dev
python download_tweets.py SemEval2013_task2_test_fixed/gold/twitter-
test-gold-A.tsv > sem_eval2103.test
```

Preprocessing text data

As we know, it is common to use URLs, user mentions, and hashtags frequently on Twitter. Thus, first we need to preprocess the tweets as follow.

Ensure that all the tokens are separated using the space. Each tweet is lowercased.

The URLs, user mentions, and hashtags are replaced by the `<url>`, `<user>`, and `<hashtag>` tokens respectively. This step is done using the `process` function, it takes a tweet as input, tokenizes it using the NLTK `TweetTokenizer`, preprocesses it, and returns the set of words (token) in the tweet:

```
import re
from nltk.tokenize import TweetTokenizer

def process(tweet):
  tknz = TweetTokenizer()
  tokens = tknz.tokenize(tweet)
  tweet = " ".join(tokens)
  tweet = tweet.lower()
  tweet = re.sub(r'http[s]?://(?:[a-z]|[0-9]|[$-_@.&amp;+]|[!*\
(\),]|(?:%[0-9a-f][0-9a-f]))+', '<url>', tweet) # URLs
  tweet = re.sub(r'(?:@[\w_]+)', '<user>', tweet)  # user-mentions
  tweet = re.sub(r'(?:\#+[\w_]+[\w\'_\-]*[\w_]+)', '<hashtag>', tweet)
# hashtags
  tweet = re.sub(r'(?:(?:\d+,?)+(?:\.?\d+)?)', '<number>', tweet)  #
numbers
  return tweet.split(" ")
```

For example, if we have the tweet `RT @mhj: just an example! :D http://`
`example.com #NLP`, the function process is as follows:

```
tweet = 'RT @mhj: just an example! :D http://example.com #NLP'
print(process(tweet))
```

returns

```
[u'rt', u'\<user\>', u':', u'just', u'an', u'example', u'!', u':d',
u'\<url\>', u'\<hashtag\>']
```

The following function is used to read the datasets and return a list of tuples, where each tuple represents one sample of (tweet, class), with the class an integer in {0, 1, or 2} defining the polarity:

```
def read_data(file_name):
    tweets = []
    labels = []
    polarity2idx = {'positive': 0, 'negative': 1, 'neutral': 2}
    with open(file_name) as fin:
        for line in fin:
            _, _, _, _, polarity, tweet = line.strip().split("\t")
            tweet = process(tweet)
            cls = polarity2idx[polarity]
            tweets.append(tweet)
            labels.append(cls)
    return tweets, labels


train_file = 'sem_eval2103.train'
dev_file = 'sem_eval2103.dev'


train_tweets, y_train = read_data(train_file)
dev_tweets, y_dev = read_data(dev_file)
```

Now, we can build the vocabulary, which is a dictionary to map each word to a fixed index. The following function receives as input a set of data and returns the vocabulary and maximum length of the tweets:

```
def get_vocabulary(data):
    max_len = 0
    index = 0
    word2idx = {'<unknown>': index}
    for tweet in data:
```

```
      max_len = max(max_len, len(tweet))
      for word in tweet:
        if word not in word2idx:
          index += 1
          word2idx[word] = index
    return word2idx, max_len

  word2idx, max_len = get_vocabulary(train_tweets)
  vocab_size = len(word2idx)
```

We also need a function to transfer each tweet or set of tweets into the indices based on the vocabulary if the words exist, or replacing **out-of-vocabulary** (**OOV**) words with the unknown token (index 0) as follows:

```
def transfer(data, word2idx):
  transfer_data = []
  for tweet in data:
    tweet2vec = []
    for word in tweet:
      if word in word2idx:
        tweet2vec.append(word2idx[word])
      else:
        tweet2vec.append(0)
    transfer_data.append(tweet2vec)
  return transfer_data

X_train = transfer(train_tweets, word2idx)
X_dev   = transfer(dev_tweets, word2idx)
```

We can save some memory:

```
del train_tweets, dev_tweets
```

Keras provides a helper method to pad the sequences to ensure they all have the same length, so that a batch of sequences can be represented by a tensor, and use optimized operations on tensors, either on a CPU or on a GPU.

By default, the method pads at the beginning, which helps get us better classification results:

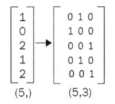

```
from keras.preprocessing.sequence import pad_sequences
X_train = pad_sequences(X_train, maxlen=max_len, truncating='post')
X_dev = pad_sequences(X_dev, maxlen=max_len, truncating='post')
```

Lastly, Keras provides a method to convert the classes into their one-hot encoding representation, by adding a dimension:

$$
\begin{bmatrix} 1 \\ 0 \\ 2 \\ 1 \\ 2 \end{bmatrix} \rightarrow \begin{bmatrix} 0\ 1\ 0 \\ 1\ 0\ 0 \\ 0\ 0\ 1 \\ 0\ 1\ 0 \\ 0\ 0\ 1 \end{bmatrix}
$$
$$
(5,) \qquad\ (5,3)
$$

With Keras to_categorical method:

```
from keras.utils.np_utils import to_categorical
y_train = to_categorical(y_train)
y_dev = to_categorical(y_dev)
```

Designing the architecture for the model

The main blocks of the model in this example will be the following:

- First, the words of the input sentence are mapped to vectors of real numbers. This step is called vector representation of words or word embedding (for more details, see *Chapter 3, Encoding Word into Vector*).

- Afterwards, this sequence of vectors is represented by one fixed-length and real-valued vector using a bi-LSTM encoder. This vector summarizes the input sentence and contains semantic, syntactic, and/or sentimental information based on the word vectors.

- Finally, this vector is passed through a softmax classifier to classify the sentence into positive, negative, or neutral.

Vector representations of words

Word embeddings are an approach to distributional semantics that represents words as vectors of real numbers. Such a representation has useful clustering properties, since the words that are semantically and syntactically related are represented by similar vectors (see *Chapter 3, Encoding Word into Vector*).

The main aim of this step is to map each word into a continuous, low-dimensional, and real-valued vector, which can later be used as an input to any model. All the word vectors are stacked into a matrix $E \in \mathbb{R}^{d \times N}$; here, N is the vocabulary size and d the vector dimension. This matrix is called the embedding layer or the lookup table layer. The embedding matrix can be initialized using a pre-trained model such as **Word2vec** or **Glove**.

In Keras, we can simply define the embedding layer as follows:

```
from keras.layers import Embedding
d = 100
emb_layer = Embedding(vocab_size + 1, output_dim=d, input_length=max_
len)
```

The first parameter represents the vocabulary size, `output_dim` is the vector dimension, and `input_length` is the length of the input sequences.

Let us add this layer as the input layer to the model and declare the model as a sequential model:

```
from keras.models import Sequential
model = Sequential()
model.add(emb_layer)
```

Sentence representation using bi-LSTM

A recurrent neural network has the ability to represent sequences such as sentences. However, in practice, learning long-term dependencies with a vanilla RNN is difficult due to vanishing/exploding gradients. As presented in the previous chapter, **Long Short-Term Memory** (**LSTM**) networks were designed to have more persistent memory (that is, state), specialized in keeping and transmitting long-term information, making them very useful for capturing long-term dependencies between the elements of a sequence.

LSTM units are the basic components of the model used in this chapter.

Keras proposes a method, `TimeDistributed`, to clone any model in multiple time steps and make it recurrent. But for commonly used recurrent units such as LSTM, there already exists a module in Keras:

```
from keras.layers import LSTM
rnn_size = 64
lstm = LSTM(rnn_size, input_shape=(max_len, d))
```

The following is identical:

```
lstm = LSTM(rnn_size, input_dim=d, input_length=max_len)
```

And for the subsequent layers, we do not need to specify the input size (this is the case since the LSTM layer comes after the embedding layer), thus we can define the `lstm` unit simply as follows:

```
lstm = LSTM(rnn_size)
```

Last but not least, in this model, we'd like to use a bidirectional LSTM. It has proved to lead to better results, capturing the meaning of the current word given the previous words, as well as words appearing after:

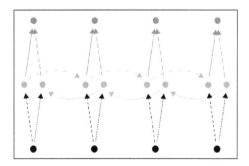

To make this unit process the input bidirectionally, we can simply use Bidirectional, a bidirectional wrapper for RNNs:

```
from keras.layers import Bidirectional
bi_lstm = Bidirectional(lstm)
model.add(bi_lstm)
```

Outputting probabilities with the softmax classifier

Finally, we can pass the vector obtained from `bi_lstm` to a softmax classifier as follows:

```
from keras.layers import Dense, Activation

nb_classes = 3
fc = Dense(nb_classes)
classifier = Activation('softmax')
model.add(fc)
model.add(classifier)
```

Now, let us print the summary of the model:

```
print(model.summary())
Which will end with the results:
Using Theano backend:
```

Layer (type)	Output Shape	Param #	Connected to
embedding_1 (Embedding)	(None, 30, 100)	10000100	embedding_input_1[0][0]
bidirectional_1 (Bidirectional)	(None, 128)	84480	embedding_1[0][0]
dense_1 (Dense)	(None, 3)	387	bidirectional_1[0][0]
activation_1 (Activation)	(None, 3)	0	dense_1[0][0]

```
Total params: 10,084,967
Trainable params: 10,084,967
Non-trainable params: 0
```

Compiling and training the model

Now that the model is defined, it is ready to be compiled. To compile the model in Keras, we need to determine the optimizer, the loss function, and optionally the evaluation metrics. As we mentioned previously, the problem is to predict if the tweet is positive, negative, or neutral. This problem is known as a multi-category classification problem. Thus, the loss (or the objective) function that will be used in this example is the `categorical_crossentropy`. We will use the `rmsprop` optimizer and the accuracy evaluation metric.

In Keras, you can find state-of-the-art optimizers, objectives, and evaluation metrics implemented. Compiling the model in Keras is very easy using the compile function:

```
model.compile(optimizer='rmsprop',
          loss='categorical_crossentropy',
          metrics=['accuracy'])
```

We have defined the model and compiled it, and it is now ready to be trained. We can train or fit the model on the defined data by calling the fit function.

The training process runs for a certain number of iterations through the dataset, called epochs, which can be specified using the `epochs` parameter. We can also set the number of instances that are fed to the model at each step using the `batch_size` argument. In this case, we will use a small number of `epochs` = 30 and use a small batch size of 10. We can also evaluate the model during training by explicitly feeding the development set using the `validation_data` parameter, or choosing a sub set from the training set using the `validation_split` parameter. In this case, we will use the development set that we defined previously:

```
model.fit(x=X_train, y=y_train, batch_size=10, epochs=30, validation_
data=[X_dev, y_dev])
```

Evaluating the model

We have trained the model on the train test and now we can evaluate the performance of the network on the test set. This can be done using the `evaluation()` function. This function returns the loss value and the metrics values for the model in test mode:

```
test_file = 'sem_eval2103.test'
test_tweets, y_test = read_data(test_file)


X_test   = transfer(test_tweets, word2idx)


del test_twee


X_test = pad_sequences(X_test, maxlen=max_len, truncating='post')


y_test = to_categorical(y_test)


test_loss, test_acc = model.evaluate(X_test, y_test)


print("Testing loss: {:.5}; Testing Accuracy: {:.2%}" .format(test_
loss, test_acc))
```

Saving and loading the model

To save the weights of the Keras model, simply call the `save` function, and the model is serialized into `.hdf5` format:

```
model.save('bi_lstm_sentiment.h5')
```

To load the model, use the `load_model` function provided by Keras as follows:

```
from keras.models import load_model
loaded_model = load_model('bi_lstm_sentiment.h5')
```

It is now ready for evaluation and does not need to be compiled. For example, on the same test set we must obtain the same results:

```
test_loss, test_acc = loaded_model.evaluate(X_test, y_test)
print("Testing loss: {:.5}; Testing Accuracy: {:.2%}" .format(test_
loss, test_acc))
```

Running the example

To run the model, we can execute the following command line:

python `bilstm.py`

Further reading

Please refer to the following articles:

- *SemEval Sentiment Analysis in Twitter* `https://www.cs.york.ac.uk/semeval-2013/task2.html`

- *Personality insights with IBM Watson demo* `https://personality-insights-livedemo.mybluemix.net/`

- *Tone analyzer* `https://tone-analyzer-demo.mybluemix.net/`

- *Keras* `https://keras.io/`

- Deep Speech: Scaling up end-to-end speech recognition, Awni Hannun, Carl Case, Jared Casper, Bryan Catanzaro, Greg Diamos, Erich Elsen, Ryan Prenger, Sanjeev Satheesh, Shubho Sengupta, Adam Coates, Andrew Y. Ng, 2014

- Speech Recognition with Deep Recurrent Neural Networks, Alex Graves, Abdel-Rahman Mohamed, Geoffrey Hinton, 2013

- Deep Speech 2: End-to-End Speech Recognition in English and Mandarin, Dario Amodei, Rishita Anubhai, Eric Battenberg, Carl Case, Jared Casper, Bryan Catanzaro, Jingdong Chen, Mike Chrzanowski, Adam Coates, Greg Diamos, Erich Elsen, Jesse Engel, Linxi Fan, Christopher Fougner, Tony Han, Awni Hannun, Billy Jun, Patrick LeGresley, Libby Lin, Sharan Narang, Andrew Ng, Sherjil Ozair, Ryan Prenger, Jonathan Raiman, Sanjeev Satheesh,David Seetapun, Shubho Sengupta, Yi Wang, Zhiqian Wang, Chong Wang, Bo Xiao, Dani Yogatama, Jun Zhan, Zhenyao Zhu, 2015

Summary

This chapter acted as a review of the basic concepts introduced in the previous chapters, while introducing a new application, sentiment analysis, and a high-level library, Keras, to simplify the development of models with the Theano engine.

Among these basic concepts were recurrent networks, word embeddings, batch sequence padding, and class one-hot encoding. Bidirectional recurrency was presented to improve the results.

In the next chapter, we'll see how to apply recurrency to images, with another library, Lasagne, which is more lightweight than Keras, and will let you mix the library modules with your own code for Theano more smoothly.

6
Locating with Spatial Transformer Networks

In this chapter, the NLP field is left to come back to images, and get an example of application of recurrent neural networks to images. In *Chapter 2, Classifying Handwritten Digits with a Feedforward Network* we addressed the case of image classification, consisting of predicting the class of an image. Here, we'll address object localization, a common task in computer vision as well, consisting of predicting the bounding box of an object in the image.

While *Chapter 2, Classifying Handwritten Digits with a Feedforward Network* solved the classification task with neural nets built with linear layers, convolutions, and non-linarites, the spatial transformer is a new module built on very specific equations dedicated to the localization task.

In order to locate multiple objects in the image, spatial transformers are composed with recurrent networks. This chapter takes the opportunity to show how to use prebuilt recurrent networks in **Lasagne**, a library on top of Theano that brings extra modules, and helps you develop your neural networks very fast with pre-built components, while not changing the way you build and handle nets with Theano.

To sum up, the list of topics is composed of:

- An introduction to the Lasagne library
- Spatial transformer networks
- Classification network with spatial transformers
- Recurrent modules with Lasagne
- Recurrent read of digits
- Unsupervised training with hinge loss functions
- Region-based object localization neural nets

MNIST CNN model with Lasagne

The Lasagne library has packaged layers and tools to handle neural nets easily. Let's first install the latest version of Lasagne:

```
pip install --upgrade https://github.com/Lasagne/Lasagne/archive/master.zip
```

Let us reprogram the MNIST model from *Chapter 2, Classifying Handwritten Digits with a Feedforward Network* with Lasagne:

```python
def model(l_input, input_dim=28, num_units=256, num_classes=10, p=.5):


    network = lasagne.layers.Conv2DLayer(
            l_input,
            num_filters=32, filter_size=(5, 5),
            nonlinearity=lasagne.nonlinearities.rectify,
            W=lasagne.init.GlorotUniform())

    network = lasagne.layers.MaxPool2DLayer(network, pool_size=(2, 2))

    network = lasagne.layers.Conv2DLayer(
            network,
            num_filters=32,
            filter_size=(5, 5),
            nonlinearity=lasagne.nonlinearities.rectify)

    network = lasagne.layers.MaxPool2DLayer(network, pool_size=(2, 2))

    if num_units > 0:
        network = lasagne.layers.DenseLayer(
                lasagne.layers.dropout(network, p=p),
                num_units=num_units,
                nonlinearity=lasagne.nonlinearities.rectify)

    if (num_units > 0) and (num_classes > 0):
        network = lasagne.layers.DenseLayer(
                lasagne.layers.dropout(network, p=p),
                num_units=num_classes,
                nonlinearity=lasagne.nonlinearities.softmax)

    return network
```

The layers are `layer0_input`, `conv1_out`, `pooled_out`, `conv2_out`, `pooled2_out`, `hidden_output`. They are built with pre-built modules, such as, `InputLayer`, `Conv2DLayer`, `MaxPool2DLayer`, `DenseLayer`, dropout non-linearities such as rectify or softmax, and initialization such as `GlorotUniform`.

To connect the network graph composed of modules with the input symbolic `var` and get the output `var`, use the following code:

```
input_var = T.tensor4('inputs')
l_input = lasagne.layers.InputLayer(shape=(None, 1, 28, 28),
        input_var=input_var)
network = mnist_cnn.model(l_input)
prediction = lasagne.layers.get_output(network)
```

Or use this code:

```
l_input = lasagne.layers.InputLayer(shape=(None, 1, 28, 28))
network = mnist_cnn.model(l_input)

input_var = T.tensor4('inputs')
prediction = lasagne.layers.get_output(network, input_var)
```

A very convenient feature is that you can print the output shape of any module:

```
print(l_input.output_shape)
```

Lasagne's `get_all_params` method lists the parameters of the model:

```
params = lasagne.layers.get_all_params(network, trainable=True)
for p in params:
    print p.name
```

Lastly, Lasagne comes with different learning rules, such as `RMSprop`, `Nesterov Momentum`, `Adam`, and `Adagrad`:

```
target_var = T.ivector('targets')
loss = lasagne.objectives.categorical_crossentropy(prediction, target_var)
loss = loss.mean()

updates = lasagne.updates.nesterov_momentum(
        loss, params, learning_rate=0.01, momentum=0.9)

train_fn = theano.function([input_var, target_var], loss,
updates=updates)
```

All other things remain unchanged.

To test our MNIST model, download the MNIST dataset:

wget `http://www.iro.umontreal.ca/~lisa/deep/data/mnist/mnist.pkl.gz -P /`
`sharedfiles`

Train an MNIST classifier for digit classification:

python `1-train-mnist.py`

The model parameters are saved in `model.npz`. The accuracy is again above 99%.

A localization network

In **Spatial Transformer Networks (STN)**, instead of applying the network directly to the input image signal, the idea is to add a module to preprocess the image and crop it, rotate it, and scale it to fit the object, to assist in classification:

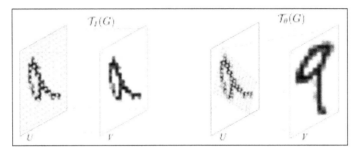

Spatial Transformer Networks

For that purpose, STNs use a localization network to predict the affine transformation parameters and process the input:

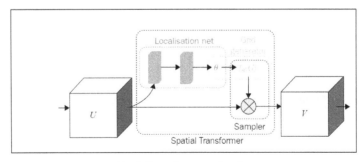

Spatial transformer networks

In Theano, differentiation through the affine transformation is automatic, we simply have to connect the localization net with the input of the classification net through the affine transformation.

First, we create a localization network not very far from the MNIST CNN model, to predict six parameters of the affine transformation:

```
l_in = lasagne.layers.InputLayer((None, dim, dim))
l_dim = lasagne.layers.DimshuffleLayer(l_in, (0, 'x', 1, 2))
l_pool0_loc = lasagne.layers.MaxPool2DLayer(l_dim, pool_size=(2, 2))
l_dense_loc = mnist_cnn.model(l_pool0_loc,
        input_dim=dim,
        num_classes=0)

b = np.zeros((2, 3), dtype=theano.config.floatX)
b[0, 0] = 1.0
b[1, 1] = 1.0

l_A_net = lasagne.layers.DenseLayer(
    l_dense_loc,
    num_units=6,
    name='A_net',
    b=b.flatten(),
    W=lasagne.init.Constant(0.0),
    nonlinearity=lasagne.nonlinearities.identity)
```

Here, we simply add to the input array, with `DimshuffleLayer`, a channel dimension that will have only value 1. Such a dimension add is named a broadcast.

The pooling layer resizes the input image to *50x50*, which is enough to determine the position of the digit.

The localization layer weight is initiated with zeros, except for the bias, which is initiated to the Identity affine parameters; the STN modules will not have any impact at the beginning and the full input image will be transmitted.

To crop given the affine parameters:

```
l_transform = lasagne.layers.TransformerLayer(
    incoming=l_dim,
    localization_network=l_A_net,
    downsample_factor=args.downsample)
```

The `down_sampling_factor` enables us to define the size of the output image with respect to the input. In this case, it is three, meaning the image will be *33x33* — not very far from our MNIST digit size of *28x28*. Lastly, we simply add our MNIST CNN model to classify the output:

```
l_out = mnist_cnn.model(l_transform,
     input_dim=dim,
     p=sh_drp,
     num_units=400)
```

To test the classifier, let us create images of *100x100* pixels, with some distortions and one digit:

```
python create_mnist_sequence.py --nb_digits=1
```

Plot the first three images (corresponding to 1, 0, 5):

```
python plot_data.py mnist_sequence1_sample_8distortions_9x9.npz
```

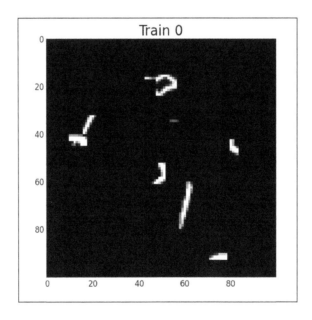

Let's run the command to train the model:

```
python 2-stn-cnn-mnist.py
```

Here again, the accuracy gets above 99% when the digit is alone without distortions, which is typically not possible with the simple MNIST CNN model alone, and above 96.9% with distortions.

The command to plot the crops is:

```
python plot_crops.py res_test_2.npz
```

It gives us the following result:

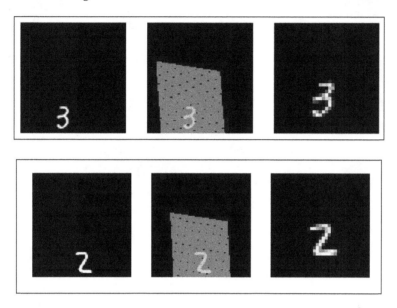

And with distortions:

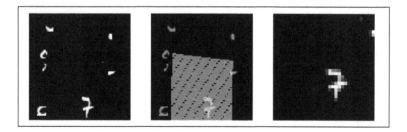

STN can be thought of as a module to include in any network, at any place between two layers. To improve the classification results further, adding multiple STNs between different layers of a classification network helps get better results.

Here is an example of a network with two branches inside the network, each with its SPN that will, when unsupervised, try to catch different parts of the image to classify it:

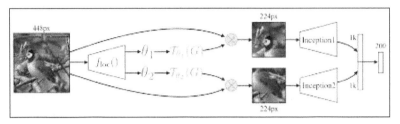

(Spatial transformer networks paper, Jaderberg et al., 2015)

Recurrent neural net applied to images

The idea is to use recurrency to read multiple digits, instead of just one:

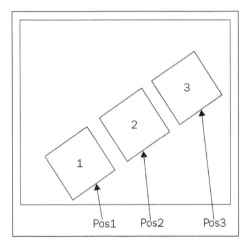

In order to read multiple digits, we simply replace the localization feedforward network with a recurrent network that will output multiple affine transformations corresponding to each digit:

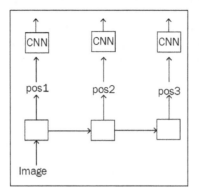

From the previous example, we replace the fully connected layer with the GRU layer:

```
l_conv2_loc = mnist_cnn.model(l_pool0_loc,
    input_dim=dim,
    p=sh_drp,
    num_units=0)

class Repeat(lasagne.layers.Layer):
    def __init__(self, incoming, n, **kwargs):
        super(Repeat, self).__init__(incoming, **kwargs)
        self.n = n

    def get_output_shape_for(self, input_shape):
        return tuple([input_shape[0], self.n] + list(input_shape[1:]))

    def get_output_for(self, input, **kwargs):
        tensors = [input]*self.n
        stacked = theano.tensor.stack(*tensors)
        dim = [1, 0] + range(2, input.ndim+1)
        return stacked.dimshuffle(dim)

l_repeat_loc = Repeat(l_conv2_loc, n=num_steps)
```

```
l_gru = lasagne.layers.GRULayer(l_repeat_loc, num_units=num_rnn_units,
unroll_scan=True)

l_shp = lasagne.layers.ReshapeLayer(l_gru, (-1, num_rnn_units))
```

This outputs a tensor of dimension (None, 3, 256), where the first dimension is the batch size, 3 is the number of steps in the GRU, and 256 is the hidden layer size. On top of this layer, we simply add the same fully connected layer as before to output three identity images at the beginning:

```
b = np.zeros((2, 3), dtype=theano.config.floatX)
b[0, 0] = 1.0
b[1, 1] = 1.0

l_A_net = lasagne.layers.DenseLayer(
    l_shp,
    num_units=6,
    name='A_net',
    b=b.flatten(),
    W=lasagne.init.Constant(0.0),
    nonlinearity=lasagne.nonlinearities.identity)

l_conv_to_transform = lasagne.layers.ReshapeLayer(
    Repeat(l_dim, n=num_steps), [-1] + list(l_dim.output_shape[-3:]))

l_transform = lasagne.layers.TransformerLayer(
    incoming=l_conv_to_transform,
    localization_network=l_A_net,
    downsample_factor=args.downsample)

l_out = mnist_cnn.model(l_transform, input_dim=dim, p=sh_drp, num_
units=400)
```

To test the classifier, let us create images of *100x100* pixels with some distortions, and three digits this time:

```
python create_mnist_sequence.py --nb_digits=3 --output_dim=100
```

Plot the first three images (corresponding to sequences **296**, **490**, **125**):

python plot_data.py mnist_sequence3_sample_8distortions_9x9.npz

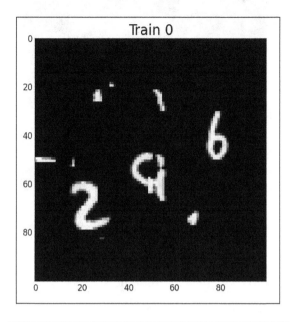

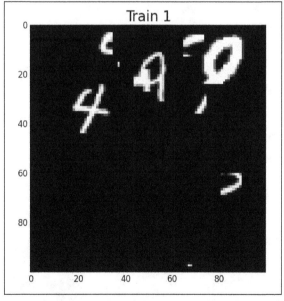

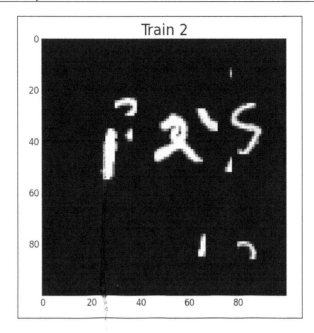

Let's run the command to train our recurrent model:

python 3-recurrent-stn-mnist.py

Epoch 0 Acc Valid 0.268833333333, Acc Train = 0.268777777778, Acc Test = 0.272466666667

Epoch 1 Acc Valid 0.621733333333, Acc Train = 0.611116666667, Acc Test = 0.6086

Epoch 2 Acc Valid 0.764066666667, Acc Train = 0.75775, Acc Test = 0.764866666667

Epoch 3 Acc Valid 0.860233333333, Acc Train = 0.852294444444, Acc Test = 0.859566666667

Epoch 4 Acc Valid 0.895333333333, Acc Train = 0.892066666667, Acc Test = 0.8977

Epoch 53 Acc Valid 0.980433333333, Acc Train = 0.984261111111, Acc Test = 0.97926666666

The classification accuracy is 99.3%.

Plot the crops:

```
python plot_crops.py res_test_3.npz
```

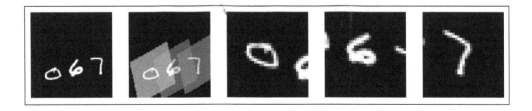

Unsupervised learning with co-localization

The first layers of the digit classifier trained in *Chapter 2, Classifying Handwritten Digits with a Feedforward Network* as an encoding function to represent the image in an embedding space, as for words:

$$I \rightarrow e(I)$$

It is possible to train unsurprisingly the localization network of the spatial transformer network by minimizing the hinge loss objective function on random sets of two images supposed to contain the same digit:

$$\sum_{m,n} max\left(0, \left\|e\left(stn\left(I_n\right)\right) - e\left(stn\left(I_m\right)\right)\right\|_2^2 - \left\|e\left(stn\left(I_n\right)\right)\right.\right.$$
$$\left.\left. - e\left(random\_crop\left(I_m\right)\right)\right\|_2^2 + 1\right)$$

Minimizing this sum leads to modifying the weights in the localization network, so that two localized digits become closer than two random crops.

Here are the results:

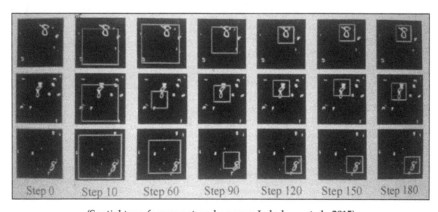

(Spatial transformer networks paper, Jaderberg et al., 2015)

Region-based localization networks

Historically, the basic approach in object localization was to use a classification network in a sliding window; it consists of sliding a window one pixel by one pixel in each direction and applying a classifier at each position and each scale in the image. The classifier learns to say if the object is present and centered. It requires a large amount of computations since the model has to be evaluated at every position and scale.

To accelerate such a process, the **Region Proposal Network (RPN)** in the Fast-R-CNN paper from the researcher Ross Girshick consists of transforming the fully connected layers of a neural net classifier such as MNIST CNN into convolutional layers as well; in fact, network dense on 28x28 image, there is no difference between a convolution and a linear layer when the convolution kernel has the same dimensions as the input. So, any fully connected layers can be rewritten as convolutional layers, with the same weights and the appropriate kernel dimensions, which enables the network to work on a wider image than 28x28, at any size, outputting a feature map with a classification score at each position. The only difference may come from the stride of the whole network, which can be set different to 1 and can be large (a few 10 pixels) with convolution kernels set to stride different to 1 in order to reduce the number of evaluation positions and thus the computations. Such a transformation is worth because the convolutions are very efficient:

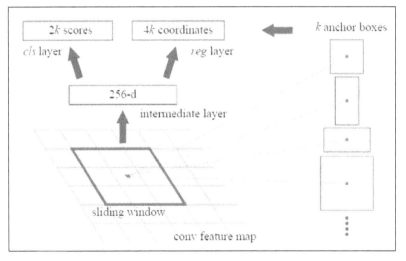

Faster R-CNN: Towards Real-Time Object Detection with Region Proposal Networks

An end-to-end network has been designed, taking ideas from deconvolution principles where an output feature map gives all bounding boxes at once: **You Only Look Once (YOLO)** architecture predicts B possible bounding boxes for each position in the feature map. Each bounding box is defined by its coordinates (x, y, w, h) in proportion to the whole image as a regression problem, and a confidence (probability) that corresponds to the **Intersection over Union (IOU)** between the box and the true box. Comparable approaches are proposed with SSD models.

Lastly, segmentation networks introduced in *Chapter 8, Translating and Explaining with Encoding – decoding Networks* can also be considered as neural net implementations towards localizing objects.

Further reading

You can further refer to these sources for more information:

- Spatial Transformer Networks, Max Jaderberg, Karen Simonyan, Andrew Zisserman, Koray Kavukcuoglu, Jun 2015

- Recurrent Spatial Transformer Networks, Søren Kaae Sønderby, Casper Kaae Sønderby, Lars Maaløe, Ole Winther, Sept 2015

- Original code: `https://github.com/skaae/recurrent-spatial-transformer-code`

- Google Street View Character Recognition, Jiyue Wang, Peng Hui How

- Reading Text in the Wild with Convolutional Neural Networks, Max Jaderberg, Karen Simonyan, Andrea Vedaldi, Andrew Zisserman, 2014

- Multi-digit Number Recognition from Street View Imagery using Deep Convolutional Neural Networks, Ian J. Goodfellow, Yaroslav Bulatov, Julian Ibarz, Sacha Arnoud, Vinay Shet, 2013

- Recognizing Characters From Google Street View Images, Guan Wang, Jingrui Zhang

- Synthetic Data and Artificial Neural Networks for Natural Scene Text Recognition, Max Jaderberg, Karen Simonyan, Andrea Vedaldi, Andrew Zisserman, 2014

- R-CNN minus R, Karel Lenc, Andrea Vedaldi, 2015

- Fast R-CNN, Ross Girshick, 2015

- Faster R-CNN: Towards Real-Time Object Detection with Region Proposal Networks, Shaoqing Ren, Kaiming He, Ross Girshick, Jian Sun, 2015

- You Only Look Once: Unified, Real-Time Object Detection, Joseph Redmon, Santosh Divvala, Ross Girshick, Ali Farhadi, Jun 2015

- YOLO demo in real time `http://pjreddie.com/darknet/yolo/`

- YOLO9000: Better, Faster, Stronger, Joseph Redmon, Ali Farhadi, Dec 2016

- SSD: Single Shot MultiBox Detector, Wei Liu, Dragomir Anguelov, Dumitru Erhan, Christian Szegedy, Scott Reed, Cheng-Yang Fu, Alexander C. Berg, Dec 2015

- Rich feature hierarchies for accurate object detection and semantic segmentation, Ross Girshick, Jeff Donahue, Trevor Darrell, Jitendra Malik, 2013

- Text Flow: A Unified Text Detection System in Natural Scene Images Shangxuan Tian, Yifeng Pan, Chang Huang, Shijian Lu, Kai Yu, Chew Lim Tan, 2016

Summary

The spatial transformer layer is an original module to localize an area of the image, crop it and resize it to help the classifier focus on the relevant part in the image, and increase its accuracy. The layer is composed of differentiable affine transformation, for which the parameters are computed through another model, the localization network, and can be learned via backpropagation as usual.

An example of the application to reading multiple digits in an image can be inferred with the use of recurrent neural units. To simplify our work, the Lasagne library was introduced.

Spatial transformers are one solution among many others for localizations; region-based localizations, such as YOLO, SSD, or Faster RCNN, provide state-of-the-art results for bounding box prediction.

In the next chapter, we'll continue with image recognition to discover how to classify full size images that contain a lot more information than digits, such as natural images of indoor scenes and outdoor landscapes. In the meantime, we'll continue with Lasagne's prebuilt layer and optimization modules.

7
Classifying Images with Residual Networks

This chapter presents state-of-the-art deep networks for image classification.

Residual networks have become the latest architecture, with a huge improvement in accuracy and greater simplicity.

Before residual networks, there had been a long history of architectures, such as **AlexNet**, **VGG**, **Inception (GoogLeNet)**, **Inception v2,v3, and v4**. Researchers were searching for different concepts and discovered some underlying rules with which to design better architectures.

This chapter will address the following topics:

- Main datasets for image classification evaluation
- Network architectures for image classification
- Batch normalization
- Global average pooling
- Residual connections
- Stochastic depth
- Dense connections
- Multi-GPU
- Data augmentation techniques

Natural image datasets

Image classification usually includes a wider range of objects and scenes than the MNIST handwritten digits. Most of them are natural images, meaning images that a human being would observe in the real world, such as landscapes, indoor scenes, roads, mountains, beaches, people, animals, and automobiles, as opposed to synthetic images or images generated by a computer.

To evaluate the performance of image classification networks for natural images, three main datasets are usually used by researchers to compare performance:

- Cifar-10, a dataset of 60,000 small images (32x32) regrouped into 10 classes only, which you can easily download:

  wget `https://www.cs.toronto.edu/~kriz/cifar-10-python.tar.gz -P /sharedfiles`

  tar `xvzf /sharedfiles/cifar-10-python.tar.gz -C /sharedfiles/`

Here are some example images for each class:

Cifar 10 dataset classes with samples https://www.cs.toronto.edu/~kriz/cifar.html

- Cifar-100, a dataset of 60,000 images, partitioned into 100 classes and 20 super-classes
- ImageNet, a dataset of 1.2 million images, labeled with a wide range of classes (1,000). Since ImageNet is intended for non-commercial use only, it is possible to download Food 101, a dataset of 101 classes of meals, and 1,000 images per class:

```
wget http://data.vision.ee.ethz.ch/cvl/food-101.tar.gz -P /
sharedfiles
```

```
tar xvzf food-101.tar.gz -C /sharedfiles/
```

Before introducing residual architectures, let us discuss two methods to improve classification net accuracy: batch normalization, and global average pooling.

Batch normalization

Deeper networks, with more than 100 layers can help image classification for a few hundred classes. The major issue with deep networks is to ensure that the flows of inputs, as well as the gradients, are well propagated from one end of the network to the other end.

Nevertheless, it is not unusual that nonlinearities in the network get saturated, and gradients become null. Moreover, each layer in the network has to adapt to constant changes in the distribution of its inputs, a phenomenon known as **internal covariate shift**.

It is known that a network trains faster with input data linearly processed to have zero mean and unit variance (known as **network input normalization**), and normalizing each input feature independently, instead of jointly.

To normalize the input of every layer in a network, it is a bit more complicated: zeroing the mean of the input will ignore the learned bias of the previous layer, and the problem is even worse with unit variance. The parameters of the previous layer may grow infinitely, while the loss stays constant, when inputs of the layer are normalized.

So, for **layer input normalization**, a **batch normalization layer** relearns the scale and the bias after normalization:

$$y^k = \gamma^k \text{Normalized}\left(x^k\right) + \beta^k$$

Rather than using the entire dataset, it uses the batch to compute the statistics for normalization, with a moving average to get closer to entire dataset statistics while training.

A batch normalization layer has the following benefits:

- It reduces the influence of bad initializations or too high learning rates
- It increases the accuracy of the net by a margin
- It accelerates the training
- It reduces overfitting, regularizing the model

When introducing batch normalization layers, you can remove dropout, increase the learning rate, and reduce L2 weight normalization.

Be careful to place nonlinearity after the BN layer, and to remove bias in the previous layer:

```
l = NonlinearityLayer(
      BatchNormLayer(
        ConvLayer(l_in,
          num_filters=n_filters[0],
          filter_size=(3,3),
          stride=(1,1),
          nonlinearity=None,
          pad='same',
          W=he_norm)
      ),
      nonlinearity=rectify
  )
```

Global average pooling

Traditionally, the two last layers of a classification net are a fully connected layer and a softmax layer. The fully connected layer outputs a number of features equal to the number of classes, and the softmax layer normalizes these values to probabilities that sum to 1.

Firstly, it is possible to replace max-pooling layers of stride 2 with new convolutional layers of stride 2: all-convolutional networks perform even better.

Secondly, removing the fully connected layer is also possible. If the number of featuremaps output by the last convolutional layer is chosen equal to the number of classes, a global spatial average reduces each featuremap to a scalar value, representing the score for the class averaged at the different *macro* spatial locations:

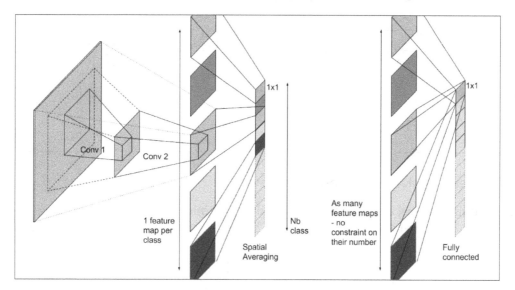

Residual connections

While very deep architectures (with many layers) perform better, they are harder to train, because the input signal decreases through the layers. Some have tried training the deep networks in multiple stages.

An alternative to this layer-wise training is to add a supplementary connection to shortcut a block of layers, named the **identity connection**, passing the signal without modification, in addition to the classic convolutional layers, named the **residuals**, forming a **residual block**, as shown in the following image:

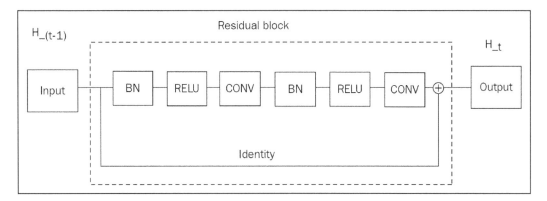

Such a residual block is composed of six layers.

A residual network is a network composed of multiple residual blocks. Input is processed by a first convolution, followed by batch normalization and non-linearity:

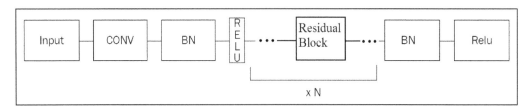

For example, for a residual net composed of two residual blocks, and eight featuremaps in the first convolution on an input image of size *28x28*, the layer output shapes will be the following:

```
InputLayer              (None, 1, 28, 28)
Conv2DDNNLayer          (None, 8, 28, 28)
BatchNormLayer          (None, 8, 28, 28)
NonlinearityLayer       (None, 8, 28, 28)
Conv2DDNNLayer          (None, 8, 28, 28)
BatchNormLayer          (None, 8, 28, 28)
NonlinearityLayer       (None, 8, 28, 28)
Conv2DDNNLayer          (None, 8, 28, 28)
ElemwiseSumLayer        (None, 8, 28, 28)
BatchNormLayer          (None, 8, 28, 28)
NonlinearityLayer       (None, 8, 28, 28)
```

```
Conv2DDNNLayer              (None, 8, 28, 28)
BatchNormLayer              (None, 8, 28, 28)
NonlinearityLayer           (None, 8, 28, 28)
Conv2DDNNLayer              (None, 8, 28, 28)
ElemwiseSumLayer            (None, 8, 28, 28)
BatchNormLayer              (None, 8, 28, 28)
NonlinearityLayer           (None, 8, 28, 28)
Conv2DDNNLayer              (None, 16, 14, 14)
BatchNormLayer              (None, 16, 14, 14)
NonlinearityLayer           (None, 16, 14, 14)
Conv2DDNNLayer              (None, 16, 14, 14)
Conv2DDNNLayer              (None, 16, 14, 14)
ElemwiseSumLayer            (None, 16, 14, 14)
BatchNormLayer              (None, 16, 14, 14)
NonlinearityLayer           (None, 16, 14, 14)
Conv2DDNNLayer              (None, 16, 14, 14)
BatchNormLayer              (None, 16, 14, 14)
NonlinearityLayer           (None, 16, 14, 14)
Conv2DDNNLayer              (None, 16, 14, 14)
ElemwiseSumLayer            (None, 16, 14, 14)
BatchNormLayer              (None, 16, 14, 14)
NonlinearityLayer           (None, 16, 14, 14)
Conv2DDNNLayer              (None, 32, 7, 7)
BatchNormLayer              (None, 32, 7, 7)
NonlinearityLayer           (None, 32, 7, 7)
Conv2DDNNLayer              (None, 32, 7, 7)
Conv2DDNNLayer              (None, 32, 7, 7)
ElemwiseSumLayer            (None, 32, 7, 7)
BatchNormLayer              (None, 32, 7, 7)
NonlinearityLayer           (None, 32, 7, 7)
Conv2DDNNLayer              (None, 32, 7, 7)
BatchNormLayer              (None, 32, 7, 7)
NonlinearityLayer           (None, 32, 7, 7)
Conv2DDNNLayer              (None, 32, 7, 7)
ElemwiseSumLayer            (None, 32, 7, 7)
BatchNormLayer              (None, 32, 7, 7)
NonlinearityLayer           (None, 32, 7, 7)
GlobalPoolLayer             (None, 32)
DenseLayer                  (None, 10)
```

The number of output featuremaps increase while the size of each output featuremap decreases: such a technique in funnel of **decreasing featuremap sizes/increasing the number of dimensions keeps the number** of parameters per layer constant which is a common best practice for building networks.

Three transitions to increase the number of dimensions occur, one before the first residual block, a second one after n residual blocks, and a third one after *2xn* residual blocks. Between each transition, the number of filters are defined in an array:

```
# 8 -> 8 -> 16 -> 32
n_filters = {0:8, 1:8, 2:16, 3:32}
```

The dimensional increase is performed by the first layer of the corresponding residual block. Since the input is not the same shape as the output, the simple identity connection cannot be concatenated with the output of layers of the block, and is replaced by a dimensional projection to reduce the size of the output to the dimension of the block output. Such a projection can be done with a convolution of kernel *1x1* with a stride of 2:

```
def residual_block(l, transition=False, first=False, filters=16):
    if transition:
        first_stride = (2,2)
    else:
        first_stride = (1,1)

    if first:
        bn_pre_relu = l
    else:
        bn_pre_conv = BatchNormLayer(l)
        bn_pre_relu = NonlinearityLayer(bn_pre_conv, rectify)

    conv_1 = NonlinearityLayer(
      BatchNormLayer(
        ConvLayer(bn_pre_relu,
          num_filters=filters,
          filter_size=(3,3),
          stride=first_stride,
          nonlinearity=None,
          pad='same',
          W=he_norm)),
        nonlinearity=rectify)

    conv_2 = ConvLayer(conv_1, num_filters=filters, filter_size=(3,3),
stride=(1,1), nonlinearity=None, pad='same', W=he_norm)


    # add shortcut connections
    if transition:
        # projection shortcut, as option B in paper
        projection = ConvLayer(bn_pre_relu, num_filters=filters,
filter_size=(1,1), stride=(2,2), nonlinearity=None, pad='same',
b=None)
```

```
    elif conv_2.output_shape == l.output_shape:
        projection=l
    else:
        projection = ConvLayer(bn_pre_relu, num_filters=filters,
 filter_size=(1,1), stride=(1,1), nonlinearity=None, pad='same',
 b=None)

    return ElemwiseSumLayer([conv_2, projection])
```

Some variants of residual blocks have been invented as well.

A wide version (Wide-ResNet) of the previous residual block simply consists of increasing the number of outputs per residual blocks by a factor as they come to the end:

```
n_filters = {0:num_filters, 1:num_filters*width, 2:num_
filters*2*width, 3:num_filters*4*width}
```

A bottleneck version consists of reducing the number of parameters per layer, to create a bottleneck that has the effect of dimension reduction, implementing the Hebbian theory *Neurons that fire together wire together*, and to help residual blocks capture particular types of pattern in the signal:

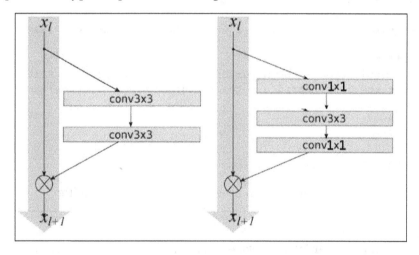

Bottlenecks are reductions in both featuremap size and number of output at the same time, not keeping the number of parameters constant per layer as in the previous practice:

```
def residual_bottleneck_block(l, transition=False, first=False,
filters=16):
    if transition:
        first_stride = (2,2)
    else:
```

```
            first_stride = (1,1)

    if first:
        bn_pre_relu = l
    else:
        bn_pre_conv = BatchNormLayer(l)
        bn_pre_relu = NonlinearityLayer(bn_pre_conv, rectify)

    bottleneck_filters = filters / 4

    conv_1 = NonlinearityLayer(BatchNormLayer(ConvLayer(bn_pre_relu,
num_filters=bottleneck_filters, filter_size=(1,1), stride=(1,1),
nonlinearity=None, pad='same', W=he_norm)),nonlinearity=rectify)

    conv_2 = NonlinearityLayer(BatchNormLayer(ConvLayer(conv_1, num_
filters=bottleneck_filters, filter_size=(3,3), stride=first_stride,
nonlinearity=None, pad='same', W=he_norm)),nonlinearity=rectify)

    conv_3 = ConvLayer(conv_2, num_filters=filters, filter_size=(1,1),
stride=(1,1), nonlinearity=None, pad='same', W=he_norm)

    if transition:
        projection = ConvLayer(bn_pre_relu, num_filters=filters,
filter_size=(1,1), stride=(2,2), nonlinearity=None, pad='same',
b=None)
    elif first:
        projection = ConvLayer(bn_pre_relu, num_filters=filters,
filter_size=(1,1), stride=(1,1), nonlinearity=None, pad='same',
b=None)
    else:
        projection = l

    return ElemwiseSumLayer([conv_3, projection])
```

Now, the full network of three stacks of residual blocks is built with:

```
def model(shape, n=18, num_filters=16, num_classes=10, width=1,
block='normal'):
  l_in = InputLayer(shape=(None, shape[1], shape[2], shape[3]))
  l = NonlinearityLayer(BatchNormLayer(ConvLayer(l_in, num_filters=n_
filters[0], filter_size=(3,3), stride=(1,1), nonlinearity=None,
pad='same', W=he_norm)),nonlinearity=rectify)

  l = residual_block(l, first=True, filters=n_filters[1])
  for _ in range(1,n):
      l = residual_block(l, filters=n_filters[1])
```

```
l = residual_block(l, transition=True, filters=n_filters[2])
for _ in range(1,n):
    l = residual_block(l, filters=n_filters[2])

l = residual_block(l, transition=True, filters=n_filters[3])
for _ in range(1,n):
    l = residual_block(l, filters=n_filters[3])

bn_post_conv = BatchNormLayer(l)
bn_post_relu = NonlinearityLayer(bn_post_conv, rectify)
avg_pool = GlobalPoolLayer(bn_post_relu)
return DenseLayer(avg_pool, num_units=num_classes, W=HeNormal(),
nonlinearity=softmax)
```

The command for a MNIST training:

```
python train.py --dataset=mnist --n=1 --num_filters=8 --batch_size=500
```

This gives a top-1 accuracy of 98%.

On Cifar 10, residual networks with more than a 100 layers require the batch size to be reduced to 64 to fit into the GPU's memory:

- For ResNet-110 (6 x 18 + 2):

  ```
  python train.py --dataset=cifar10 --n=18 --num_filters=16
  --batch_size=64
  ```

- ResNet-164 (6 x 27 + 2):

  ```
  python train.py --dataset=cifar10 --n=27 --num_filters=16
  --batch_size=64
  ```

- Wide ResNet-110:

  ```
  python train.py --dataset=cifar10 --n=18 --num_filters=16
  --width=4 --batch_size=64
  ```

- With ResNet-bottleneck-164:

  ```
  python train.py --dataset=cifar10 --n=18 --num_filters=16
  --block=bottleneck --batch_size=64
  ```

- For Food-101, I reduce further the batch size for ResNet 110:

  ```
  python train.py --dataset=food101 --batch_size=10 --n=18 --num_
  filters=16
  ```

Stochastic depth

Since the propagation of the signal through the layers might be prone to errors in any of the residual blocks, the idea of stochastic depth is to train the network to robustness by randomly removing some of the residual blocks, and replacing them with an identity connection.

First, the training is much faster, since the number of parameters is lower. Second, in practice, the robustness is proven and it provides better classification results:

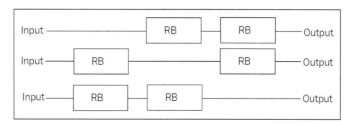

Dense connections

Stochastic depth skips some random layers by creating a direct connection. Going one step further, instead of removing some random layers, another way to do the same thing is to add an identity connection with previous layers:

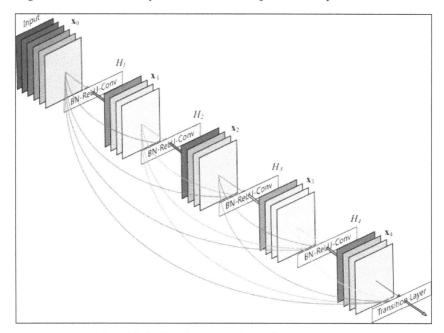

A dense block (densely connected convolutional networks)

As for residual blocks, a densely connected convolutional network consists of repeating dense blocks to create a stack of layer blocks:

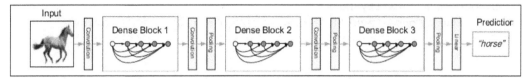

A network with dense blocks (densely connected convolutional networks)

Such an architecture choice follows the same principles as those seen in *Chapter 10, Predicting Times Sequence with Advanced RNN,* with highway networks: the identity connection helps the information to be correctly propagated and back-propagated through the network, reducing the effect of *exploding/vanishing gradients* when the number of layers is high.

In Python, we replace our residual block with a densely connected block:

```
def dense_block(network, transition=False, first=False, filters=16):
    if transition:
        network = NonlinearityLayer(BatchNormLayer(network),
nonlinearity=rectify)
        network = ConvLayer(network,network.output_shape[1], 1,
pad='same', W=he_norm, b=None, nonlinearity=None)
        network = Pool2DLayer(network, 2, mode='average_inc_pad')

    network = NonlinearityLayer(BatchNormLayer(network),
nonlinearity=rectify)
    conv = ConvLayer(network,filters, 3, pad='same', W=he_norm,
b=None, nonlinearity=None)
    return ConcatLayer([network, conv], axis=1)
```

Note also that batch normalization is done feature by feature and, since the output of every block is already normalized, a second renormalization is not necessary. Replacing the batch normalization layer by a simple affine layer learning the scale and bias on the concated normalized features is sufficient:

```
def dense_fast_block(network, transition=False, first=False,
filters=16):
    if transition:
        network = NonlinearityLayer(BiasLayer(ScaleLayer(network)),
nonlinearity=rectify)
        network = ConvLayer(network,network.output_shape[1], 1,
pad='same', W=he_norm, b=None, nonlinearity=None)
        network = BatchNormLayer(Pool2DLayer(network, 2,
mode='average_inc_pad'))
```

```
    network = NonlinearityLayer(BiasLayer(ScaleLayer(network)),
nonlinearity=rectify)
    conv = ConvLayer(network,filters, 3, pad='same', W=he_norm,
b=None, nonlinearity=None)
    return ConcatLayer([network, BatchNormLayer(conv)], axis=1)
```

For training DenseNet-40:

```
python train.py --dataset=cifar10 --n=13 --num_filters=16 --block=dense_
fast --batch_size=64
```

Multi-GPU

Cifar and MNIST images are still small, below 35x35 pixels. Training on natural images requires the preservation of details in the images. So, for example, a good input size is 224x224, which is 40 times more. When image classification nets with such input size have a few hundred layers, GPU memory limits the batch size to a dozen images and so training a batch takes a long time.

To work in multi-GPU mode:

1. The model parameters are in a shared variable, meaning shared between CPU / GPU 1 / GPU 2 / GPU 3 / GPU 4, as in single GPU mode.

2. The batch is divided into four splits, and each split is sent to a different GPU for the computation. The network output is computed on the split, and the gradients retro-propagated to each weight. The GPU returns the gradient values for each weight.

3. The gradients for each weight are fetched back from the multiple GPU to the CPU and stacked together. The stacked gradients represent the gradient of the full initial batch.

4. The update rule applies to the batch gradients and updates the shared model weights.

See the following figure:

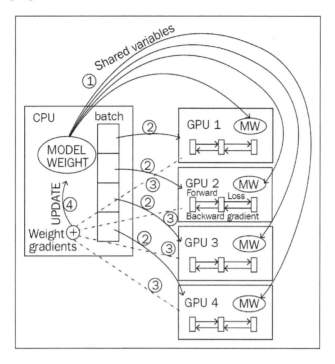

Theano stable version supports only one GPU per process, so use the first GPU in your main program and launch sub-processes for each GPU to train on. Note that the cycle described in the preceding image requires the synchronization of the update of the model to avoid each GPU training on unsynchronized models. Instead of reprogramming it yourself, a Platoon (`https://github.com/mila-udem/platoon`) framework is dedicated to train your models across multiple GPUs inside one node.

Note, too, that it would also be more accurate to synchronize the batch normalization mean and variance across multiple GPUs.

Data augmentation

Data augmentation is a very important technique to improve classification accuracy. Data augmentation consists of creating new samples from existing samples, by adding some jitters such as:

- Random scale
- Random sized crop
- Horizontal flip

- Random rotation

- Lighting noise

- Brightness jittering

- Saturation jittering

- Contrast jittering

This will help the model to be more robust to different lighting conditions that are very common in real life.

Instead of always seeing the same dataset, the model discovers different samples at each epoch.

Note that input normalization is also important to get better results.

Further reading

You can refer to the following titles for further insights:

- Densely Connected Convolutional Networks, by Gao Huang, Zhuang Liu, Kilian Q. Weinberger, and Laurens van der Maaten, Dec 2016

- Code has been inspired by the Lasagne repository:
    ○ `https://github.com/Lasagne/Recipes/blob/master/papers/`
      `deep_residual_learning/Deep_Residual_Learning_CIFAR-10.`
      `py`
    ○ `https://github.com/Lasagne/Recipes/tree/master/papers/`
      `densenet`

- Inception-v4, Inception-ResNet and the Impact of Residual Connections on Learning, Christian Szegedy, Sergey Ioffe, Vincent Vanhoucke, and Alex Alemi, 2016

- Deep Residual Learning for Image Recognition, Kaiming He, Xiangyu Zhang, and Shaoqing Ren, Jian Sun 2015

- Rethinking the Inception Architecture for Computer Vision, Christian Szegedy, Vincent Vanhoucke, Sergey Ioffe, Jonathon Shlens, and Zbigniew Wojna, 2015

- Wide Residual Networks, Sergey Zagoruyko, and Nikos Komodakis, 2016

- Identity Mappings in Deep Residual Networks, Kaiming He, Xiangyu Zhang, Shaoqing Ren, and Jian Sun, Jul 2016

- Network In Network, Min Lin, Qiang Chen, Shuicheng Yan, 2013

Summary

New techniques have been presented to achieve state-of-the-art classification results, such as batch normalization, global average pooling, residual connections, and dense blocks.

These techniques have led to the building residual networks, and densely connected networks.

The use of multiple GPUs helps training image classification networks, which have numerous convolutional layers, large reception fields, and for which the batched inputs of images are heavy in memory usage.

Lastly, we looked at how data augmentation techniques will enable an increase of the size of the dataset, reducing the potential of model overfitting, and learning weights for more robust networks.

In the next chapter, we'll see how to use the early layers of these networks as features to build encoder networks, as well as how to reverse the convolutions to reconstruct an output image to perform pixel-wise predictions.

8
Translating and Explaining with Encoding – decoding Networks

Encoding-decoding techniques occur when inputs and outputs belong to the same space. For example, image segmentation consists of transforming an input image into a new image, the segmentation mask; translation consists of transforming a character sequence into a new character sequence; and question-answering consists of replying to a sequence of words with a new sequence of words.

To address these challenges, encoding-decoding networks are networks composed of two symmetric parts: an encoding network and a decoding network. The encoder network encodes the input data into a vector, which will be used by the decoder network to produce an output, such as a *translation*, an *answer* to the input question, an *explanation*, or an *annotation* of an input sentence or an input image.

An encoder network is usually composed of the first layers of a network of the type of the ones presented in the previous chapters, without the last layers for dimensionality reduction and classification. Such a truncated network produces a multi-dimensional vector, named *features*, that gives an *internal state representation* to be used by the decoder to produce the output representation.

This chapter decomposes into the following key concepts:

- Sequence-to-sequence networks
- Application to machine translation
- Application to chatbots
- Deconvolutions
- Application to image segmentation

- Application to image captioning
- Refinements in decoding techniques

Sequence-to-sequence networks for natural language processing

Rule-based systems are being replaced by end-to-end neural networks because of their increase in performance.

An end-to-end neural network means the network directly infers all possible rules by example, without knowing the underlying rules, such as syntax and conjugation; the words (or the characters) are directly fed into the network as input. The same is true for the output format, which can be directly the word indexes themselves. The architecture of the network takes care of learning the rules with its coefficients.

The architecture of choice for such end-to-end encoding-decoding networks applied to **Natural Language Processing (NLP)**, is the **sequence-to-sequence network**, displayed in the following figure:

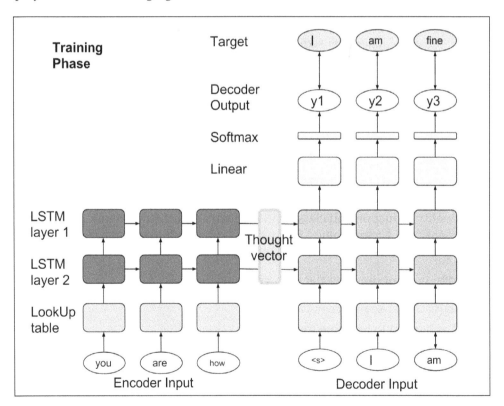

Word indexes are converted into their continuous multi-dimensional values in the embedded space with a lookup table. This conversion, presented in *Chapter 3, Encoding Word into Vector* is a crucial step to encode the discrete word indexes into a high dimensional space that a neural network can process.

Then, a first stack of LSTM is run on the input word embeddings, to encode the inputs and produce the thought vector. A second stack of LSTM is initiated with this vector as an initial internal state, and is expected to produce the next word for each word in the target sentence.

At the core, is our classical step function for the LSTM cell, with input, forget, output, and cell gates:

```python
def LSTM( hidden_size):
  W = shared_norm((hidden_size, 4*hidden_size))
  U = shared_norm((hidden_size, 4*hidden_size))
  b = shared_zeros(4*hidden_size)

  params = [W, U, b]

  def forward(m, X, h_, C_ ):
    XW = T.dot(X, W)
    h_U = T.dot(h_, U)
    bfr_actv = XW + h_U + b

    f = T.nnet.sigmoid( bfr_actv[:, 0:hidden_size] )
    i = T.nnet.sigmoid( bfr_actv[:, 1*hidden_size:2*hidden_size] )
    o = T.nnet.sigmoid( bfr_actv[:, 2*hidden_size:3*hidden_size] )
    Cp = T.tanh( bfr_actv[:, 3*hidden_size:4*hidden_size] )

    C = i*Cp + f*C_
    h = o*T.tanh( C )
    C = m[:, None]*C + (1.0 - m)[:, None]*C_
    h = m[:, None]*h + (1.0 - m)[:, None]*h_

    h, C = T.cast(h, theano.config.floatX), T.cast(h, theano.config.floatX)
    return h, C

  return forward, params
```

A simple closure is better than a class. There are not enough methods and parameters to go for a class. Writing classes impose to add lots of `self`. Before all variables, an __init__ method.

To reduce computational cost, the full stack of layers is built into a one-step function and the recurrency is added to the top of the full stack step function that the output of the last layer produces for each timestep. Some other implementations have every layer independently recurrent, which is a lot less efficient (more than two times slower).

On top of the X input, a mask variable, m, stops the recurrency when set to zero: hidden and cell states are kept constant when there is no more data (mask value is zero). Since the inputs are processed in batches, sentences in each batch can have different lengths and, thanks to the mask, all sentences in a batch can be processed in parallel with the same number of steps, corresponding to the maximal sentence length. The recurrency stops at a different position for each row in the batch.

The reason for a closure of a class is because the model cannot be applied directly to some symbolic input variables as in previous examples: indeed, the model is applied to the sequences inside a recurrency loop (with the scan operator). For this reason, in many high level deep learning frameworks, each layer is designed as a module that exposes a forward/backward method, to be added in various architectures (parallel branches and recurrency), as in this example.

The full stack step function of the encoder/decoder to be placed inside their respective recurrency loop can be designed as follows:

```python
def stack( voca_size, hidden_size, num_layers, embedding=None, target_
voca_size=0):
    params = []

    if embedding == None:
        embedding = shared_norm( (voca_size, hidden_size) )
        params.append(embedding)

    layers = []
    for i in range(num_layers):
        f, p = LSTM(hidden_size)
        layers.append(f)
        params += p

    def forward( mask, inputs, h_, C_, until_symbol = None):
        if until_symbol == None :
            output = embedding[inputs]
        else:
            output = embedding[T.cast( inputs.argmax(axis=-1), "int32"
)]

        hos = []
```

```
            Cos = []
        for i in range(num_layers):
            hs, Cs = layers[i](mask, output, h_[i], C_[i])
            hos.append(hs)
            Cos.append(Cs)
            output = hs

        if target_voca_size != 0:
            output_embedding = shared_norm((hidden_size, target_voca_
size))
            params.append(output_embedding)
            output = T.dot(output, output_embedding)

        outputs = (T.cast(output, theano.config.floatX),T.cast(hos,
theano.config.floatX),T.cast(Cos, theano.config.floatX))

        if until_symbol != None:
            return outputs, theano.scan_module.until( T.eq(output.
argmax(axis=-1)[0], until_symbol) )

        return outputs

    return forward, params
```

The first part is the conversion of the input to the embedding space. The second part is the stack of LSTM layers. For the decoder (when `target_voca_size != 0`), a linear layer is added to compute the output.

Now that we have our encoder/decoder step function, let's build the full encoder-decoder network.

First, the encoder-decoder network has to encode the input into the internal state representation:

```
encoderInputs, encoderMask = T.imatrices(2)
h0,C0 = T.tensor3s(2)

encoder, encoder_params = stack(valid_data.source_size, opt.hidden_
size, opt.num_layers)

([encoder_outputs, hS, CS], encoder_updates) = theano.scan(
  fn = encoder,
  sequences = [encoderMask, encoderInputs],
  outputs_info = [None, h0, C0])
```

To encode the input, the encoding stack step function is run recurrently on each word.

When `outputs_info` is composed of three variables, the scan operator considers that the output of the scan operation is composed of three values.

These outputs come from the encoding stack step function and correspond to:

- The output of the stack
- The hidden states of the stack, and
- The cell states for the stack, for each step/word of the input sentence

In `outputs_info`, `None` indicates to consider that the encoder will produce three outputs, but only the last two will be fed back into the step function (`h0 -> h_` and `C0 -> C_`).

Given that sequences point to two sequences, the step function for the scan operation has to handle four arguments.

Then, once the input sentence has been encoded into a vector, the encoder-decoder network decodes it:

```
decoderInputs, decoderMask, decoderTarget = T.imatrices(3)

decoder, decoder_params = stack(valid_data.target_size, opt.hidden_
size, opt.num_layers, target_voca_size=valid_data.target_size)

([decoder_outputs, h_vals, C_vals], decoder_updates) = theano.scan(
    fn = decoder,
    sequences = [decoderMask, decoderInputs],
    outputs_info = [None, hS[-1], CS[-1]])

params = encoder_params + decoder_params
```

The last states `hS[-1], CS[-1]]` of the encoder network are fed as initial hidden and cell states of the decoder network.

Computing the log likelihood on top of the output is the same as in the previous chapter on sequences.

For evaluation, the last predicted word has to be fed into the input of the decoder to predict the next word, which is a bit different from training, where input and output sequences are known:

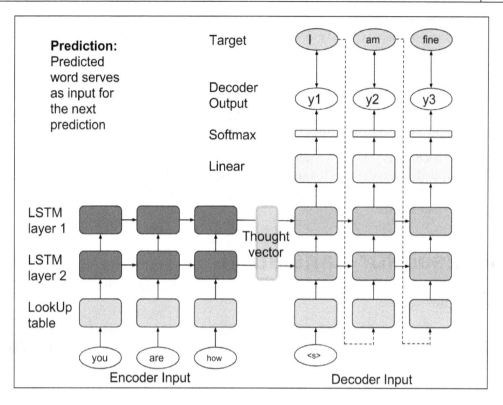

In this case, None in outputs_info can be replaced with an initial value, prediction_start, the start token. Since it is not None anymore, this initial value will be fed into the step function of the decoder, as long as it is with h0 and c0. The scan operator considers that there are three previous values to feed into the decoder function (and not two as before) at each step. Since the decoderInputs is removed from the input sequences, the number of arguments to the decoder stack step function remains four: the previous predicted output value is used in place of the fed input value. That way, the same decoder function can be used for both training and prediction:

```
prediction_mask = theano.shared(np.ones(( opt.max_sent_size, 1),
dtype="int32"))

prediction_start = np.zeros(( 1, valid_data.target_size),
dtype=theano.config.floatX)
prediction_start[0, valid_data.idx_start] = 1
prediction_start = theano.shared(prediction_start)

([decoder_outputs, h_vals, C_vals], decoder_updates) = theano.scan(
    fn = decoder,
```

```
    sequences = [prediction_mask],
    outputs_info = [prediction_start, hS[-1], CS[-1]],
    non_sequences = valid_data.idx_stop
    )
```

The non-sequence parameter, `valid_data.idx_stop`, indicates to the decoder step function that it is in prediction mode, meaning the input is not a word index, but its previous output (requires finding the max index).

Also in prediction mode, one sentence at a time is predicted (batch size is 1). The loop is stopped when the `end` token is produced, thanks to the `theano.scan_module.until` output in the decoder stack step function, and does not need to decode further words.

Seq2seq for translation

Sequence-to-sequence (Seq2seq) networks have their first application in language translation.

A translation task has been designed for the conferences of the **Association for Computational Linguistics (ACL)**, with a dataset, WMT16, composed of translations of news in different languages. The purpose of this dataset is to evaluate new translation systems or techniques. We'll use the German-English dataset.

1. First, preprocess the data:

    ```
    python 0-preprocess_translations.py --srcfile data/src-train.txt
    --targetfile data/targ-train.txt --srcvalfile data/src-val.txt
    --targetvalfile data/targ-val.txt --outputfile data/demo
    ```

    First pass through data to get vocab...

    Number of sentences in training: 10000

    Number of sentences in valid: 2819

    Source vocab size: Original = 24995, Pruned = 24999

    Target vocab size: Original = 35816, Pruned = 35820

    (2819, 2819)

    Saved 2819 sentences (dropped 181 due to length/unk filter)

    (10000, 10000)

    Saved 10000 sentences (dropped 0 due to length/unk filter)

    Max sent length (before dropping): 127

2. Train the `Seq2seq` network:

   python `1-train.py --dataset translation`

   At first glance, you notice the GPU time for one epoch is *445.906425953*, hence ten times faster than on the CPU (*4297.15962195*).

3. Once trained, translate your sentences in English to German, loading the trained model :

   python `1-train.py --dataset translation --model model_translation_` `e100_n2_h500`

Seq2seq for chatbots

A second target application of sequence-to-sequence networks is question-answering, or chatbots.

For that purpose, download the Cornell Movie--Dialogs Corpus and preprocess it:

wget `http://www.mpi-sws.org/~cristian/data/cornell_movie_dialogs_corpus.` `zip -P /sharedfiles/`

unzip `/sharedfiles/cornell_movie_dialogs_corpus.zip -d /sharedfiles/` `cornell_movie_dialogs_corpus`

python `0-preprocess_movies.py`

This corpus contains a large metadata-rich collection of fictional conversations extracted from raw movie scripts.

Since source and target sentences are in the same language, they use the same vocabulary, and the decoding network can use the same word embedding as the encoding network:

```
if opt.dataset == "chatbot":
    embeddings = encoder_params[0]
```

The same commands are true for `chatbot` dataset:

python `1-train.py --dataset chatbot # training`

python `1-train.py --dataset chatbot --model model_chatbot_e100_n2_h500 #` `answer my question`

Improving efficiency of sequence-to-sequence network

A first interesting point to notice in the chatbot example is the reverse ordered input sequence: such a technique has been shown to improve results.

For translation, it is very common then to use a bidirectional LSTM to compute the internal state as seen in *Chapter 5, Analyzing Sentiment with a Bidirectional LSTM*: two LSTMs, one running in the forward order, the other in the reverse order, run in parallel on the sequence, and their outputs are concatenated:

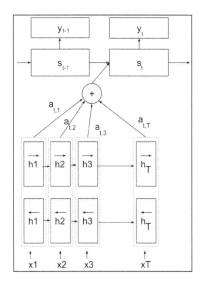

Such a mechanism captures better information given future and past.

Another technique is the *attention mechanism* that will be the focus of the next chapter.

Lastly, *refinement techniques* have been developed and tested with two-dimensional Grid LSTM, which are not very far from stacked LSTM (the only difference is a gating mechanism in the depth/stack direction):

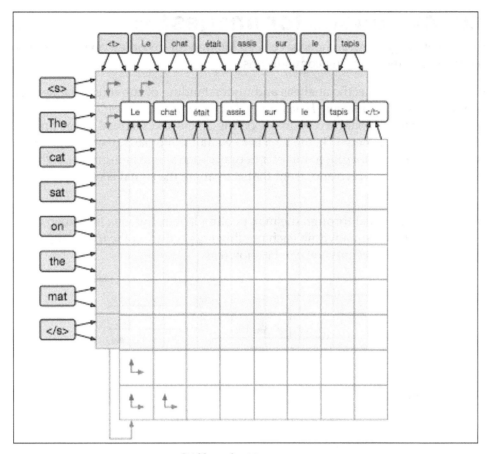

Grid long short-term memory

The principle of refinement is to run the stack in both orders on the input sentence as well, sequentially. The idea behind this formulation is to have the encoder network revisit or re-encode the sentence, after having encoded it in the forward direction, and implicitly capture some time patterns. Also, note that the 2D-grid gives more possible interactions for this re-encoding, re-encoding the vector at each prediction step, using previously outputted words as an orientation for the next predicted word. All this improvement is linked to a bigger computational capacity, in **O(n m)** for this re-encoder network (*n* and *m* represent the length of input and target sentences), while being of **O(n+m)** for the encoder-decoder network.

All these techniques decrease perplexity. When the model is trained, consider also using the **beam search algorithm** that will keep track of the top-N possible predictions with their probabilities, instead of one, at each time step, to avoid the possibility that one bad prediction ranking at first position could lead to further erroneous predictions.

Deconvolutions for images

In the case of images, researchers have been looking for decoding operations acting as the inverse of the encoding convolutions.

The first application was the analysis and understanding of convolutional networks, as seen in *Chapter 2, Classifying Handwritten Digits with a Feedforward Network*, composed of convolutional layers, max-pooling layers and rectified linear units. To better understand the network, the idea is to visualize the parts of an image that are most discriminative for a given unit of a network: one single neuron in a high level feature map is left non-zero and, from that activation, the signal is retro-propagated back to the 2D input.

To reconstruct the signal through the max pooling layers, the idea is to keep track of the position of the maxima within each pooling region during the forward pass. Such architecture, named **DeConvNet** can be shown as:

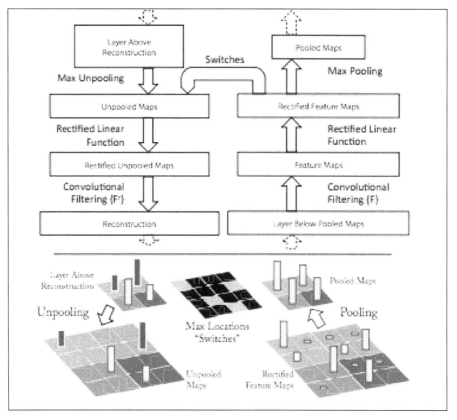

Visualizing and understanding convolutional networks

The signal is retro-propagated to the position that had the maximal value during the forward pass.

To reconstruct the signal through the ReLU layers, three methods have been proposed:

- *Back-propagation* retro-propagates only to the positions that have been positive
- *Backward DeconvNet* retro-propagates only the positive gradients
- *Guided back-propagation* retro-propagates only to a position that satisfies both previous conditions, positive input during forward pass and positive gradient

The methods are illustrated in the following figure:

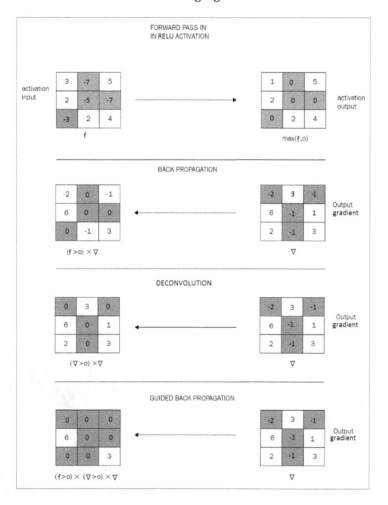

The retro-propagation from the first layers gives various sorts of filter:

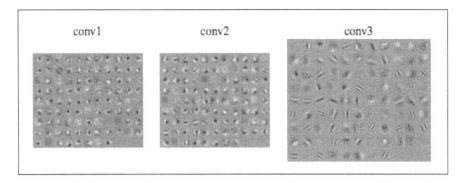

However, from higher layers in the network, the guided back-propagation gives much better results:

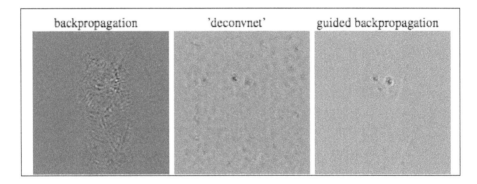

It is also possible to condition the back-propagation on an input image, that will activate more than one neuron, from which the retro-propagation will be applied, to get a more precise input visualization:

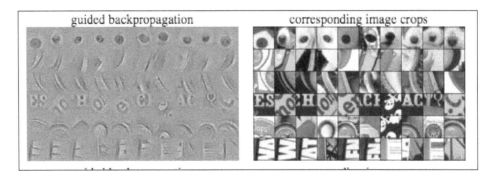

The back-propagation can also be applied to the original input image rather than a blank one, a process that has been named **Inceptionism** by Google research, when retro-propagation is used to augment the output probability:

But the main purpose of deconvolution is for scene segmentation or image semantic analysis, where the deconvolution is replaced by a learned upsampling convolution, such as in the **SegNet network**:

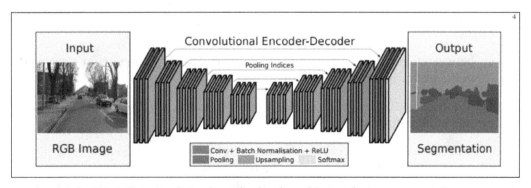

SegNet: A deep convolutional encoder-decoder architecture for image segmentation

At every step in the deconvolution process, lower input features are usually concatenated to the current features for upsampling.

The **DeepMask network** takes a mixed approach, deconvolutioning only the patches containing the objects. For that purpose, it is trained on input patches of 224x224 containing the objects (+/- 16 pixels in translation) instead of the full image:

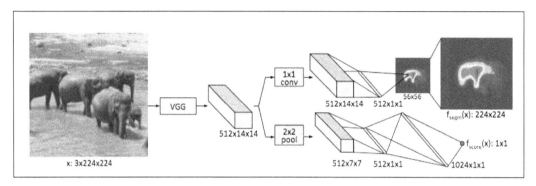

Learning to segment object candidates

The convolutions of the encoder (VGG-16) network have a downsampling of factor 16, leading to a feature map of 14x14.

A joint learning trains two branches, one for segmentation, one for scoring if the object is present, centered, and at the right scale in the patch.

The branch of interest is the semantic branch that upsamples to a 56x56 segmentation map of the object in the patch from the 14x14 feature map.
To upsample, is possible if:

- A fully connected layer, meaning that each position in the upsampled map depends on all features and has the global picture to predict the value

- A convolution (or locally connected layer), reducing the number of parameters, but also predicting each position score with a partial view

- A mixed approach, consisting of two linear layers with no non-linearity between them, in a way to perform a dimensionality reduction, as presented in the preceding figure

The output mask is then upsampled back to the original patch dimensions 224x224 by a simple bilinear upsampling layer.

To deal with the full input image, fully connected layers can be transformed into convolutions with a kernel size equal to the fully connected layer input size and the same coefficients, so that the network becomes fully convolutional, with stride 16, when applied to the full image.

As sequence-to-sequence networks have been refined with a bidirectional reencoding mechanism, the **SharpMask** approach improves the sharpness of the upsampling deconvolutional process using the input convolutional features at the equivalent scale:

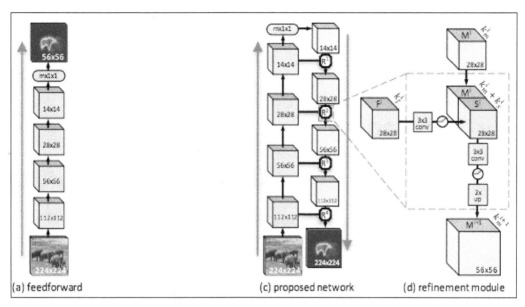

Learning to refine object segments

While the SegNet approach only learns to deconvolve from an up-sampled map produced by keeping track of the max pooling indices, the SharpMask approach directly reuses the input feature maps, a very usual technique for coarse-to-finegrained approaches.

Lastly, bear in mind that it is possible to improve the results one step further with the application of a **Conditional Random Fields (CRF)** post-processing step, either for one-dimensional inputs such as texts, or two-dimensional inputs such as segmentation images.

Multimodal deep learning

To open the possible applications further, the encoding-decoding framework can be applied with different modalities, such as, for example, for image captioning.

Image captioning consists of describing the content of the image with words. The input is an image, naturally encoded into a thought vector with a deep convolutional network.

The text to describe the content of the image can be produced from this internal state vector with the same stack of LSTM networks as a decoder, as in Seq2seq networks:

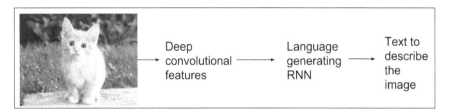

Further reading

Please refer to the following topics for better insights:

- *Sequence to Sequence Learning with Neural Networks*, Ilya Sutskever, Oriol Vinyals, Quoc V. Le, Dec 2014

- *Learning Phrase Representations using RNN Encoder–Decoder for Statistical Machine Translation*, Kyunghyun Cho, Bart van Merrienboer, Caglar Gulcehre, Dzmitry Bahdanau, Fethi Bougares, Holger Schwenk, Yoshua Bengio, Sept 2014

- *Neural Machine Translation by Jointly Learning to Align and Translate*, Dzmitry Bahdanau, Kyunghyun Cho, Yoshua Bengio, May 2016

- *A Neural Conversational Model*, Oriol Vinyals, Quoc Le, July 2015

- *Fast and Robust Neural Network Joint Models for Statistical Machine Translation*, Jacob Devlin, Rabih Zbib, Zhongqiang Huang,Thomas Lamar, Richard Schwartz, John Mkahoul, 2014

- *SYSTRAN's Pure Neural Machine Translation Systems*, Josep Crego, Jungi Kim, Guillaume Klein, Anabel Rebollo, Kathy Yang, Jean Senellart, Egor Akhanov, Patrice Brunelle, Aurelien Coquard, Yongchao Deng, Satoshi Enoue, Chiyo Geiss, Joshua Johanson, Ardas Khalsa, Raoum Khiari, Byeongil Ko, Catherine Kobus, Jean Lorieux, Leidiana Martins, Dang-Chuan Nguyen, Alexandra Priori, Thomas Riccardi, Natalia Segal, Christophe Servan, Cyril Tiquet, Bo Wang, Jin Yang, Dakun Zhang, Jing Zhou, Peter Zoldan, 2016

- *Blue: a method for automatic evaluatoin of machine translation,* Kishore Papineni, Salim Roukos, Todd Ward, and Wei-Jing Zhu, 2002

- ACL 2016 translation task

- *Chameleons in imagined conversations: A new approach to understanding coordination of linguistic style in dialogs*, Cristian Danescu-NiculescuMizil and Lillian Lee2011 at: `https://research.googleblog.com/2015/06/inceptionism-going-deeper-into-neural.html`

- *Semantic Image Segmentation with Deep Convolutional Nets and Fully Connected CRFs*, Liang-Chieh Chen, George Papandreou, Iasonas Kokkinos, Kevin Murphy, Alan L., Yuille 2014

- *SegNet: A Deep Convolutional Encoder-Decoder Architecture for Image Segmentation*, Vijay Badrinarayanan, Alex Kendall, Roberto Cipolla, Oct 2016

- *R-FCN: Object Detection via Region-based Fully Convolutional Networks*, Jifeng Dai, Yi Li, Kaiming He, Jian Sun2016

- *Learning to segment object candidates*, Pedro O. Pinheiro, Ronan Collobert, Piotr Dollar, June 2015

- *Learning to refine object segments*, Pedro O. Pinheiro, Tsung-Yi Lin, Ronan Collobert, Piotr Dollàr, Mar 2016

- *Visualizing and Understanding Convolutional Networks*, Matthew D Zeiler, Rob Fergus, Nov 2013

- *Show and tell: A Neural Image Caption Generator*, Oriol Vinyals, Alexander Toshev, Samy Bengio, Dumitru Erhan, 2014

Summary

As for love, head-to-toe positions provide exciting new possibilities: encoder and decoder networks use the same stack of layers but in their opposite directions.

Although it does not provide new modules to deep learning, such a technique of *encoding-decoding* is quite important because it enables the training of the networks 'end-to-end', that is, directly feeding the inputs and corresponding outputs, without specifying any rules or patterns to the networks and without decomposing encoding training and decoding training into two separate steps.

While image classification was a one-to-one task, and sentiment analysis a many-to-one task, encoding-decoding techniques illustrate many-to-many tasks, such as translation or image segmentation.

In the next chapter, we'll introduce an *attention mechanism* that provides the ability for encoder-decoder architecture to focus on some parts of the input in order to produce a more accurate output.

9
Selecting Relevant Inputs or Memories with the Mechanism of Attention

This chapter introduces a mechanism of attention to neural network performance, and enables networks to improve their performance by focusing on relevant parts of their inputs or memories.

With such a mechanism, translations, annotations, explanations, and segmentations, as seen in previous chapter, enjoy greater accuracy.

Inputs and outputs of a neural network may also be connected to *reads* and *writes* to an external memory. These networks, **memory networks**, are enhanced with an external memory and capable of deciding what information, and from where, to store or retrieve.

In this chapter, we'll discuss:

- The mechanism of attention
- Aligning translations
- Focus in images
- Neural Turing Machines
- Memory networks
- Dynamic memory networks

Differentiable mechanism of attention

When translating a sentence, describing the content of an image, annotating a sentence, or transcribing an audio, it sounds natural to focus on one part at a time of the input sentence or image, to get the sense of the block and transform it, before moving to the next part, under a certain order for global understanding.

For example, in the German language, under certain conditions, verbs come at the end of the sentence, so, when translating to English, once the subject has been read and translated, a good machine translation neural network could move its focus to the end of the sentence to find the verb and translate it into English. This process of matching input positions to current output predictions is possible through the *mechanism of attention*.

First, let's come back to classification networks that have been designed with a softmax layer (see *Chapter 2, Classifying Handwritten Digits with a Feedforward Network*) that outputs a non-negative weight vector $\vec{v}$ that sums to 1 given an input X:

$$w_i(X) \geq 0$$

Then:

$$\sum_i w_i(X) = 1$$

The objective of classification is to have $w_i(X)$ as close as possible to 1 for the correct class k, and near zero for the other classes.

But $w_i(X)$ is a probability distribution, and can also be used as a weight vector to pay attention to some values of a memory vector $\vec{m}(X)$ at a position k:

$$\text{attention output} = \sum_i w_i(X) m_i(X)$$

It returns m_k if the weights focus on position k. Depending on the sharpness of the weights, the output will be more or less blurry.

This mechanism of addressing the value of the vector *m* at a particular position is an **attention mechanism**: that is, it's linear, differentiable, and has a back-propagation gradient descent for training on specific tasks.

Better translations with attention mechanism

The applications for attention mechanisms are very large. To get a better understanding, let us first illustrate it with the example of machine translation. Attention mechanism aligns the source sentence and the target sentence (predicted translation), and avoids translation degradation for long sentences:

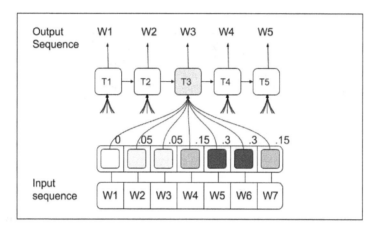

In the previous chapter, we addressed the machine translation with an encoder-decoder framework and a fixed-length encoded vector *c* provided by the encoder to the decoder. With the attention mechanism, if each step of the encoding recurrent network produces a hidden state h_i, the vector provided to the decoder at each decoding time step *t* will be variable and given by:

$$c_t = \sum_i^T \alpha_{t,i} h_i$$

With $\alpha_{t,i}$ the alignment coefficients produced by a softmax function:

$$\alpha_{t,i} = \mathrm{softmax}\left(\left(W_s \cdot s_{t-1} \right)^T \left(W_h \cdot h_i \right) \right)$$

Depending on the previous hidden state of the decoder s_{t-1} and the encoding hidden states h_i , the embedded dot product between the previous decoder hidden state and each encoder hidden state produces a weight that describes how they should match:

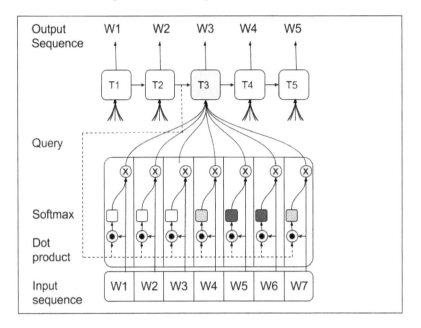

After a few epochs of training, the model predicts each next word by focusing on a part of the input:

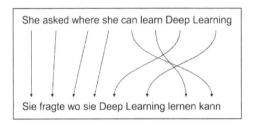

To learn to align better, it is possible to use the alignment annotations present in the dataset, and add a cross entropy loss for the weights produced by the attention mechanism, to be used in the first epochs of training.

Better annotate images with attention mechanism

The same mechanism of attention can be applied to the tasks of annotating images or transcribing audio.

For images, the attention mechanism focuses on the relevant part of the features at each predicting time step:

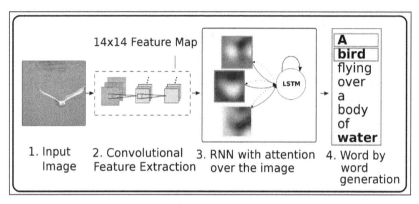

Show, attend and tell: neural image caption generation with visual attention

Let's have a look at the point of attention on images for a trained model:

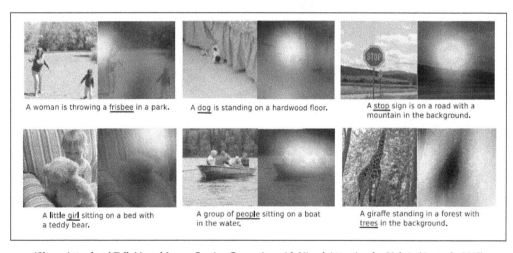

(*Show, Attend and Tell: Neural Image Caption Generation with Visual Attention*, by Kelvin Xu et al., 2015)

Store and retrieve information in Neural Turing Machines

Attention mechanism can be used as an access to a part of memory in the memory-augmented networks.

The concept of memory in Neural Turing Machines has been inspired by both neuroscience and computer hardware.

RNN hidden states to store information is not capable of storing sufficiently large amounts of data and retrieving it, even when the RNN is augmented with a memory cell, such as in the case of LSTM.

To solve this problem, **Neural Turing Machines (NTM)** have been first designed with an **external memory bank** and read/write heads, whilst retaining the magic of being trained via gradient descent.

Reading the memory bank is given by an attention on the variable memory bank as the attention on inputs in the previous examples:

$$r = \sum_i w_i^r M_i$$

Which can be illustrated the following way:

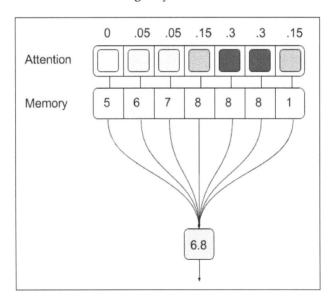

While writing a value to the memory bank consists of assigning our new value to part of the memory, thanks to another attention mechanism:

$$M_t(i) = M_{t-1}(i)\left(1 - w_t^w(i)e_t\right) + w_t^w(i)a_t$$

a_t describes the information to store, and e_t the information to erase, and are each the size of the memory bank:

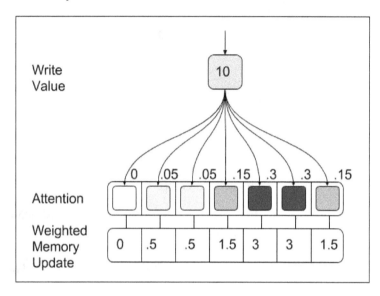

The read and write heads are designed as in a hard drive and their mobility is imagined by the attention weights w_t^r and w_t^w.

The memory M_t will evolve at every timestep as the cell memory of a LSTM; but, since the memory bank is designed to be large, the network tends to store and organize the incoming data at every timestep with less interference than for any classical RNN.

The process to work with the memory is naturally been driven with a recurrent neural network acting as a **controller** at each time step:

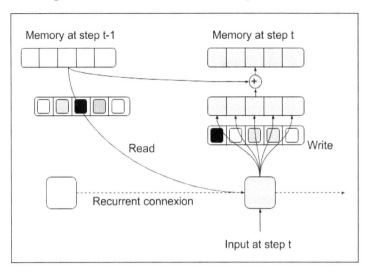

The controller network outputs at each timestep:

- The positioning or attention coefficients for each write/read head
- The value to store or erase for the write heads

The original NTM proposes two approaches to define the *head positioning*, also named *addressing*, defined by the weights w_t:

- A content-based positioning, to place similar content in the same area of the memory, which is useful for retrieval, sorting or counting tasks:

$$w_t(i) = \text{softmax}\left(\beta_t \text{similarity}\left(x_t, M_t(i)\right)\right)$$

- A location-based positioning, which is based on previous position of the head, and can be used in copy tasks. A gate g_t defines the influence of the previous weights versus newly generated weights to compute the position of the head. A shift weight s_t defines how much to translate from the position with respect to this position.

Last, a sharpening weight γ_t reduces the blur on the head position:

$$w_t^g(i) = g_t w_t^c + \left(1 - g_t\right) w_{t-1}$$

$$w_t(i) = \mathsf{softmax}\left(\left(\sum_k w_t^g(k) s_t(i+k)\right)^{\gamma_t}\right)$$

All operations are differentiable.

Many more than two heads are possible, in particular for tasks such as the addition of two stored values where a single read head would be limiting.

These NTM have demonstrated better capability than LSTM in tasks such as retrieving the next item in an input sequence, repeating the input sequence many times, or sampling from distribution.

Memory networks

Answering questions or resolving problems given a few facts or a story have led to the design of a new type of networks, **memory networks**. In this case, the facts or the story are embedded into a memory bank, as if they were inputs. To solve tasks that require the facts to be ordered or to create transitions between the facts, memory networks use a recurrent reasoning process in multiple steps or hops on the memory banks.

First, the query or question q is converted into a constant input embedding:

$$u_0 = B \cdot q$$

While, at each step of the reasoning, the facts X to answer the question are embedded into two memory banks, where the embedding coefficients are a function of the timestep:

$$M1_t = A_t \cdot X$$

To compute attention weights:

$$p_t = \mathsf{softmax}\left(M1_t \cdot (B_t \cdot u_{t-1})\right)$$

And:

$$M2_t = C_t \cdot X$$

Selected with the attention:

$$o_t = p_t \cdot M2_t$$

The output at each reasoning time step is then combined with the identity connection, as seen previously to improve the efficiency of the recurrency:

$$u_t = o_t + u_{t-1}$$

A linear layer and classification softmax layer are added to the last u_k:

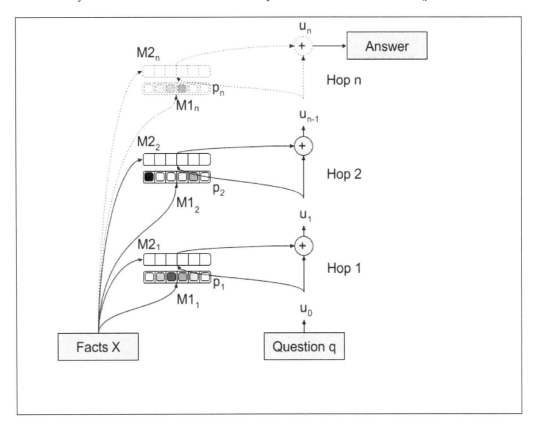

Episodic memory with dynamic memory networks

Another design has been introduced with dynamic memory networks. First, the N facts are concatenated with a separator token and then encoded with a RNN: the output of the RNN at each separation c_i is used as input embedding. This way to encode facts is more natural and also preserves time dependency. The question is also encoded with an RNN to produce a vector q.

Secondly, the memory bank is replaced with an episodic memory, relying on an attention mechanism mixed with an RNN, in order to preserve time dependency between the facts as well:

$$h_i^t = g_i^t GRU\left(c_i, h_{i-1}^t\right) + \left(1 - g_i^t\right)h_{i-1}^t$$

The gates g_i^t are given by a multilayer perceptron depending on the previous state of reasoning u_{t-1}, the question and the input embedding c_i as inputs.

The reasoning occurs the same way with a RNN:

$$u_t = GRU\left(h_N^t, u_{t-1}\right)$$

The following picture illustrates the interactions between inputs and outputs to compute the episodic memories:

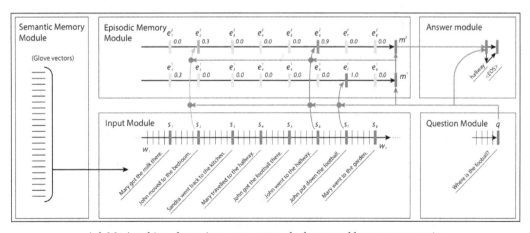

Ask Me Anything: dynamic memory networks for natural language processing

To benchmark these networks, Facebook research has synthetized the bAbI dataset, using NLP tools to create facts, questions, and answers for some random modeled stories. The dataset is composed of different tasks to test different reasoning skills, such as reasoning on one, two, or three facts, in time, size, or position, counting, listing, or understanding relations between arguments, negations, motivations, and finding paths.

As for guided alignment in machine translation, when the dataset also contains the annotations for the facts leading to the answer, it is also possible to use supervised training for:

- The attention mechanism
- When to stop the reasoning loop, producing a stop token, when the number of facts used is sufficient to answer the question

Further reading

You can refer to these topics for more insights:

- *Ask Me Anything: Dynamic Memory Networks for Natural Language Processing*, Ankit Kumar, Ozan Irsoy, Peter Ondruska, Mohit Iyyer, James Bradbury, Ishaan Gulrajani, Victor Zhong, Romain Paulus, Richard Socher, 2015

- *Attention and Augmented Recurrent Neural Networks*, Chris Olah, Shan Carter, Sept 2016 http://distill.pub/2016/augmented-rnns/

- *Guided Alignment training for Topic Aware Neural Machine Translation*, Wenhu Chen, Evgeny Matusov, Shahram Khadivi, Jan-Thorsten Peter, Jul 2016

- *Show, Attend and Tell: Neural Image Caption Generation with Visual Attention*, Kelvin Xu, Jimmy Ba, Ryan Kiros, Kyunghyun Cho, Aaron Courville, Ruslan Salakhutdinov, Richard Zemel, Yoshua Bengio, Fev 2015

- *Towards AI-Complete Question Answering: A Set of Prerequisite Toy Tasks*, Jason Weston, Antoine Bordes, Sumit Chopra, Alexander M. Rush, Bart van Merriënboer, Armand Joulin, Tomas Mikolov,2015

- *Memory Networks*, Jason Weston, Sumit Chopra, Antoine Bordes,2014

- *End-To-End Memory Networks*, Sainbayar Sukhbaatar, Arthur Szlam, Jason Weston, Rob Fergus, 2015

- *Neural Turing Machines*, Alex Graves, Greg Wayne, Ivo Danihelka, 2014

- *Deep Visual-Semantic Alignments for Generating Image Descriptions*, Andrej Karpathy, Li Fei-Fei, 2014

Summary

The attention mechanism is a smart option to help neural networks select the right information and focus to produce the correct output. It can be placed either directly on the inputs or the features (inputs processed by a few layers). Accuracies in the cases of translation, image annotation, and speech recognition, are increased, in particular when the dimension of the inputs is important.

Attention mechanism has led to new types of networks enhanced with external memory, working as an input/output, from which to read or to which to write. These networks have proved to be very powerful in question-answering challenges, into which most tasks in natural language processing can can be cast: tagging, classification, sequence-to-sequence, or question answering tasks.

In the next chapter, we'll see more advanced techniques and their application to the more general case of recurrent neural networks, to improve accuracy.

10
Predicting Times Sequences with Advanced RNN

This chapter covers advanced techniques for recurrent neural networks.

The techniques seen in *Chapter 2, Classifying Handwritten Digits with a Feedforward Network*, for feedforward networks, such as going deeper with more layers, or adding a dropout layer, have been more challenging for recurrent networks and require some new design principles.

Since adding new layers increases the vanishing/exploding gradient issue, a new technique based on identity connections as for *Chapter 7, Classifying Images with Residual Networks* has proved to provide state-of-the-art results.

The topics covered are:

* Variational RNN
* Stacked RNN
* Deep Transition RNN
* Highway connections and their application to RNN

Dropout for RNN

The application of dropout inside neural networks has long been a subject of research, since the naïve application of dropout to the recurrent connection introduced lots more instability and difficulties to training the RNN.

A solution has been discovered, derived from the variational **Bayes Network** theory. The resulting idea is very simple and consists of preserving the same dropout mask for the whole sequence on which the RNN is training, as shown in the following picture, and generating a new dropout mask at each new sequence:

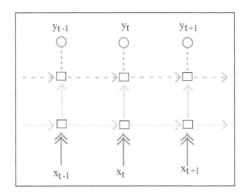

Such a technique is called **variational RNN.** For the connections that have the same arrows in the preceding figure, we'll keep the noise mask constant for the all sequence.

For that purpose, we'll introduce the symbolic variables _is_training and _noise_x to add a random (variational) noise (dropout) to input, output, and recurrent connection during training:

```
_is_training = T.iscalar('is_training')
_noise_x = T.matrix('noise_x')
inputs = apply_dropout(_is_training, inputs, T.shape_padright(_
noise_x.T))
```

Deep approaches for RNN

The core principle of deep learning to improve the representative power of a network is to add more layers. For RNN, two approaches to increase the number of layers are possible:

- The first one is known as **stacking** or **stacked recurrent network**, where the output of the hidden layer of a first recurrent net is used as input to a second recurrent net, and so on, with as many recurrent networks on top of each other:

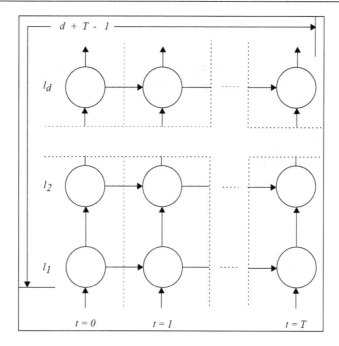

For a depth d and T time steps, the maximum number of connections between input and output is $d + T - 1$:

- The second approach is the **deep transition network**, consisting of adding more layers to the recurrent connection:

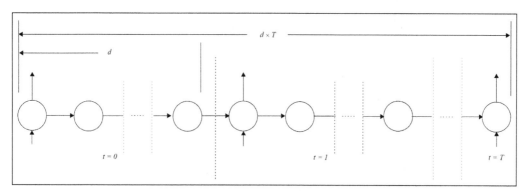

Figure 2

In this case, the maximum number of connections between input and output is $d \times T$, which has been proved to be a lot more powerful.

Both approaches provide better results.

However, in the second approach, as the number of layers increases by a factor, the training becomes much more complicated and unstable since the signal fades or explodes a lot faster. We'll address this problem later by tackling the principle of recurrent highway connections.

First, as usual, sequences of words, represented as an array of index values in the vocabulary, and of dimension (`batch_size, num_steps`), are embedded into an input tensor of dimension (`num_steps, batch_size, hidden_size`):

```
embedding = shared_uniform(( config.vocab_size,config.hidden_size),
config.init_scale)
params = [embedding]
inputs = embedding[_input_data.T]
```

The symbolic input variable `_lr` enables the decrease of the learning rate during training:

```
_lr = theano.shared(cast_floatX(config.learning_rate), 'lr')
```

Let's begin with the first approach, the stacked recurrent networks.

Stacked recurrent networks

To stack recurrent networks, we connect the hidden layer of the following recurrent network, to the input of the preceding recurrent network:

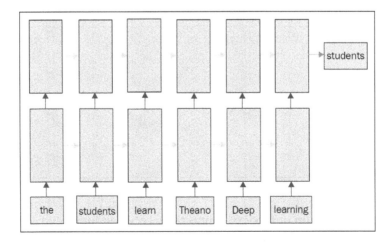

When the number of layers is one, our implementation is a recurrent network as in the previous chapter.

First we implement dropout in our simple RNN model:

```
def model(inputs, _is_training, params, batch_size, hidden_size,
drop_i, drop_s, init_scale, init_H_bias):
    noise_i_for_H = get_dropout_noise((batch_size, hidden_size),
drop_i)
        i_for_H = apply_dropout(_is_training, inputs, noise_i_for_H)
        i_for_H = linear.model(i_for_H, params, hidden_size,
                        hidden_size, init_scale, bias_init=init_H_bias)


    # Dropout noise for recurrent hidden state.
    noise_s = get_dropout_noise((batch_size, hidden_size), drop_s)


    def step(i_for_H_t, y_tm1, noise_s):
        s_lm1_for_H = apply_dropout(_is_training,y_tm1, noise_s)
        return T.tanh(i_for_H_t + linear.model(s_lm1_for_H,
                    params, hidden_size, hidden_size, init_scale))


    y_0 = shared_zeros((batch_size, hidden_size), name='h0')
    y, _ = theano.scan(step, sequences=i_for_H, outputs_info=[y_0],
non_sequences = [noise_s])


    y_last = y[-1]
    sticky_state_updates = [(y_0, y_last)]


    return y, y_0, sticky_state_updates
```

We do the same in our LSTM model:

```
def model(inputs, _is_training, params, batch_size, hidden_size,
drop_i, drop_s, init_scale, init_H_bias, tied_noise):
    noise_i_for_i = get_dropout_noise((batch_size, hidden_size),
drop_i)
    noise_i_for_f = get_dropout_noise((batch_size, hidden_size),
drop_i) if not tied_noise else noise_i_for_i
    noise_i_for_c = get_dropout_noise((batch_size, hidden_size),
drop_i) if not tied_noise else noise_i_for_i
    noise_i_for_o = get_dropout_noise((batch_size, hidden_size),
drop_i) if not tied_noise else noise_i_for_i

    i_for_i = apply_dropout(_is_training, inputs, noise_i_for_i)
    i_for_f = apply_dropout(_is_training, inputs, noise_i_for_f)
    i_for_c = apply_dropout(_is_training, inputs, noise_i_for_c)
    i_for_o = apply_dropout(_is_training, inputs, noise_i_for_o)

    i_for_i = linear.model(i_for_i, params, hidden_size, hidden_size,
init_scale, bias_init=init_H_bias)
```

```
    i_for_f = linear.model(i_for_f, params, hidden_size, hidden_size,
init_scale, bias_init=init_H_bias)
    i_for_c = linear.model(i_for_c, params, hidden_size, hidden_size,
init_scale, bias_init=init_H_bias)
    i_for_o = linear.model(i_for_o, params, hidden_size, hidden_size,
init_scale, bias_init=init_H_bias)

    # Dropout noise for recurrent hidden state.
    noise_s = get_dropout_noise((batch_size, hidden_size), drop_s)
    if not tied_noise:
        noise_s = T.stack(noise_s, get_dropout_noise((batch_size,
hidden_size), drop_s),
 get_dropout_noise((batch_size, hidden_size), drop_s), get_dropout_
noise((batch_size, hidden_size), drop_s))


    def step(i_for_i_t,i_for_f_t,i_for_c_t,i_for_o_t, y_tm1, c_tm1,
noise_s):
        noise_s_for_i = noise_s if tied_noise else noise_s[0]
        noise_s_for_f = noise_s if tied_noise else noise_s[1]
        noise_s_for_c = noise_s if tied_noise else noise_s[2]
        noise_s_for_o = noise_s if tied_noise else noise_s[3]

        s_lm1_for_i = apply_dropout(_is_training,y_tm1, noise_s_for_i)
        s_lm1_for_f = apply_dropout(_is_training,y_tm1, noise_s_for_f)
        s_lm1_for_c = apply_dropout(_is_training,y_tm1, noise_s_for_c)
        s_lm1_for_o = apply_dropout(_is_training,y_tm1, noise_s_for_o)

        i_t = T.nnet.sigmoid(i_for_i_t + linear.model(s_lm1_for_i,
params, hidden_size, hidden_size, init_scale))
        f_t = T.nnet.sigmoid(i_for_o_t + linear.model(s_lm1_for_f,
params, hidden_size, hidden_size, init_scale))
        c_t = f_t * c_tm1 + i_t * T.tanh(i_for_c_t + linear.model(s_
lm1_for_c, params, hidden_size, hidden_size, init_scale))
        o_t = T.nnet.sigmoid(i_for_o_t + linear.model(s_lm1_for_o,
params, hidden_size, hidden_size, init_scale))
        return o_t * T.tanh(c_t), c_t

    y_0 = shared_zeros((batch_size,hidden_size), name='h0')
    c_0 = shared_zeros((batch_size,hidden_size), name='c0')
    [y, c], _ = theano.scan(step, sequences=[i_for_i,i_for_f,i_
for_c,i_for_o], outputs_info=[y_0,c_0], non_sequences = [noise_s])

    y_last = y[-1]
    sticky_state_updates = [(y_0, y_last)]

    return y, y_0, sticky_state_updates
```

Running our stacked networks:

```
python train_stacked.py --model=rnn
python train_stacked.py --model=lstm
```

We get 15,203,150 parameters for the RNN, with 326 **words per seconds** (WPS) on a CPU and 4,806 WPS on a GPU.

For LSTM, the number of parameters is 35,882,600 with a speed of 1,445 WPS on a GPU.

The stacked RNN do not converge, as we might have imagined: the vanishing/exploding gradient issue is increased with depth.

LSTM, designed to reduce such as an issue, do converge a lot better when stacked, than as a single layer.

Deep transition recurrent network

Contrary to stacked recurrent network, a deep transition recurrent network consists of increasing the depth of the network along the time direction, by adding more layers or *micro-timesteps* inside the recurrent connection.

To illustrate this, let us come back to the definition of a transition/recurrent connection in a recurrent network: it takes as input the previous state y^{t-1} and the input data x^t at time step t, to predict its new state y^t.

In a deep transition recurrent network (figure 2), the recurrent transition is developed with more than one layer, up to a recurrency depth L: the initial state is set to the output of the last transition:

$$s_0^t = y^{t-1}$$

Furthermore, inside the transition, multiple states or steps are computed:

$$s_l^t = H_l\left(x^t, s_{l-1}^t\right) = \tanh\left(W_l^H x^t 1_{l=1} + R_l^H s_{l-1}^t + b_l^H\right)$$

The final state is the output of the transition:

$$y^t = s_L$$

Highway networks design principle

Adding more layers in the transition connections increases the vanishing or exploding gradient issue during backpropagation in long term dependency.

In the *Chapter 4, Generating Text with a Recurrent Neural Net*, LSTM and GRU networks have been introduced as solutions to address this issue. Second order optimization techniques also help overcome this problem.

A more general principle, based on **identity connections**, to improve the training in deep networks *Chapter 7, Classifying Images with Residual Networks*, can also be applied to deep transition networks.

Here is the principle in theory:

Given an input x to a hidden layer H with weigh W_H :

$$y = H\left(W_H, x\right)$$

A highway networks design consists of adding the original input information (with an identity layer) to the output of a layer or a group of layers, as a shortcut:

$$y = x$$

Two mixing gates, the *transform gate* $T(W_T, x)$ and the *carry gate*, $C(W_C, x)$ learn to modulate the influence of the transformation in the hidden layer, and the amount of original information to allow to pass through:

$$y = H\left(W_H, x\right) \cdot T\left(W_T, x\right) + x \cdot C\left(W_c, x\right)$$

Usually, to reduce the total number of parameters in order to get faster-to-train networks, the carry gate is taken as the complementary to 1 for the transform gate:

$$C\left(W_c, x\right) = 1 - T\left(W_T, x\right)$$

Recurrent Highway Networks

So, let's apply the highway network design to deep transition recurrent networks, which leads to the definition of **Recurrent Highway Networks (RHN)**, and predict the output y^t given y^{t-1} the input of the transition:

$$s_0^t = y^{t-1}$$

The transition is built with multiple steps of highway connections:

$$s_l^t = H_l\left(x^t, s_{l-1}^t\right) \cdot T_l\left(x^t, s_{l-1}^t\right) + s_{l-1}^t \cdot C_l\left(x^t, s_{l-1}^t\right)$$

$$y^t = s_L$$

Here the transform gate is as follows:

$$T_l\left(x^t, s_{l-1}^t\right) = \sigma\left(W_l^T x^t 1_{l=1} + R_l^T s_{l-1}^t + b_l^T\right)$$

And, to reduce the number of weights, the carry gate is taken as the complementary to the transform gate:

$$C\left(W_c, x\right) = 1 - T\left(W_T, x\right)$$

For faster computation on a GPU, it is better to compute the linear transformation on inputs over different time steps $W_l^H x^t$ and $W_l^T x^t$ in a single big matrix multiplication, all-steps input matrices $i\_for\_H = W_l^H x$ and $i\_for\_T = W_l^T x$ at once, since the GPU will use a better parallelization, and provide these inputs to the recurrency:

```
y_0 = shared_zeros((batch_size, hidden_size))
y, _ = theano.scan(deep_step_fn, sequences = [i_for_H, i_for_T],
         outputs_info = [y_0], non_sequences = [noise_s])
```

With a deep transition between each step:

```
def deep_step_fn(i_for_H_t, i_for_T_t, y_tm1, noise_s):
  s_lm1 = y_tm1
  for l in range(transition_depth):
    if l == 0:
       H = T.tanh(i_for_H_t + linear(s_lm1, params, hidden_size,
hidden_size, init_scale))
       Tr = T.nnet.sigmoid(i_for_T_t + linear(s_lm1, params, hidden_
size, hidden_size, init_scale))
    else:
       H = T.tanh(linear(s_lm1, params, hidden_size, hidden_size, init_
scale, bias_init=init_H_bias))
```

```
        Tr = T.nnet.sigmoid(linear(s_lm1, params, hidden_size, hidden_
size, init_scale, bias_init=init_T_bias))
    s_l = H * Tr + s_lm1 * ( 1 - Tr )
    s_lm1 = s_l
  y_t = s_l
  return y_t
```

The recurrent hidden state of the RHN is sticky (the last hidden state of one batch is carried over to the next batch, to be used as an initial hidden state). These states are kept in a shared variable.

Let's run the mode:

```
python train_stacked.py
```

The number of parameters of the stacked RHN is *84,172,000*, its speed *420* wps on the GPU.

This model is the new state-of-the-art model for recurrent neural network accuracy on texts.

Further reading

You can refer to the following topics for more insights:

- *Highway Networks* at: https://arxiv.org/abs/1505.00387
- *Depth-Gated LSTM* at: https://arxiv.org/abs/1508.03790
- *Learning Longer Memory in Recurrent Neural Networks* at: https://arxiv.org/abs/1412.7753
- *Grid Long Short-Term Memory*, Nal Kalchbrenner, Ivo Danihelka, Alex Graves
- Zilly, J, Srivastava, R, Koutnik, J, Schmidhuber, J., *Recurrent Highway Networks*, 2016
- Gal, Y, *A Theoretically Grounded Application of Dropout in Recurrent Neural Networks*, 2015.
- Zaremba, W, Sutskever, I, Vinyals, O, *Recurrent neural network regularization*, 2014.
- Press, O, Wolf, L, *Using the Output Embedding to Improve Language Models*, 2016.
- Gated Feedback Recurrent Neural Networks: Junyoung Chung, Caglar Gulcehre, Kyunghyun Cho, Yoshua Bengio 2015
- A Clockwork RNN: Jan Koutník, Klaus Greff, Faustino Gomez, Jürgen Schmidhuber 2014

Summary

A classic dropout method to improve network robustness may be applied to recurrent network sequence-wise or batch-wise to avoid instability and destruction of the recurrent transition. For example, when applied on word inputs/outputs, it is equivalent to removing the same words from the sentence, replacing them with a blank value.

The principle of stacking layers in deep learning to improve accuracy applies to recurrent networks that can be stacked in the depth direction without burden.

Applying the same principle in the transition of the recurrent nets increases the vanishing/exploding issue, but is offset by the invention of the highway networks with identity connections.

Advanced techniques for recurrent neural nets give state-of-the-art results in sequence prediction.

11
Learning from the Environment with Reinforcement

Supervised and unsupervised learning describe the presence or the absence of labels or targets during training. A more natural learning environment for an agent is to receive rewards when the correct decision has been taken. This reward, such as *playing correctly tennis* for example, may be attributed in a complex environment, and the result of multiple actions, delayed or cumulative.

In order to optimize the reward from the environment for an artificial agent, the **Reinforcement Learning** (**RL**) field has seen the emergence of many algorithms, such as Q-learning, or Monte Carlo Tree Search, and with the advent of deep learning, these algorithms have been revised into new methods, such as deep-Q-networks, policy networks, value networks, and policy gradients.

We'll begin with a presentation of the reinforcement learning frame, and its potential application to virtual environments. Then, we'll develop its algorithms and their integration with deep learning, which has solved the most challenging problems in artificial intelligence.

The points covered in this chapter are the following:

- Reinforcement learning
- Simulation environments
- Q-learning
- Monte Carlo Tree Search
- Deep Q-networks

- Policy gradients
- Asynchronous gradient descents

To simplify the development of our neural nets in this chapter, we'll use Keras, the high level deep learning library on top of Theano I presented in *Chapter 5, Analyzing Sentiment with a Bidirectional LSTM*.

Reinforcement learning tasks

Reinforcement learning consists of training an **agent,** that just needs occasional feedback from the **environment**, to learn to get the best feedback at the end. The agent performs **actions**, modifying the **state** of the environment.

The actions to navigate in the environment can be represented as directed edges from one state to another state as a graph, as shown in the following figure:

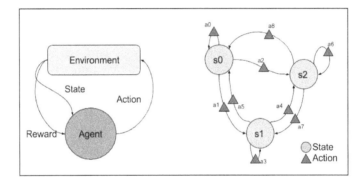

A robot, working in a real environment (walking robots, control of motors, and so on) or a virtual environment (video game, online games, chat room, and so on) has to decide which movements (or keys to strike) to receive the maximum reward:

Simulation environments

Virtual environments make it possible to simulate thousands to millions of gameplays, at no other cost than the computations. For the purpose of benchmarking different reinforcement learning algorithms, simulation environments have been developed by the research community.

In order to find the solutions that generalize well, the Open-AI non-profit artificial intelligence research company, associated with business magnate Elon Musk, that aims to carefully promote and develop friendly AI in such a way as to benefit humanity as a whole, has gathered in its open source simulation environment, **Open-AI Gym** (https://gym.openai.com/), a collection of reinforcement tasks and environments in a Python toolkit to test our own approaches on them. Among these environments, you'll find:

- Video games from Atari 2600, a home video game console released by Atari Inc in 1977, wrapping the simulator from the Arcade Learning Environment, one of the most common RL benchmark environment:

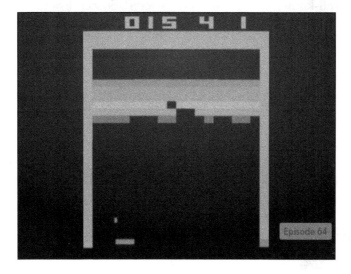

- MuJoCo, a physics simulator for evaluating agents on continuous control tasks:

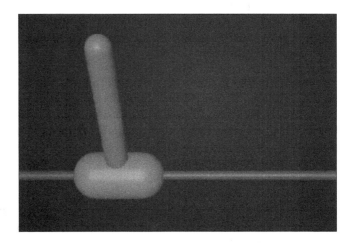

- Other well-known games such as Minecraft, Soccer, Doom, and many others:

Let's install Gym and its Atari 2600 environment:

```
pip install gym
pip install gym[atari]
```

It is also possible to install all environments with:

```
pip install gym[all]
```

Interacting with the gym environment is pretty simple with the env.step() method that, given an action we choose for the agent, returns the new state, the reward, and whether the game has terminated.

For example, let's sample a random action:

```
import gym

env = gym.make('CartPole-v0')
env.reset()

for _ in range(1000):
    env.render()
    action = env.action_space.sample()
    next_state, reward, done, info = env.step(action)
    if done:
        env.reset()
```

Gym also provides sophisticated monitoring methods, to record videos and algorithm performance. The records can be uploaded to Open-AI API for scoring with other algorithms.

One might also look at:

- 3D car racing simulator Torcs (http://torcs.sourceforge.net/), which is more realistic with smaller discretization of actions, but with less sparse rewards than simple Atari games, and also fewer possible actions than continuous motor control in MuJoCo:

- 3D environment called Labyrinth for randomly generated mazes:

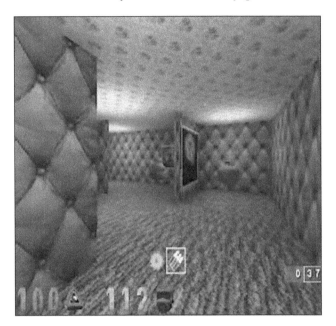

Q-learning

A major approach to solve games has been the Q-learning approach. In order to fully understand the approach, a basic example will illustrate a simplistic case where the number of states of the environment is limited to 6, state **0** is the entrance, state **5** is the exit. At each stage, some actions make it possible to jump to another state, as described in the following figure:

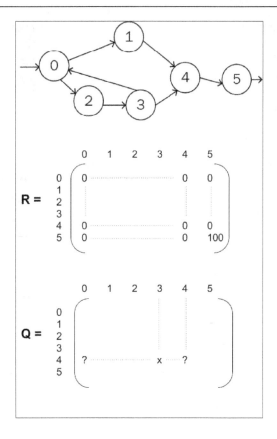

The reward is, let's say, 100, when the agent leaves state **4** to state **5**. There isn't any other reward for other states since the goal of the game in this example is to find the exit. The reward is time-delayed and the agent has to scroll through multiple states from state 0 to state 4 to find the exit.

In this case, Q-learning consists of learning a matrix Q, representing the **value of a state-action pair**:

- Each row in the Q-matrix corresponds to a state the agent would be in
- Each column the target state from that state

the value representing how much choosing that action in that state will move us close to the exit. If there isn't any action from state i leading to state j, we define a zero or negative value at position (i,j) in the Q-matrix. If there are one or more possible actions from state i to state j, then the value in the Q-matrix will be chosen to represent how state j will help us to achieve our goal.

For example, leaving state **3** for state **0**, will move the agent away from the exit, while leaving state **3** for state **4** gets us closer to the goal. A commonly used algorithm, known as a *greedy* algorithm, to estimate **Q** in the discrete space, is given by the recursive *Bellman equation* which is demonstrated to converge:

$$Q(S,a) = r + \gamma \max_{a'} Q(S',a')$$

Here, S' is the new state when taking action a on state S; r defines the reward on the path from state S to S' (in this case it is null) and γ is the discounting factor to discourage actions to states too far in the graph. The application of this equation multiple times will result in the following Q values:

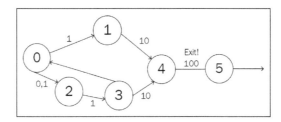

In Q-learning, Q stands for *quality* representing the power of the action to get the best rewards. Since late rewards are discounted, the values correspond to **maximum discounted future rewards** for each (state, action) couple.

Note that the full graph outcome is not required as soon as we know the **state values** for the output nodes of the search subtree:

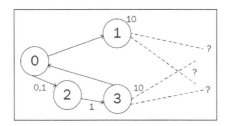

In this figure, the value **10** for nodes **1** and **3** are the **optimal state value function v(s);** that is, the outcome of a game under perfect play / optimal path. In practice, the exact value function is not known but approximated.

Such an approximation is used in combination with a **Monte Carlo Tree Search (MCTS)** in the **DeepMind** algorithm **AlphaGo** to beat the world champion in Go. MCTS consists of sampling actions given a policy, so that only the most likely actions from the current node to estimate its Q-value are retained in the Bellman equation:

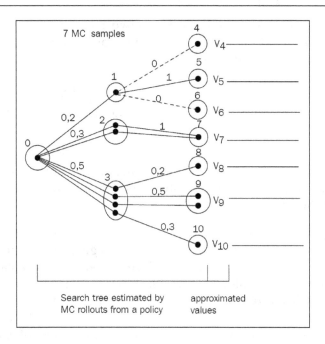

Search tree estimated by   approximated
MC rollouts from a policy   values

Deep Q-network

While the number of possible actions is usually limited (number of keyboard keys
or movements), the number of possible states can be dramatically huge, the search
space can be enormous, for example, in the case of a robot equipped with cameras
in a real-world environment or a realistic video game. It becomes natural to use a
computer vision neural net, such as the ones we used for classification in *Chapter 7,
Classifying Images with Residual Networks*, to represent the value of an action given an
input image (the state), instead of a matrix:

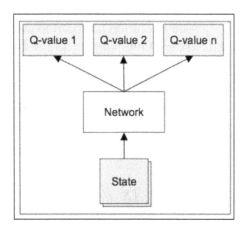

The Q-network is called a **state-action value network** and predicts action values given a state. To train the Q-network, one natural way of doing it is to have it fit the Bellman equation via gradient descent:

$$\mathcal{L} = \left(r + \gamma \max_{a'} Q_\theta \left(S', a' \right) - Q_\theta \left(S, a \right) \right)^2 / 2$$

Note that, $\max_a Q_\theta(S', a')$ is evaluated and fixed, while the descent is computed for the derivatives in, $Q_\theta(S, a)$ and that the value of each state can be estimated as the maximum of all state-action values.

After initializing the Q-network with random weights, the initial predictions are random, but as the network converges, the action given a particular state will become more and more predictable, so the exploration of new states drops. Exploiting a model trained online requires the forcing of the algorithm to **continue to explore**: the ε **greedy approach** consists of doing a random action with a probability epsilon, otherwise following the maximum-reward action given by the Q-network. It is a kind of learning by trial-and-error. After a certain number of epochs, ε is decayed to reduce exploration.

Training stability

Different methods are possible to improve stability during training. **Online training**, that is, training the model while playing the game, forgetting previous experiences, just considering the last one, is fundamentally unstable with deep neural networks: states that are close in time, such as the most recent states, are usually strongly similar or correlated, and taking the most recent states during training does not converge well.

To avoid such a failure, one possible solution has been to store the experiences in a **replay memory** or to use a database of human gameplays. Batching and shuffling random samples from the replay memory or the human gameplay database leads to more stable training, but **off-policy** training.

A second solution to improve stability is to fix the value of the parameter θ in the **target evaluation** $\max_a Q_\theta(S', a')$ for several thousands of updates of $Q_\theta(S, a)$, reducing the correlations between the target and the Q-values:

$$\mathcal{L} = \left(r + \gamma \max_{a'} Q_{\theta^-} \left(S', a' \right) - Q_\theta \left(S, a \right) \right)^2 / 2$$

It is possible to train more efficiently with n-steps Q-learning, propagating the rewards on n preceding actions instead of one:

Q learning formula:

$$
S_1 \xrightarrow{\text{action a}} S_2 \xrightarrow{\hspace{2cm}}
$$

$$
+ \text{ reward } \textcircled{r}
$$

$$
\xleftarrow{\text{update state value}}
$$

$$
y = \textcircled{r} + \gamma \max_{a_2} Q(s_2, a_2)
$$

n-steps Q-learning formula:

$$
S_1 \xrightarrow{a_1} S_2 \xrightarrow{a_2} S_3 \xrightarrow{a_3} S_4
$$

$$
+\textcircled{r_1} \qquad +\textcircled{r_2} \qquad +\textcircled{r_3}
$$

$$
y_3 = \textcircled{r_3} + \gamma \max_{a_4} Q(s_4, a_4)
$$

$$
y_2 = \textcircled{r_2} + \gamma \; \textcircled{r_3} + \gamma^2 \max_{a_4} Q(s_4, a_4)
$$

$$
y_1 = \textcircled{r_1} + \gamma \; \textcircled{r_2} + \gamma^2 \; \textcircled{r_3} + \gamma^3 \max_{a_4} Q(s_4, a_4)
$$

Here, each step will benefit from n next rewards:

$$
y_i = \sum_{k=0}^{n-1} \gamma^k r_{i+k} + \gamma^n \max_a Q(s_{i+n}, a)
$$

A last solution for training stability and efficiency is an **asynchronous gradient descent** with multiple agents executing in parallel, on multiple instances of the environment, with different exploration policies, so that each gradient update is less correlated: each learning agent runs in a different thread on the same machine, sharing its model and target model parameters with other agents, but computing the gradients for a different part of the environment. The parallel actor learners have a stabilization effect, enable on-policy reinforcement, a reduction in training time, and comparable performances on GPU or multi-core CPU, which is great!

The stabilization effect leads to better **data efficiency**: the data efficiency is measured by the number of epochs (an epoch is when the full training dataset has been presented to the algorithm) required to converge to a desired training loss or accuracy. Total training time is impacted by data efficiency, parallelism (number of threads or machines), and the parallelism overhead (it is sublinear in the number of threads, given the number of cores, machines and algorithm distribution efficiency).

Let's see it in practice. To implement multiple agents exploring different parts of the environment, we'll run multiple processes with the Python multiprocessing module, one process for the model to update (GPU), and *n* processes for the agents exploring (CPU). The manager object of the multiprocessing module controls a server process holding the weights of the Q-network to share between processes. The communication channel to store the experiences of the agents and serve them once for the model update, is implemented with a process-safe queue:

```
from multiprocessing import *
manager = Manager()
weight_dict = manager.dict()
mem_queue = manager.Queue(args.queue_size)

pool = Pool(args.processes + 1, init_worker)

for i in range(args.processes):
    pool.apply_async(generate_experience_proc, (mem_queue, weight_
dict, i))

pool.apply_async(learn_proc, (mem_queue, weight_dict))

pool.close()
pool.join()
```

Now, let's generate experiences and enqueue them in the common queue object.

For that purpose, where each agent creates its game environment, compile the Q-network and load the weights from the manager:

```
env = gym.make(args.game)

load_net = build_networks(observation_shape, env.action_space.n)

load_net.compile(optimizer='rmsprop',
                 loss='mse',
                 loss_weights=[0.5, 1.])

while 'weights' not in weight_dict:
    time.sleep(0.1)
load_net.set_weights(weight_dict['weights'])
```

To generate one experience, the agent chooses an action and executes it in its environment:

```
observation, reward, done, _ = env.step(action)
```

Each experience by the agent is stored in a list until the game is terminated or the list is longer than *n_step*, to evaluate the state-action value with *n-steps* Q-learning :

```
if done or counter >= args.n_step:
    r = 0.
    if not done:
        r = value_net.predict(observations[None, ...])[0]
    for i in range(counter):
        r = n_step_rewards[i] + discount * r
        mem_queue.put((n_step_observations[i], n_step_actions[i], r))
```

Once in a while, the agent updates its weights from the learning process:

```
load_net.set_weights(weight_dict['weights'])
```

Let's see now how to update the weights in the learning agent.

Policy gradients with REINFORCE algorithms

The idea of **Policy Gradients (PG)** / REINFORCE algorithms is very simple: it consists in re-using the classification loss function in the case of reinforcement learning tasks.

Let's remember that the classification loss is given by the negative log likelihood, and minimizing it with a gradient descent follows the negative log-likelihood derivative with respect to the network weights:

$$\frac{\partial}{\partial \theta}\left(\ln g\left(y\right)\right)$$

Here, y is the select action, $g(y)$ the predicted probability of this action given inputs X and weights θ.

The REINFORCE theorem introduces the equivalent for reinforcement learning, where r is the reward. The following derivative:

$$(r-b)\frac{\partial \ln g(y)}{\partial \theta}$$

represents an unbiased estimate of the derivative of the expected reward with respect to the network weights:

$$\frac{\partial E(r\,|\,\theta)}{\partial \theta}$$

So, following the derivative will encourage the agent to maximize the reward.

Such a gradient descent enables us to optimize a **policy network** for our agents: a policy $p(a\,|\,s)$ is a probability distribution over legal actions, to sample actions to execute during online learning, and can be approximated with a parameterized neural net as well.

It is particularly useful in the continuous case, for example for motor control, where discretization of the action space might lead to some suboptimal artifacts and the maximization over an action-value network Q is not possible under infinite action space.

Moreover, it is possible to enhance the policy network with recurrency (LSTM, GRU,) so that the agent selects its actions with respect to multiple previous states.

The REINFORCE theorem gives us a gradient descent to optimize the parametrized policy network. To encourage exploration in this policy-based case, it is also possible to add a regularization term, the entropy of the policy, to the loss function.

Under this policy, it is possible to compute the value of every state $v^{\pi}(s)$:

- Either by playing the game from that state with the policy
- Or, if parameterized into a **state value network**, by gradient descent, the current parameter serving as target, as for the state-action value network seen in the previous section with discounted rewards:

$$V^{\pi}(s) = r + \gamma V^{\pi}(s')$$

This value is usually chosen as reinforcement baseline b to reduce the variance of the estimate of the policy gradient, and the Q-value can be used as the expected reward:

$$R = Q(s,a) = r + \gamma V^{\pi}(s')$$

The first factor in the REINFORCE derivative:

$$R - b = Q(s,a) - V^{\pi}(s) = A(a,s)$$

is called the **advantage of action a in state** s.

Both gradient descents, for the policy network and for the value network, can be performed asynchronously with our parallel actor learners.

Let's create our policy network and state value network, sharing their first layers, in Keras:

```
from keras.models import Model
from keras.layers import Input, Conv2D, Flatten, Dense

def build_networks(input_shape, output_shape):
    state = Input(shape=input_shape)
    h = Conv2D(16, (8, 8) , strides=(4, 4), activation='relu', data_
format="channels_first")(state)
    h = Conv2D(32, (4, 4) , strides=(2, 2), activation='relu', data_
format="channels_first")(h)
    h = Flatten()(h)
    h = Dense(256, activation='relu')(h)

    value = Dense(1, activation='linear', name='value')(h)
    policy = Dense(output_shape, activation='softmax', name='policy')
(h)

    value_network = Model(inputs=state, outputs=value)
    policy_network = Model(inputs=state, outputs=policy)
    train_network = Model(inputs=state, outputs=[value, policy])

    return value_network, policy_network, train_network
```

Our learning process builds the model as well, shares the weights to other processes, and compiles them for training with their respective losses:

```
_, _, train_network = build_networks(observation_shape, env.action_
space.n)
weight_dict['weights'] = train_net.get_weights()

from keras import backend as K

def policy_loss(advantage=0., beta=0.01):
    def loss(y_true, y_pred):
        return -K.sum(K.log(K.sum(y_true * y_pred, axis=-1) + \
                K.epsilon()) * K.flatten(advantage)) + \
                beta * K.sum(y_pred * K.log(y_pred + K.epsilon())))
    return loss

def value_loss():
    def loss(y_true, y_pred):
        return 0.5 * K.sum(K.square(y_true - y_pred))
    return loss

train_net.compile(optimizer=RMSprop(epsilon=0.1, rho=0.99),
            loss=[value_loss(), policy_loss(advantage, args.beta)])
```

The policy loss is a REINFORCE loss plus an entropy loss to encourage exploration. The value loss is a simple mean square error loss.

De-queueing the experiences into a batch, our learning process trains the model on the batch and updates the weights dictionary:

```
loss = train_net.train_on_batch([last_obs, advantage], [rewards,
targets])
```

To run the full code:

```
pip install -r requirements.txt

python 1-train.py --game=Breakout-v0 --processes=16
python 2-play.py --game=Breakout-v0 --model=model-
Breakout-v0-35750000.h5
```

Learning took about 24 hours.

A policy-based advantage actor critic usually outperforms value-based methods.

Related articles

You can refer to the following articles:

- *Simple Statistical Gradient-Following Algorithms for Connectionist Reinforcement Learning*, Ronald J. Williams, 1992

- *Policy Gradient Methods for Reinforcement Learning with Function Approximation*, Richard S. Sutton, David McAllester, Satinder Singh, Yishay Mansour, 1999

- *Playing Atari with Deep Reinforcement Learning*, Volodymyr Mnih, Koray Kavukcuoglu, David Silver, Alex Graves, Ioannis Antonoglou, Daan Wierstra, Martin Riedmiller, 2013

- *Mastering the Game of Go with Deep Neural Networks and Tree Search*, David Silver, Aja Huang, Chris J. Maddison, Arthur Guez, Laurent Sifre, George van den Driessche, Julian Schrittwieser, Ioannis Antonoglou, Veda Panneershelvam, Marc Lanctot, Sander Dieleman, Dominik Grewe, John Nham, Nal Kalchbrenner, Ilya Sutskever, Timothy Lillicrap, Madeleine Leach, Koray Kavukcuoglu, Thore Graepel & Demis Hassabis, 2016

- *Asynchronous Methods for Deep Reinforcement Learning*, Volodymyr Mnih, Adrià Puigdomènech Badia, Mehdi Mirza, Alex Graves, Tim Harley, Timothy P. LilliCrap, David Silver, Koray Kavukcuoglu, Feb 2016

- *Deep Reinforcement Learning Radio Control and Signal Detection with KeRLym, a Gym RL Agent* Timothy J. O'Shea and T. Charles Clancy, 2016

Summary

Reinforcement learning describes the tasks of optimizing an agent stumbling into rewards episodically. Online, offline, value-based, or policy-based algorithms have been developed with the help of deep neural networks for various games and simulation environments.

Policy-gradients are a brute-force solution that require the sampling of actions during training and are better suited for small action spaces, although they provide first solutions for continuous search spaces.

Policy-gradients also work to train non-differentiable stochastic layers in a neural net and back propagate gradients through them. For example, when propagation through a model requires to sample following a parameterized submodel, gradients from the top layer can be considered as a reward for the bottom network.

In more complex environments, when there is no obvious reward (for example understanding and inferring possible actions from the objects present in the environment), reasoning helps humans optimize their actions, for which research does not provide any solution currently. Current RL algorithms are particularly suited for precise plays, fast reflexes, but no long term planning and reasoning. Also, RL algorithms require heavy datasets, which simulation environments provide easily. But this opens up the question of scaling in the real world.

In the next chapter, we'll explore the latest solutions to generate new data undistinguishable from real-world data.

12
Learning Features with Unsupervised Generative Networks

This chapter focuses on a new type of model, the generative models, which include **Restricted Boltzmann Machines**, **Deep Belief Networks**, **Variational Auto Encoders**, **Autoregressive models, and Generative Adversarial** Networks. For the first nets, we've limited the presentation to the theory, while the last is explained in detail with practical code and advice.

These nets do not require any labels to be trained, which is called *unsupervised learning*. Unsupervised learning helps compute features from the data, without the bias of the labels. These models are generative in the sense that they are trained to generate new data that sounds real.

The following points will be covered:

- Generative models
- Unsupervised learning
- Restricted Boltzmann Machines
- Deep belief networks
- Generative adversarial models
- Semi-supervised learning

Generative models

A generative model in neural processing is a model that generates data given a noise vector z as input:

$$x \leftarrow G\left(z, \theta^G\right)$$

The purpose of the training is to find the parameters to generate data as close as possible to the real data.

Applications of generative networks include data dimensionality reduction, synthetic data generation, unsupervised feature learning, and pre-training / training efficiency. Pre-training helps generalization because pre-training focuses on the patterns in the data, and less on the data-label relation.

Restricted Boltzmann Machines

A Restricted Boltzmann Machine is the simplest generative net, composed of one fully connected hidden layer, as shown in the picture:

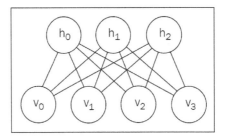

The full Boltzmann Machines have also hidden-to-hidden and visible-to-visible loop connections, while the *Restricted* version does not have any.

In the general case, RBM are defined as *energy-based models*, which means that they define a probability distribution through an energy function:

$$p(v) = \frac{e^{-E(v)}}{Z} = \sum_h p(v, h) = \sum_h \frac{e^{-E(v,h)}}{Z}$$

$$Z = \sum_x e^{-E(x)} = \sum_{x,y} e^{-E(x,y)}$$

Z is the **partition function**, and $E(v)$ is the **free energy** function (does not depend on the hidden state).

[📝 Minimizing the negative log likelihood is equivalent to minimizing the energy function.]

The RBM defines the energy function as a linearity in the parameters of the model:

$$E(v,h) = -b \cdot v - c \cdot h - h \cdot W \cdot v$$

$$E(v,h) = -\sum_i b_i v_i - \sum_i c_i h_i - \sum_{i,j} h_i W_{i,j} v_j$$

The relation between the energy and the free energy is given by:

$$E(v) = -\log Zp(v) = -\log \sum_h Zp(v,h)$$

$$E(v) = -\log \sum_h e^{-E(v,h)}$$

In the case of the RBM:

$$E(v) = -b \cdot v - \sum_i \log \sum_{h_i} e^{h_i \, (c_i + W_{i,.} \cdot v)}$$

Here $\sum_{h_i}$ denotes the sum over possible values of the i-th hidden neuron.

The RBM are usually considered in the particular case where v and h are binomial values in {0,1}, so:

$$P(v_j = 1 | h) = \sigma(b_j + h \cdot W_{.,j})$$

The model is symmetric, following the symmetry in the model: hidden and visible have the same place in the energy function:

$$P\left(h_i = 1 \middle| v\right) = \sigma\left(c_i + W_{i,\cdot} \cdot v\right)$$

RBM works as a simple stochastic fully connected layer in both directions (from input to hidden, and from hidden to input).

The gradient or derivative of the negative log-likelihood for the RBM has two terms, defined as **positive and negative phases**, where the first term increases the probability of data, and the second term decreases the probability of generated samples:

$$-\frac{\partial \log p\left(v\right)}{\partial \theta} = \frac{\partial E\left(v\right)}{\partial \theta} - \sum_{\bar{v}} p\left(\bar{v}\right) \frac{\partial E\left(\bar{v}\right)}{\partial \theta}$$

Here, the sum is over all possible inputs $\bar{v}$ weighted by its probability (the expectation). At the minima, any increase in the free energy of our data sample will decrease the expectation of the total data.

Empirically, such a sum in the negative phase can be transformed into a sum over N observed (v,h):

$$\frac{1}{N}\sum_{x} \frac{\partial E\left(x\right)}{\partial \theta}$$

To compute such a sum in practice, the probability of observing the sample (v,h) has to satisfy $p(v \mid h)$ given by the above formula as well as $p(h \mid v)$.

Sampling is performed via the contrastive divergence algorithm, in practice: v is sampled from the dataset, while h is drawn following its above distribution given v. This operation is repeated, to produce a new v given h, then a new h given v. In practice, this is sufficient to achieve samples closely distributed to the real distribution. These observed samples for v and h are referred to as **negative particles**, and the second term in the cost function decreases the probability of these generated samples, while the first term increases the probability of the data.

Here is what the computation of the partition function with the negative particules would look like:

```
W = shared_glorot_uniform((n_visible, n_hidden), name='W')
hbias = shared_zeros(n_hidden, name='hbias')
vbias = shared_zeros(n_visible, name='vbias')
params = [W, hbias, vbias]


def sample_h_given_v(v0_sample):
    pre_sigmoid_h1 = T.dot(v0_sample, W) + hbias
    h1_mean = T.nnet.sigmoid(pre_sigmoid_h1)
    h1_sample = theano_rng.binomial(size=h1_mean.shape, n=1, p=h1_
mean, dtype=theano.config.floatX)
    return [pre_sigmoid_h1, h1_mean, h1_sample]


def sample_v_given_h(h0_sample):
    pre_sigmoid_v1 = T.dot(h0_sample, W.T) + vbias
    v1_mean = T.nnet.sigmoid(pre_sigmoid_v1)
    v1_sample = theano_rng.binomial(size=v1_mean.shape, n=1, p=v1_
mean, dtype=theano.config.floatX)
    return [pre_sigmoid_v1, v1_mean, v1_sample]


def gibbs_hvh(h0_sample):
    pre_sigmoid_v1, v1_mean, v1_sample = sample_v_given_h(h0_sample)
    pre_sigmoid_h1, h1_mean, h1_sample = sample_h_given_v(v1_sample)
    return [pre_sigmoid_v1, v1_mean, v1_sample,
            pre_sigmoid_h1, h1_mean, h1_sample]


chain_start = persistent_chain
(
    [
        pre_sigmoid_nvs,
        nv_means,
        nv_samples,
        pre_sigmoid_nhs,
        nh_means,
        nh_samples
    ],
    updates
) = theano.scan(
    gibbs_hvh,
```

```
        outputs_info=[None, None, None, None, None, chain_start],
        n_steps=k,
        name="gibbs_hvh"
    )

chain_end = nv_samples[-1]

def free_energy(v_sample):
    wx_b = T.dot(v_sample, W) + hbias
    vbias_term = T.dot(v_sample, vbias)
    hidden_term = T.sum(T.log(1 + T.exp(wx_b)), axis=1)
    return -hidden_term - vbias_term

cost = T.mean(free_energy(x)) - T.mean(free_energy(chain_end))
```

The pictures of the filters trained on MNIST dataset after 15 epochs:

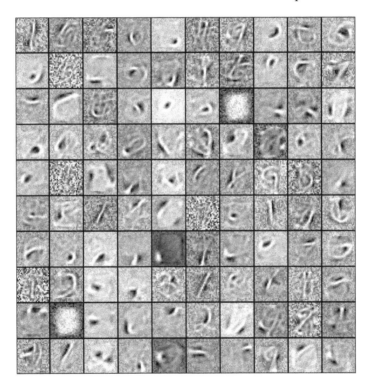

And a mini-batch of negative particles (1,000 steps of sampling between each row):

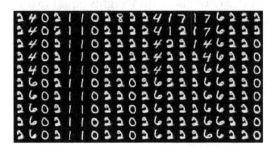

Deep belief bets

A **deep belief network (DBN)** is a stack of multiple RBMs to increase their representative power and better capture patterns in the data.

The training occurs layer by layer, first considering there is only one RBM with the hidden state h_1. Once the weights of the RBM have been trained, these weights are kept fixed and the hidden layer of the first RBM h_1 is considered as the visible layer for a second RBM, with one hidden state h_2. Each new RBM will capture patterns that have not been captured by the previous RBM as in the following diagram:

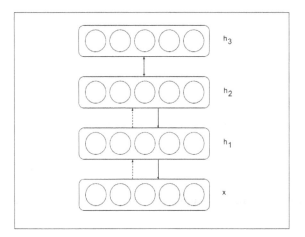

It can be shown that each add-on of a new RBM on top of the stack decreases the negative log likelihood.

As last step, it is possible to use these weights in a classification network, by simply adding a linear layer and a softmax layer on top of the final hidden state, and fine-tuning all the weights via gradient descent training, as usual.

The application to data dimensionality remains the same, with the unrolling of all layers to produce a decoder network, with weights equal to the transpose of the weights in the encoder network (initial multi-layer RBM):

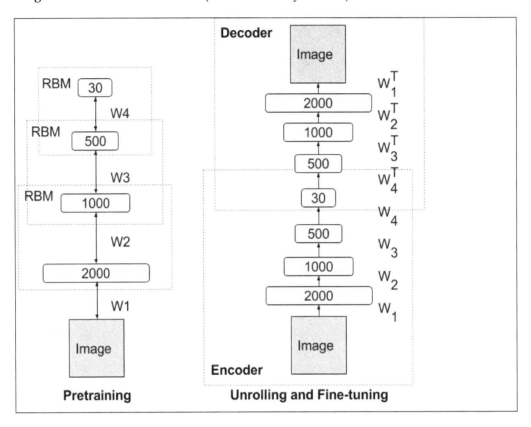

Such an unrolled network is called an **auto encoder**.

In practice, training directly via a gradient descent without the greedy layer by layer training would require finding the right initialization, which could be a lot trickier, as the weight initialization has to be close enough to the solution. That is why the commonly used approach for auto encoders is to train each RBM separately.

Generative adversarial networks

Since the partition function in the previous models is untractable and requires contrastive divergence algorithm with Gibbs sampling, game theory has recently delivered a new class of methods for learning generative models, the **Generative adversarial networks** (**GANs**), which enjoys great success today.

Generative adversarial networks are composed of two models that are alternatively trained to compete with each other. The generator network **G** is optimized to reproduce the true data distribution, by generating data that is difficult for the discriminator **D** to differentiate from real data. Meanwhile, the second network D is optimized to distinguish real data and synthetic data generated by G. Overall, the training procedure is similar to a two-player min-max game with the following objective function:

$$\min_{\theta_G} \max_{\theta_D} \mathbb{E}_{x \sim p_{\text{data}}} D_{\theta_D}(x) + \mathbb{E}_{z \sim p_z}(1 - D_{\theta_D}(G_{\theta_G}(z)))$$

Here, x is real data sampled from real data distribution, and z the noise vector of the generative model. In some ways, the discriminator and the generator can be seen as the police and the thief: to be sure the training works correctly, the police is trained twice as much as the thief.

Let's illustrate GANs with the case of images as data. In particular, let's again take our example from *Chapter 2, Classifying Handwritten Digits with a Feedforward Network* about MNIST digits, and consider training a generative adversarial network, to generate images, conditionally on the digit we want.

The GAN method consists of training the generative model using a second model, the discriminative network, to discriminate input data between real and fake. In this case, we can simply reuse our MNIST image classification model as discriminator, with two classes, `real` or `fake`, for the prediction output, and also condition it on the label of the digit that is supposed to be generated. To condition the net on the label, the digit label is concatenated with the inputs:

```
def conv_cond_concat(x, y):
    return T.concatenate([x, y*T.ones((x.shape[0], y.shape[1],
x.shape[2], x.shape[3]))], axis=1)

def discrim(X, Y, w, w2, w3, wy):
    yb = Y.dimshuffle(0, 1, 'x', 'x')
    X = conv_cond_concat(X, yb)
    h = T.nnet.relu(dnn_conv(X, w, subsample=(2, 2), border_mode=(2,
2)), alpha=0.2 )
    h = conv_cond_concat(h, yb)
    h2 =  T.nnet.relu(batchnorm(dnn_conv(h, w2, subsample=(2, 2),
border_mode=(2, 2))), alpha=0.2)
    h2 = T.flatten(h2, 2)
    h2 = T.concatenate([h2, Y], axis=1)
```

```
h3 = T.nnet.relu(batchnorm(T.dot(h2, w3)))
h3 = T.concatenate([h3, Y], axis=1)
y = T.nnet.sigmoid(T.dot(h3, wy))
return y
```

 Note the use of two leaky rectified linear units, with a leak of 0.2, as activation for the first two convolutions.

To generate an image given noise and label, the generator network consists of a stack of deconvolutions, using an input noise vector z that consists of 100 real numbers ranging from 0 to 1:

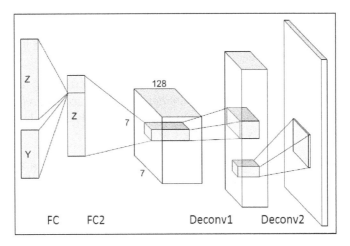

To create a deconvolution in Theano, a dummy convolutional forward pass is created, which gradient is used as deconvolution:

```
def deconv(X, w, subsample=(1, 1), border_mode=(0, 0), conv_
mode='conv'):
    img = gpu_contiguous(T.cast(X, 'float32'))
    kerns = gpu_contiguous(T.cast(w, 'float32'))
    desc = GpuDnnConvDesc(border_mode=border_mode,
subsample=subsample,
conv_mode=conv_mode)(gpu_alloc_empty(img.shape[0], kerns.shape[1],
img.shape[2]*subsample[0], img.shape[3]*subsample[1]).shape, kerns.
shape)
    out = gpu_alloc_empty(img.shape[0], kerns.shape[1], img.
shape[2]*subsample[0], img.shape[3]*subsample[1])
    d_img = GpuDnnConvGradI()(kerns, img, out, desc)
    return d_img
```

```
def gen(Z, Y, w, w2, w3, wx):
    yb = Y.dimshuffle(0, 1, 'x', 'x')
    Z = T.concatenate([Z, Y], axis=1)
    h = T.nnet.relu(batchnorm(T.dot(Z, w)))
    h = T.concatenate([h, Y], axis=1)
    h2 = T.nnet.relu(batchnorm(T.dot(h, w2)))
    h2 = h2.reshape((h2.shape[0], ngf*2, 7, 7))
    h2 = conv_cond_concat(h2, yb)
    h3 = T.nnet.relu(batchnorm(deconv(h2, w3, subsample=(2, 2),
border_mode=(2, 2))))
    h3 = conv_cond_concat(h3, yb)
    x = T.nnet.sigmoid(deconv(h3, wx, subsample=(2, 2), border_
mode=(2, 2)))
    return x
```

Real data is given by the tuple (X,Y), while generated data is built from noise and label (Z,Y):

```
X = T.tensor4()
Z = T.matrix()
Y = T.matrix()

gX = gen(Z, Y, *gen_params)
p_real = discrim(X, Y, *discrim_params)
p_gen = discrim(gX, Y, *discrim_params)
```

Generator and discriminator models compete during adversarial learning:

- The discriminator is trained to label real data as real (1) and label generated data as generated (0), hence minimizing the following cost function:

```
d_cost = T.nnet.binary_crossentropy(p_real,
                    T.ones(p_real.shape)).mean() \
         + T.nnet.binary_crossentropy(p_gen, T.zeros(p_gen.shape)).
mean()
```

- The generator is trained to deceive the discriminator as much as possible. The training signal for the generator is provided by the discriminator network (p_gen) to the generator:

```
g_cost = T.nnet.binary_crossentropy(p_gen,T.ones(p_gen.shape)).
mean()
```

The same as usual follows. Cost with respect to the parameters for each model is computed and training optimizes the weights of each model alternatively, with two times more the discriminator. In the case of GANs, competition between discriminator and generator does not lead to decreases in each loss.

From the first epoch:

To the 45th epoch:

Generated examples look closer to real ones:

Improve GANs

GANs are recent and very promising but still undergoing heavy research today. Yet, there are ways to improve the previous results.

First, as for RBM and other networks, GANs can be stacked in order to increase their generative power. As an example, the StackGan model proposes to use two stacked GANs for high quality image generation: the first GAN generates a coarse and low resolution image, while the second uses this generated sample as the input to generate an image of higher definition and realism, in which details of the objects are precised.

One of the main issues with GAN is the **model collapse**, which makes them difficult to train. Model collapse occurs when the generator begins to ignore the input noise and learns to generate only one sample, always the same. Diversity in the generation has collapsed. One very nice way to deal with this comes from the S-GAN model, and consists of adding a third net to train with the generator. The purpose of this net is to predict back the noise given the input:

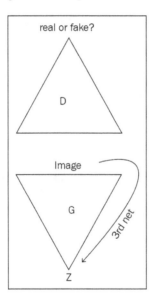

To optimize this third net with the generator, an entropy loss is added to the generator loss, to encourage the generated images x to be sufficiently dependent on the noise z. In other words, the conditional entropy $H(x \mid z)$ has to be as low as possible:

$$\mathop{\mathbb{E}}_{z \sim p_z} \mathop{\mathbb{E}}_{x \sim G(z)} - \log Q(z|x)$$

This third net predicts an auxiliary distribution Q to approximate the true posterior $P(z \mid x)$ and can be proved to be a variational higher bound for $H(x \mid z)$. Such a loss function helps the generator not to ignore the input noise.

Semi-supervised learning

Last but not least, such generative adversarial networks can be used to enhance supervised learning itself.

Suppose the objective is to classify K classes, for which an amount of labeled data is available. It is possible to add some generated samples to the dataset, which come from a generative model, and consider them as belonging to a *(K+1)th* class, the fake data class.

Decomposing the training cross-entropy loss of the new classifier between the two sets (real data and fake data) leads to the following formula:

$$
\begin{aligned}
L &= - \mathop{\mathbb{E}}_{x,y} \log p_{model}(y|x) \\
&= - \mathop{\mathbb{E}}_{x,y \sim p_{data}} \log p_{model}(y|x) \\
&\quad - \mathop{\mathbb{E}}_{x \sim G} \log p_{model}(y = K+1|x)
\end{aligned}
$$

Here, P_{model} is the probability predicted by the model:

$$
p_{model}(y = j|x) = \frac{e^{o_j}}{\sum_{k}^{K+1} e^{o_k}}
$$

Note that if we know that the data is real:

$$
p(y|x, y < K+1) = \frac{p_{model}(y|x)}{p_{model}(y < K+1|x)}
$$

And training on real data (K classes) would have led to the loss:

$$L_{supervised} = - \operatorname*{\mathbb{E}}_{x,y} \log p_{model}(y|x, y < K+1)$$

Hence the loss of the global classifier can be rewritten:

$$L = L_{supervised} - \operatorname*{\mathbb{E}}_{x,y \sim pdata} \log(1 - p_{model}(y = K+1|x))$$
$$- \operatorname*{\mathbb{E}}_{x \sim G} \log p_{model}(y = K+1|x)$$

The second term of the loss corresponds to the standard unsupervised loss for GAN:

$$L_{unsupervised} = - \operatorname*{\mathbb{E}}_{x,y \sim pdata} \log D(x)$$
$$- \operatorname*{\mathbb{E}}_{z \sim noise} \log(1 - D(G(z)))$$

The interaction introduced between the supervised and the unsupervised loss is still not well understood but, when the classification is not trivial, an unsupervised loss helps.

Further reading

You can refer to the following topics for more insights:

- *Deeplearning.net tutorial on RBM*: http://deeplearning.net/tutorial/rbm.html

- *Deeplearning.net tutorial on Deep Belief Nets*: http://deeplearning.net/tutorial/DBN.html

- *Deeplearning.net tutorial on generating with RBM-RNN*: http://deeplearning.net/tutorial/rnnrbm.html

- *Modeling Temporal Dependencies in High-Dimensional Sequences: Application to Polyphonic Music Generation and Transcription*, Nicolas Boulanger-Lewandowski, Yoshua Bengio, Pascal Vincent, 2012

- Generative Adversarial Networks, Ian J. Goodfellow, Jean Pouget-Abadie, Mehdi Mirza, Bing Xu, David Warde-Farley, Sherjil Ozair, Aaron Courville, Yoshua Bengio, 2014

- *Gans will change the world*, Nikolai Yakovenko, 2016 https://medium.com/@Moscow25/

- *Pixel Recurrent Neural Networks*, Aaron van den Oord, Nal Kalchbrenner, Koray Kavukcuoglu, 2016

- *InfoGAN: Interpretable Representation Learning by Information Maximizing Generative Adversarial Nets,* Xi Chen, Yan Duan, Rein Houthooft, John Schulman, Ilya Sutskever, Pieter Abbeel, 2016

- *StackGAN: Text to Photo-realistic Image Synthesis with Stacked Generative Adversarial Networks*, Han Zhang, Tao Xu, Hongsheng Li, Shaoting Zhang, Xiaolei Huang, Xiaogang Wang, Dimitris Metaxas, 2016

- *Stacked Generative Advanced Networks*, Xun Huang, Yixuan Li, Omid Poursaeed, John Hopcroft, Serge Belongie, 2016

- *Adversarial Learning for Neural Dialogue Generation*, Jiwei Li, Will Monroe, Tianlin Shi, Sébastien Jean, Alan Ritter, Dan Jurafsky, 2017

- *Improved Techniques for Training GANs*, Tim Salimans, Ian Goodfellow, Wojciech Zaremba, Vicki Cheung, Alec Radford, Xi Chen, 2016

- *Unsupervised Representation Learning with Deep Convolutional Generative Adversarial Networks*, Alec Radford, Luke Metz, Soumith Chintala, 2015

Summary

Generative adversarial networks are a very active area of research today. They belong to the family of generative models, which includes RBM and deep belief networks.

Generative models aim at generating more data, or learning better features for supervised and other tasks in an unsupervised way.

Generative models can be conditioned on some environmental input, and try to find the hidden variables behind the real data.

These models, the most advanced, complete the overview of deep learning nets with Theano. The next chapter will look at some advanced concepts to extend Theano and the future of deep learning.

13
Extending Deep Learning with Theano

This chapter gives clues to go further with both Theano and Deep Learning. First, it presents how to create new operators for the Theano computation graph in Python or C, either for the CPU or the GPU. Then, interactions with other Deep Learning frameworks are studied with the support of code repositories and libraries that enable back-and-forth conversion with other technologies.

Lastly, to complete the possibilities offered by the field of Deep Learning with Theano, we develop the concepts of a new **General Artificial Intelligence** field.

The topics covered in this chapter are as follows:

- Writing new operators for Theano computation graphs
- Python code for CPU and GPU
- The C API for CPU and GPU
- Sharing models with other Deep Learning frameworks
- Cloud GPUs
- Meta learning, gradual learning, and guided learning
- General Artificial Intelligence

This chapter gives a complete overview of Deep Learning with Theano.

Theano Op in Python for CPU

As a mathematical compilation engine, Theano's purpose is to compile a graph of computations in an optimal way for a target platform.

The development of new operators is possible in Python or C for compilation either on the CPU or GPU.

First, we address the simplest case, in Python for CPU, which will enable you to add new operations very easily and quickly.

To fix the ideas, let's implement a simple affine operator that performs the affine transformation $a * x + b$, given x as the input.

The operator is defined by a class deriving from the generic `theano.Op` class:

```python
import theano, numpy

class AXPBOp(theano.Op):
    """
    This creates an Op that takes x to a*x+b.
    """
    __props__ = ("a", "b")

    def __init__(self, a, b):
        self.a = a
        self.b = b
        super(AXPBOp, self).__init__()

    def make_node(self, x):
        x = theano.tensor.as_tensor_variable(x)
        return theano.Apply(self, [x], [x.type()])

    def perform(self, node, inputs, output_storage):
        x = inputs[0]
        z = output_storage[0]
        z[0] = self.a * x + self.b

    def infer_shape(self, node, i0_shapes):
        return i0_shapes
    def grad(self, inputs, output_grads):
        return [self.a * output_grads[0]]
```

```
mult4plus5op = AXPBOp(4,5)

x = theano.tensor.matrix()
y = mult4plus5op(x)
f = theano.function([x], y)

res = f(numpy.random.rand(3,2))
```

Let's understand this example.

The __props__ property is set to the two parameter names, a and b, on which the operator depends. It will automatically generate the __eq__(), __hash__(), and __str__() methods for us so that if we create two different objects with the same values for parameters a and b, Theano will consider them as equal operators:

```
>>> mult4plus5op2 = AXPBOp(4,5)

>>> mult4plus5op == mult4plus5op2
True

>>> hash(mult4plus5op)
-292944955210390262

>>> hash(mult4plus5op2)
-292944955210390262
```

Also, the parameters a and b will appear when printing the op:

```
>>> theano.printing.pprint(y)
AXPBOp{a=4, b=5}.0

>>> theano.printing.pydotprint(y)
```

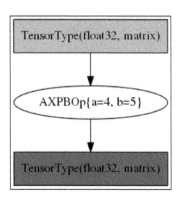

If __props__ is not specified, it is required to define the __eq__(), __hash__(), and __str__() methods manually.

The make_node() method creates the node to be included in the graph and is run when the mult4plus5op object is applied to the input x. Node creation is performed with the theano.Apply() method that takes as arguments the input variables and the type of the output. To enforce that the inputs are variables, the as_tensor_variable() method is called on the input to transform any NumPy array into a variable. This is the place where we define the type of the output given the input as well as to check whether the inputs are compatible with the operator and raise a TypeError otherwise.

Note that it is possible to generate the make_node() method automatically, as we did previously with the __props__ attribute for the __eq__() method, but in this case, with the itypes and otypes properties defining the types of the inputs and outputs:

```
itypes = [theano.tensor.dmatrix]
otypes = [theano.tensor.dmatrix]
```

The perform() method defines the computations in Python to be performed for this operator. Since it is possible to implement operators on multiple inputs that return multiple outputs, the inputs and outputs are given as lists. A second output would be stored in output_storage[1][0]. Outputs might be already allocated by previous values in order to reuse memory. They will always be of the good dtype object, but not necessary of the right shape and stride. It is good to re-allocate them when they are not of the good shape.

The last two methods, infer_shape() and grad(), are optional. The first one is used when the output does not need to be computed, but only a shape information is necessary to perform the computation—such a case occurs during Theano optimization procedures. The second is used when the output needs to be differentiated under the grad() method:

```
>>> dy=theano.tensor.grad(y.sum(), x)

>>> theano.printing.pprint(dy)
'(TensorConstant{4} * fill(AXPBOp{a=4, b=5}(<TensorType(float32,
matrix)>), fill(Sum{acc_dtype=float64}(AXPBOp{a=4, b=5}
(<TensorType(float32, matrix)>)), TensorConstant{1.0}))))'
```

```
>>> df = theano.function([x], dy)

>>> theano.printing.debugprint(df)
Alloc [id A] ''    2
 |TensorConstant{(1, 1) of 4.0} [id B]
 |Shape_i{0} [id C] ''    1
 | |<TensorType(float32, matrix)> [id D]
 |Shape_i{1} [id E] ''    0
   |<TensorType(float32, matrix)> [id D]
```

In the same way, it is possible to define the R-operator function of the operator.

Theano Op in Python for the GPU

Let's take a look at what happens when we run this operator in a graph in the GPU `config` mode:

```
>>> y = mult4plus5op(2 * x) + 4 * x

>>> f = theano.function([x], y)

>>> theano.printing.debugprint(f)
HostFromGpu(gpuarray) [id A] ''    6
 |GpuElemwise{Composite{(i0 + (i1 * i2))}}[(0, 0)]<gpuarray> [id B] ''
5
   |GpuFromHost<None> [id C] ''    4
   | |AXPBOp{a=4, b=5} [id D] ''    3
   |   |HostFromGpu(gpuarray) [id E] ''    2
   |     |GpuElemwise{mul,no_inplace} [id F] ''    1
   |       |GpuArrayConstant{[[ 2.]]} [id G]
   |       |GpuFromHost<None> [id H] ''    0
   |         |<TensorType(float32, matrix)> [id I]
   |GpuArrayConstant{[[ 4.]]} [id J]
   |GpuFromHost<None> [id H] ''    0
```

Since we have only defined a CPU implementation of the new operator in Python and the full graph is running on GPU, the data is transferred back and forth to CPU in the middle of the graph to apply our new CPU operator:

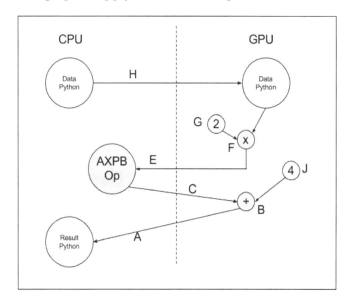

To avoid the inefficiency of the transfers inside the graph, let's create the same operator in Python for the GPU.

For this, you will have to simply modify the `make_node()` and `perform()` methods of the operator, as follows:

```python
from theano.gpuarray.type import get_context

def make_node(self, x):
    x = as_gpuarray_variable(x, self.context_name)

    x_arg = pygpu.elemwise.arg('x', 'float32', read=True)
    c_arg = pygpu.elemwise.arg('c', 'float32', read=True, write=True)
    self.my_op = pygpu.elemwise.GpuElemwise(get_context(self.context_
name), "c = " + str(self.a) + " * x + " + str(self.b), [x_arg, c_arg],
convert_f16=True)

    return Apply(self, [x], [x.type()])


def perform(self, node, inputs, output_storage):
    x = inputs[0]
    z = output_storage[0]
```

```
    z[0] = pygpu.empty(x.shape, dtype=x.dtype, context=get_
context(self.context_name))
    self.my_op( x, z[0])
```

Not many changes.

In the `make_node()` method, `as_tensor_variable()` is replaced by `as_gpuarray_variable()`, which requires the context that is one part of the type definition of a GPU variable. The `get_context()` method transforms the context name we have chosen for the device into a `GPUContext` for the `pygpu` library.

In the `perform()` method, computations are performed on GPU thanks to the `pygpu` library that contains an element-wise operator on GPU as well as the **Basic Linear Algebra Subprograms (BLAS)** methods, such as the **GEneral Matrix to Matrix Multiplication (GEMM)** and **General Matrix to Vector Multiplication (GEMV)** operations.

Let's now take a look at the compiled graph when this new operator is inside a bigger graph on GPU:

```
HostFromGpu(gpuarray) [id A] ''    4
 |GpuElemwise{Add}[(0, 1)]<gpuarray> [id B] ''    3
   |GpuArrayConstant{[[ 4.]]} [id C]
   |GpuAXPBOp{a=4, b=5, context_name='dev0'} [id D] ''    2
     |GpuElemwise{Mul}[(0, 1)]<gpuarray> [id E] ''    1
       |GpuArrayConstant{[[ 2.]]} [id F]
       |GpuFromHost<dev0> [id G] ''    0
         |<TensorType(float32, matrix)> [id H]
```

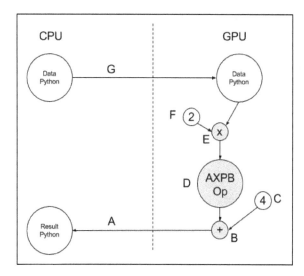

For readability, we have prefixed the name of the class of the operator for GPU with Gpu; for example, GpuAXPBOp.

Theano Op in C for CPU

Another inefficiency arises from the fact the Python implementation of an operator adds a significant overhead each time computations are performed, that is, for each instance of our operator in the graph. The Python code is not compiled as the rest of the graph by Theano in C and the overhead occurs when the C implementation is wrapped into Python and data is exchanged.

To remedy this, it is possible to directly write some C code that will be incorporated into the code of the rest of the graph and compiled together.

When implementing an operator directly in C, NumPy is the underlying library to manage arrays, with the the NumPy-API extending Python C-API. The Python class defining the new C operator does not have to implement the `perform()` method; instead, it returns the C code to incorporate in the `c_code()`, `c_support_code()` and `c_support_code_apply()` methods:

```python
def c_code_cache_version(self):
    return (6, 0)


def c_support_code(self):
    c_support_code = """
    bool same_shape(PyArrayObject* arr1, PyArrayObject* arr2)
    {
        if( PyArray_NDIM(arr1) != PyArray_NDIM(arr2)) {
            return false;
        }
        for(int i = 0; i < PyArray_NDIM(arr2) ; i++) {
            if (PyArray_DIMS(arr1)[0] == PyArray_DIMS(arr2)[0]) {
                return false;
            }
        }
        return true;
    }
    """


    return c_support_code
```

```python
def c_support_code_apply(self, node, name):
    dtype_x = node.inputs[0].dtype
    dtype_z = node.outputs[0].dtype

    a = self.a
    b = self.b

    c_support_code = """
    void elemwise_op_%(name)s(npy_%(dtype_x)s* x_ptr, npy_intp* x_str,
int itemsize_x,
        npy_%(dtype_z)s* z_ptr, npy_intp* z_str, int itemsize_z,
        int nbDims, npy_intp* dims)
    {
        npy_intp stride_x = (npy_intp)(1);
        npy_intp stride_z = (npy_intp)(1);
        for (int i = 0; i < nbDims; i ++) {
            stride_x = stride_x * x_str[i] / itemsize_x;
            stride_z = stride_z * z_str[i] / itemsize_z;
        }
        for (int i=0; i < dims[0]; i++)
            if (nbDims==1) {
                z_ptr[i * z_str[0]/itemsize_z] = x_ptr[i * x_str[0] /
itemsize_x] * ((npy_%(dtype_z)s) %(a)s) + ((npy_%(dtype_z)s)%(b)s);
            } else {
                elemwise_op_%(name)s( x_ptr + i * stride_x , x_str +
1, itemsize_x,
                    z_ptr + i * stride_z , z_str + 1, itemsize_z,
                    nbDims - 1, dims + 1 );
            }
    }
    """

    return c_support_code % locals()

def c_code(self, node, name, inp, out, sub):
    x = inp[0]
    z = out[0]

    dtype_x = node.inputs[0].dtype
    dtype_z = node.outputs[0].dtype
```

```
    itemsize_x = numpy.dtype(dtype_x).itemsize
    itemsize_z = numpy.dtype(dtype_z).itemsize

    typenum_z = numpy.dtype(dtype_z).num

    fail = sub['fail']

    c_code = """
    // Validate that the output storage exists and has the same
    // dimension as x.
    if (NULL == %(z)s || !(same_shape(%(x)s, %(z)s)))
    {
        /* Reference received to invalid output variable.
        Decrease received reference's ref count and allocate new
        output variable */
        Py_XDECREF(%(z)s);
        %(z)s = (PyArrayObject*)PyArray_EMPTY(PyArray_NDIM(%(x)s),
                                              PyArray_DIMS(%(x)s),
                                              %(typenum_z)s,
                                              0);

        if (!%(z)s) {
            %(fail)s;
        }
    }

    // Perform the elemwise operation
    ((npy_%(dtype_z)s *)PyArray_DATA(%(z)s))[0] = 0;
    elemwise_op_%(name)s((npy_%(dtype_x)s*)PyArray_DATA(%(x)s),
PyArray_STRIDES(%(x)s), %(itemsize_x)s,
                            (npy_%(dtype_z)s*)PyArray_DATA(%(z)s),
PyArray_STRIDES(%(z)s), %(itemsize_z)s,
                            PyArray_NDIM(%(x)s), PyArray_DIMS(%(x)s)
    );

    """

    return c_code % locals()
```

Let's now discuss the different parts:

When the `c_code_cache_version()` is implemented, Theano will cache the compiled code to save some compilation time the next time the operator is incorporated into a graph, but whenever we modify the code of the C op, the version number has to be incremented.

The code placed in the `c_support_code()` and `c_support_code_apply()` methods is included in the global scope of the C program. The code placed in the `c_support_code_apply()` and `c_code()` methods has to be specific to each apply of the op in the graph; in particular, in this case, they depend on the type of the input. And since the `c_support_code_apply()` code is included in the global scope, the methods are named after the op name.

`PyArray_NDIM`, `PyArray_DIMS`, `PyArray_STRIDES`, and `PyArray_DATA` are the macros to access the number of dimensions, the dimensions, the strides of the array, and the data in the array, respectively, for each NumPy array in C, `PyArrayObject`. `PyArray_EMPTY` is the equivalent to the Python `numpy.empty()` method in C.

The NumPy `PyArrayObject` class inherits from the `PyObject` class from the Python C-API. The `Py_XDECREF` macro enables us to decrement the reference count to the output before memory is allocated for a new output array. As in the Python C-API, the NumPy C-API requires to correctly count references to objects. Theano does not guarantee that the output array has been allocated, nor does it guarantee if it has been allocated with the correct shape. This is why a test is performed at the beginning of the `c_code()`.

Note that arrays can be strided, since they can be a view (or a subtensor) of an array (a tensor). It is possible to implement ops that create views or modify the inputs, as well.

There exist a few other possible methods to go further in the C implementation: `c_libraries()` and `c_lib_dirs()` to use external libraries, `c_code_cleanup()` to destroy memory allocations, and `c_init_code()` to execute some code at initialization.

Lastly, it is also possible to reference some C files inside the code to reduce the burden on the Python class. We do not detail these three last specificities.

Theano Op in C for GPU

As you could have imagined, it is possible to combine both optimizations:

- Reduce the Python/C overhead by programming directly in C
- Write the code for the GPU

To write CUDA code for GPU, the code that will be run in parallel on the numerous cores of the GPU has to be packaged into a special function type named **kernel**.

For that purpose, the __init__(), make_node(), and c_code_cache_version() methods stay the same as for our Python example for GPU, but with a new gpu_kernels() method to define new GPU kernels and the c_code() method (which replaces the perform() method again) to implement the C code, also named the **host code**, that orchestrates how and when to call the different kernels on GPU:

```
def gpu_kernels(self, node, name):
    code = """
KERNEL void axpb(GLOBAL_MEM %(ctype)s *x, GLOBAL_MEM  %(ctype)s *z,
ga_size n, ga_size m) {
for (ga_size i = LID_0; i < n; i += LDIM_0) {
    for (ga_size j = LID_0; j < m; j += LDIM_0) {
        z[i*m + j] = %(write_a)s( 2 * x[i*m + j] );
    }
}
}""" % dict(ctype=pygpu.gpuarray.dtype_to_ctype(self.dtype),
        name=name, write_a=write_w(self.dtype))
    return [Kernel(
            code=code, name="axpb",
            params=[gpuarray.GpuArray, gpuarray.GpuArray, gpuarray.
SIZE, gpuarray.SIZE],
            flags=Kernel.get_flags(self.dtype),
            objvar='k_axpb_' + name)]

def c_code(self, node, name, inp, out, sub):
    n, = inp
    z, = out
    dtype_n = node.inputs[0].dtype
    fail = sub['fail']
    ctx = sub['params']
    typecode = pygpu.gpuarray.dtype_to_typecode(self.dtype)
    sync = bool(config.gpuarray.sync)
```

```
kname = self.gpu_kernels(node, name)[0].objvar
s = """
size_t dims[2] = {0, 0};
size_t ls, gs;
int err;
dims[0] = %(n)s->ga.dimensions[0];
dims[1] = %(n)s->ga.dimensions[1];
Py_CLEAR(%(z)s);
%(z)s = pygpu_zeros(2, dims,
                    %(typecode)s,
                    GA_C_ORDER,
                    %(ctx)s, Py_None);
if (%(z)s == NULL) {
    %(fail)s
}
ls = 1;
gs = 256;
err = axpb_call(1, &gs, &ls, 0, %(n)s->ga.data, %(z)s->ga.data,
dims[0], dims[1]);
if (err != GA_NO_ERROR) {
    PyErr_Format(PyExc_RuntimeError,
                "gpuarray error: kEye: %%s. n%%lu, m=%%lu.",
                GpuKernel_error(&%(kname)s, err),
                (unsigned long)dims[0], (unsigned long)dims[1]);
    %(fail)s;
}
if(%(sync)d)
    GpuArray_sync(&%(z)s->ga);
""" % locals()


return s
```

Let's review this code snippet.

A new GPU computation kernel is defined under the name axpb, and it is a simple C code with special GPU types and two macros: KERNEL to designate the kernel function (hiding the CUDA __global__ declaration for kernels) and GLOBAL_MEM for the variables defined globally, available both on the CPU and the GPU (in opposition to variables inside the kernel function that, by default, are local to the thread executed on a GPU core).

Note that I implemented the operator for matrix (that is, two-dimensional) inputs only and the 256 threads will execute the same operations in parallel, while the operations could have been split into different groups and assigned to different threads.

The host code run on the CPU manages memory on both the CPU and GPU, and also launches kernels which are functions executed on the GPU device.

The allocation of a new GPU array is performed with the `pygpu_zeros()` method, which will from behind call the `cudamalloc()` method when using CUDA to allocate the array directly in the GPU memory. The operator instance does not need to manage the release of the memory allocated to outputs as well as data transfer between GPU and CPU since this is the role of Theano optimization to decide when to insert the transfer operators `HostFromGpu` and `GpuFromHost`.

The call to the kernel in the C code is performed via `axpb_call()`, that is, the name of the kernel followed by `_call()`. Note that there are four more arguments in the call than in the definition of the kernel method. These four arguments define how `libgpuarray` will execute or deploy the kernel on the cores.

To understand the GPU execution configuration for parallel programming, let's precise some basic concepts about a GPU first. A CUDA GPU is composed of **Streaming Multiprocessors** (**SM**), with a specification given by the compute capability in warp size, grid size, block size, the maximum number of threads per SM and per block, shared and local memory size, and maximum number of registrars:

Technical specifications	1.0	1.1	1.2	1.3	2.x	3.0	3.2	3.5	3.7	5.0	5.2	5.3	6.0	6.1	6.2
Maximum dimensionality of grid of thread blocks		2								3					
Maximum x-dimension of a grid of thread blocks		65535								$2^{31}-1$					
Maximum y-, or z-dimension of a grid of thread blocks									65535						
Maximum dimensionality of thread block									3						
Maximum x- or y-dimension of a block		512								1024					
Maximum z-dimension of a block									64						
Maximum number of threads per block		512								1024					
Warp size									32						
Maximum number of resident blocks per multiprocessor		8					16					32			
Maximum number of resident warps per multiprocessor	24		32		48					64					
Maximum number of resident threads per multiprocessor	768		1024		1536					2048					
Number of 32-bit registers per multiprocessor	8 K		16 K		32 K		64 K		128 K			64 K			
Maximum number of 32-bit registers per thread block	N/A				32 K	64 K	32 K		64 K			32 K	64 K		32 K
Maximum number of 32-bit registers per thread		124			63						255				
Maximum amount of shared memory per multiprocessor		16 KB					48 KB		112 KB	64 KB	96 KB	64 KB	96 KB		64 KB
Maximum amount of shared memory per thread block									48 KB						
Number of shared memory banks		16							32						
Amount of local memory per thread		16 KB								512 KB					

(Source: https://en.wikipedia.org/wiki/CUDA)

During execution, multiprocessors execute instructions for a group of 32 threads (as described in the preceding table), named warp, in the **Single Instruction Multiple Data (SIMD)** manner. When programming for parallel execution, you need to organize your threads into blocks that are as close as possible to the underlying architecture. For example, for an element-wise operation on matrices, as our AXPBOp, you could say that each thread is going to perform the operation on one element of the matrix. So, a computation on a 224 x 224 image will require 50,176 threads. Let's say that the GPU has 8 multiprocessors with 1024 cores each. In the execution configuration, you can, for example, define a block size of 256 threads, and the number of blocks required to perform the complete computation will be 196 blocks. In order to simplify the development of parallel programs, blocks can be organized into a multidimensional grid (up to 3 dimensions for a CC above 2.0, as shown in the preceding table), and in the case of an image input, it would be natural to use a two-dimensional grid of 14 x 14 blocks. It is up to you to organize the threads into blocks organized on a grid, but the best way to organize the threads is to follow the dimensionality of the underlying data, since it will be easier to split the data and affect it to different threads.

Each thread execution is provided with values to access its position in the grid that you can use inside the code:

- `gridDim.x`, `gridDim.y`, `gridDim.z` the dimensions of the grid of blocks of threads

- `blockIdx.x`, `blockIdx.y`, `blockIdx.z` the coordinate of the block on the grid

- `blockDim.x`, `blockDim.y`, `blockDim.z` the dimensions of the block

- `threadIdx.x`, `threadIdx.y`, `threadIdx.z` the coordinate of the thread in the block

In the case of our element-wise AXPBOp with one thread per element, the thread can fetch the data element given by the following row indice:

```
int i = blockIdx.x*blockDim.x + threadIdx.x;
```

To deploy, the first new four parameters in the kernel call correspond to:

- Dimensionality of the grid/blocks, in this case 2 for an image/matrice as input

- The sizes of launch grid, in this case is {14, 14}. Once the number of threads per block is defined (256 in our case), the number of blocks per grid is then determined by the problem size (here, the size of the matrix).

- The sizes of launch blocks, in this case {16, 16} to go for 256 threads per block, as it is usually set to 128 or 256. It is better to choose a multiple of the warp size, since execution is performed per warp; if you set it to 250, then, 201 of our blocks will underperform: one warp of each block will not be used at its full parallel potential. It is possible to try different multiples of 32 and make the choice on the most efficient runs.

- The amount of dynamic shared memory to allocate, which is required when you define a shared memory (with the LOCAL_MEM macro) that is dynamic (when the amount of shared memory is not known at compile time). Shared memory designates memory shared between threads belonging to the same block of threads. On devices of compute capability 2.x and 3.x, each multiprocessor has 64 KB of on-chip memory that can be partitioned between L1 cache and shared memory (16, 32, or 48K). The L1 cache coalesces global memory accesses by threads in a warp into as few cache lines as possible. The alignment differences between each thread have a negligible effect on performance thanks to the cache. Inefficiencies arise in the strided access for second and third dimensions; in this case, the use of shared memory enables you to extract a 2D tile of a multidimensional array from global memory in a coalesced fashion into shared memory and have contiguous threads stride through the shared memory tile:

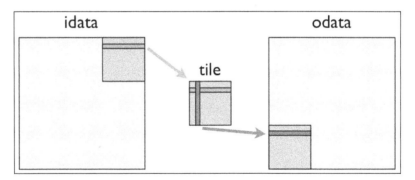

Coalesced transpose via shared memory, NVIDIA parallel for all

When the dimension of the data is not divisible into a block size times a grid size, threads dealing with data at the border will execute faster than other threads, and the kernel code has to be written in a way to check for out-of-bounds memory accesses.

When programming in parallel, race conditions, as well as memory bank conflicts in shared memory, and data that cannot stay local to the thread in the available registrars are some new pains to check. Coalescing global memory accesses is by far the most critical aspect of achieving good performance. The NVIDIA® Nsight™ tool will help you develop, debug, and profile the code that executes on CPU and GPU.

Model conversions

When a model is saved, the resulting data is simply a list of arrays, that is, weight vectors (for biases) and matrices (for multiplications) and a name for each layer. It is quite simple to convert a model from one framework to another: it consists of loading a numerical array and checking the layer names. Here are a few conversion examples from and to Caffe Deep Learning framework written in C++:

* `https://github.com/an-kumar/caffe-theano-conversion`
* `https://github.com/kencoken/caffe-model-convert`
* `https://github.com/piergiaj/caffe-to-theano`

To convert variables between the Torch Deep Learning framework (written in Lua) and Theano, you simply need a tool to convert data from Lua to Python NumPy:

`https://github.com/imodpasteur/lutorpy`

To convert models between Tensorflow and Theano, I would advise you to use the Keras library, which will stay up-to-date and enable to train models either in Theano or Tensorflow. For example, to convert a model from Tensorflow to Theano, keep your Keras install configured with Theano as we have seen in *Chapter 5, Analyzing Sentiment with a Bidirectional LSTM,* load the Tensorflow weights, and modify the layer names as follows:

```
from keras import backend as K
from keras.utils.conv_utils import convert_kernel
from keras.models import Model

# build your Keras model HERE
# then
model.load_weights('my_weights_tensorflow.h5')
```

```
for layer in model.layers:
    if layer.__class__.__name__ in ['Convolution1D', 'Convolution2D']:
        original_w = K.get_value(layer.W)
        converted_w = convert_kernel(original_w)
        K.set_value(layer.W, converted_w)

model.save_weights('my_weights_theano.h5')
```

A mirror sequence of operations enables us to do the contrary, from Theano to Tensorflow.

Another advantage of designing networks in Keras is the possibility to train them directly in the cloud, using the Google Cloud Machine Learning Engine, built with **Tensor Processing Units** (TPU), an alternative to GPU, designed from the ground for machine learning.

Let's take our example from *Chapter 5, Analyzing Sentiment with a Bidirectional LSTM*.

To train the model in the cloud, I create a project named *DeepLearning Theano* in the Google console `https://console.cloud.google.com/iam-admin/projects`, and in the API manager of the project, enable the Machine Learning Engine API. A few installation requirements might be checked with instructions at: `https://cloud.google.com/ml-engine/docs/quickstarts/command-line`, such as the Google Cloud SDK and the project configuration. With `gcloud init` command, your SDK configuration can be re-initialize to switch to the *DeepLearning Theano* project.

Let's upload the data in a newly created bucket in the cloud, given the region you choose (here `europe-west1`):

gsutil `mb -l europe-west1 gs://keras_sentiment_analysis`

gsutil `cp -r sem_eval2103.train gs://keras_sentiment_analysis/sem_eval2103.train`

gsutil `cp -r sem_eval2103.dev gs://keras_sentiment_analysis/sem_eval2103.dev`

gsutil `cp -r sem_eval2103.test gs://keras_sentiment_analysis/sem_eval2103.test`

Since the model is executed on a instance in the cloud, it is required:

- To modify the Python script to load the file stream from the remote bucket instead of a local directory, with the library `tensorflow.python.lib.io.file_io.FileIO(train_file, mode='r')` rather than the standard method `open(train_file, mode='r')`, with the same usage of the mode argument for both, 'r' for reading, w for writing,

- To define a `setup.py` file to configure the libraries required in the cloud instance environment:

```
from setuptools import setup, find_packages

setup(name='example5',
    version='0.1',
    packages=find_packages(),
    description='keras on gcloud ml-engine',
    install_requires=[
        'keras',
        'h5py',
        'nltk'
    ],
    zip_safe=False)
```

- To define a cloud deployment configuration file, `cloudml-gpu.yaml`:

```
trainingInput:
  scaleTier: CUSTOM
  # standard_gpu provides 1 GPU. Change to complex_model_m_gpu
for 4 GPUs
  masterType: standard_gpu
  runtimeVersion: "1.0"
```

To check the training works locally before submitting it to Google ML Cloud, run the following command:

```
gcloud ml-engine local train --module-name 7-google-cloud.bilstm \
  --package-path ./7-google-cloud  -- --job-dir ./7-google-cloud \
  -t sem_eval2103.train -d sem_eval2103.dev -v sem_eval2103.test
```

If everything works fine locally, let's submit it to the cloud:

```
JOB_NAME="keras_sentiment_analysis_train_$(date +%Y%m%d_%H%M%S)"

gcloud ml-engine jobs submit training $JOB_NAME \
        --job-dir gs://keras_sentiment_analysis/$JOB_NAME \
        --runtime-version 1.0 \
        --module-name 7-google-cloud.bilstm  \
        --package-path ./7-google-cloud \
        --region europe-west1 \
        --config=7-google-cloud/cloudml-gpu.yaml \
        -- \
```

```
        -t gs://keras_sentiment_analysis/sem_eval2103.train \
        -d gs://keras_sentiment_analysis/sem_eval2103.dev \
        -v gs://keras_sentiment_analysis/sem_eval2103.test
```

```
gcloud ml-engine jobs describe $JOB_NAME
```

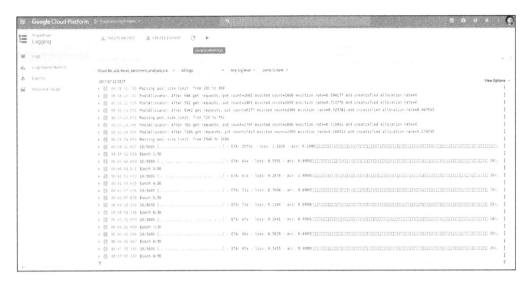

 Note that Google ML Cloud uses Tensorflow as backend.

The future of artificial intelligence

Chapter 2, Classifying Handwritten Digits with a Feedforward Network presented diverse optimization techniques (Adam, RMSProp, and so on) and mentioned second order optimization techniques. A generalization would be to also learn the update rule:

$$\theta_{t+1} = \theta_t + g_t\left(\nabla f\left(\theta_t\right), \phi\right)$$

Here, ϕ is the parameter of the optimizer g_t to learn from different problem instances, a sort of *generalization* or *transfer learning* of the optimizer from problems to learn better on new problems. The objective to minimize under this *learning to learn* or *meta-learning* framework has to optimize the time to learn correctly and, consequently, be defined on multiple timesteps:

$$\sum_{t=1}^{T} f(\theta_t(f, \phi))$$

Where:

$$\theta_{t+1}(f, \phi) = \theta_t(f, \phi) + g_t(\nabla f(\theta_t(f, \phi)), \phi)$$

A recurrent neural network can be used as the optimizer model g_t. Such a generalization technique that solves a multi-objective optimization problem improves the learning rate of the neural networks in general.

Researchers have been looking one step further, searching for general artificial intelligence, which aims for a human-level skill set with the capacity to improve itself and acquire new skills in a gradual way, using its **intrinsic** and previously learned skills to search for the solutions of new optimization problems.

A **skill** could be defined as a tool of intelligence to narrow or constrain the search space and restrict the behavior of the robot in the infinite world of possibilities.

Building a **General Artificial Intelligence** requires you to define the architecture of the intelligence with the intrinsic skills, which will be hardcoded by programmers into the robot and help solve smaller subproblems, as well as to define the order in which new skills will be acquired, the **curriculum roadmap** that could be taught in a **School for AI**. While **gradual learning** learns skill incrementally using simpler skills, **guided learning** involves a teacher who has already discovered the skills and will teach them to other AI.

On natural language translation tasks, smaller networks have been proven to learn faster and better from a bigger network, the *mentor*, which would have learned to translate and produce the translations for the smaller network to learn from, rather than learning directly from a real set of human translations.

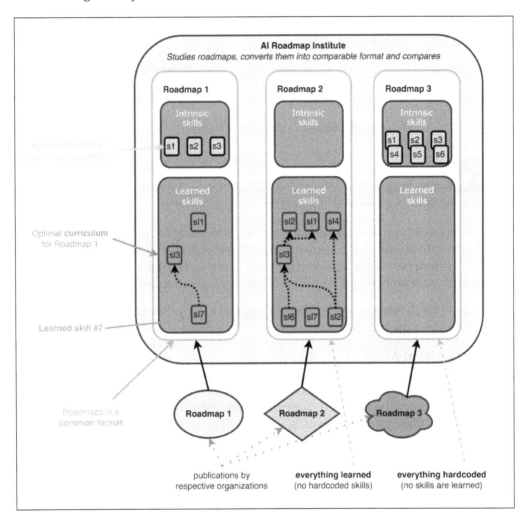

The preceding figure represents GoodAI Roadmap Institute to evaluate the learning roadmaps for AI.

Self exploration, communication with the mentor, and incorporation of negative and positive feedback are among the ideas toward autonomous intelligence that will develop itself, and the current Deep Learning networks open the way toward this future.

Among the companies that work toward this goal, it would be worth to quote GoodAI, as well as Amazon with its Echo product and the underlying voice control assistant technology, Alexa, that has already learned more than 10,000 skills in order to help you organize your life. Alexa's knowledge has become so vast that it becomes hard to dive deep into it and find its limitations. A test environment for developers enables them to insert these skills into intelligence tools of higher level:

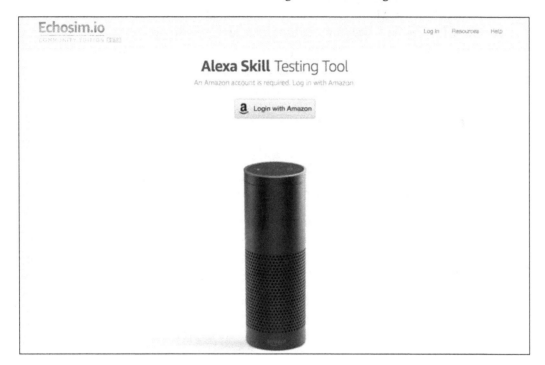

Further reading

You can refer to the following articles to learn more:

- *An Easy Introduction to CUDA C and C++,* https://devblogs.nvidia.com/parallelforall/easy-introduction-cuda-c-and-c/

- *How to Access Global Memory Efficiently in CUDA C/C++ Kernels,* https://devblogs.nvidia.com/parallelforall/how-access-global-memory-efficiently-cuda-c-kernels/

- *Using Shared Memory in CUDA C/C++*, `https://devblogs.nvidia.com/parallelforall/using-shared-memory-cuda-cc/`

- *Just another Tensorflow beginner guide (Part4 - Google Cloud ML + GUP + Keras)*, `http://liufuyang.github.io/2017/04/02/just-another-tensorflow-beginner-guide-4.html`

- Learning to learn by gradient descent by gradient descent, Marcin Andrychowicz, Misha Denil, Sergio Gomez, Matthew W. Hoffman, David Pfau, Tom Schaul, Brendan Shillingford, and Nando de Freitas, 2016

- A Framework for Searching for General Artificial Intelligence, Marek Rosa, and Jan Feyereisl, The GoodAI Collective, 2016

Summary

This chapter concludes our overview of Deep Learning with Theano.

The first set of extensions of Theano, in Python and C for the CPU and GPU, has been exposed here to create new operators for the computation graph.

Conversion of the learned models from one framework to another is not a complicated task. Keras, a high-level library presented many times in this book as an abstraction on top of the Theano engine, offers a simple way to work with Theano and Tensorflow as well as to push the training of models in the Google ML Cloud.

Lastly, all the networks presented in this book are at the base of General Intelligence, which can use these first skills, such as vision or language understanding and generation, to learn a wider range of skills, still from experiences on real-world data or generated data.

Index

A

AdaDelta 71
Adagrad 71
Adam 72
AlexNet 149
AlphaGo 220
analogical reasoning 90-93
architecture
  designing, for model 125, 126
  outputting probabilities,
      with softmax classifier 128
  sentence representation, using bi-LSTM 127
  vector representations, of words 126
artificial intelligence
  future 266-269
Association for Computational
      Linguistics (ACL) 174
asynchronous gradient descent 223
attention mechanism
  about 189
  annotate images 191
  differentiable 188, 189
  translations 189, 190
auto encoder 238
automatic differentiation 26, 27
Autoregressive models 231

B

backpropagation 45-47
Backpropagation Through Time (BPTT) 104
Basic Linear Algebra Subprograms
      (BLAS) 253
batch normalization layer 151, 152

Bayes Network theory 202
beam search algorithm 177
Bi-directional Recurrent Neural
      Networks (BRNN) 118
broadcasting 18

C

Character Error Rate (CER) 108
coalesced transpose
  model conversions 263-265
  via NVIDIA parallel 262, 263
  via shared memory 262, 263
Conditional Random Fields (CRF) 183
Continuous Bag of Words (CBOW) 77, 80-84
controller 193
Convolutional Neural Network
      (CNN) 37, 77
convolutions 56-60
cost function 44
CUDA
  URL, for downloading 4

D

data augmentation 163, 164
dataset
  about 78, 79
  character level 99
  for natural language 99-101
  word level 99
DeConvNet 178
deep belief bets 237, 238
deep belief network (DBN) 231, 237

Deeplearning.net Theano
  references 73
DeepMask network 182
DeepMind algorithm 220
Deep Q-network 221, 222
deep transition network 203
deep transition recurrent network 207
dense connections 160-162
dimension manipulation operators 16
dropout 67

E

elementwise operators 17-20
embedding 76-78
encoding 76-78
episodic memory
  with dynamic memory networks 197, 198
errors 44
external memory bank 192

F

functions 25, 27

G

gated recurrent network 107, 108
General Artificial Intelligence 247
GEneral Matrix to Matrix Multiplication
    (GEMM) 253
General Matrix to Vector Multiplication
    (GEMV) 253
generative adversarial networks (GANs)
  about 231, 238-242
  improving 243
generative model
  about 232
  deep belief bets 237, 238
  generative adversarial networks
      (GANs) 238-242
  Restricted Boltzmann Machine 232-237
global average pooling 152
Graphical Computation Unit (GPU) 1
graphs 10-13
greedy approach 222

H

highway networks design principle 208
host code 258

I

identity connection 154, 208
images
  deconvolutions 178-183
Inception (GoogLeNet) 149
Inceptionism 181
Inception v2 149
Inception v3 149
Inception v4 149
Independent Component Analysis (ICA) 88
inference 68
internal covariate shift 151
Intersection over Union (IOU) 147

K

Keras
  configuring 118, 119
  installing 118, 119
  model, compiling 129
  model, training 129
  programming 119, 120
  SemEval 2013 dataset 121
kernel 258

L

Lasagne 133
  MNIST CNN model 134-136
Latent Sementic Analysis / Indexing
    (LSA / LSI) 88
layer input normalization 151
learned embeddings
  visualizing 88, 89
linear algebra operators 21-23
Linear Discriminant Analysis (LDA) 88
localization network
  about 136-140
  recurrent neural net,
      applied to images 140-144

model, building 40
script environment, setting up 40
structure 40, 41
training 40

U

unsupervised learning
  with co-localisation 145
update rules 68, 69

V

validation dataset
  training 60-67
variables 23, 24

Variational Auto Encoders 231
variational RNN 202
VGG 149

W

weight tying (WT) 94
word embeddings
  application 93
Word Error Rate (WER) 108

Y

You Only See Once (YOLO)
    architecture 147

www.ingramcontent.com/pod-product-compliance
Lightning Source LLC
Chambersburg PA
CBHW060516060326
40690CB00017B/3300